NATO's Approach to the Civil Dimensions of War

"An excellent account of NATO's civilian defence with an astute understanding of the relevant conceptual issues and the contemporary political dimensions of resilience".

—Jonathan Jospeh, *Professor in Politics and International Relations, University of Bristol.*

"Finally, a tracing of the world's longest-lasting alliance's understanding of civil defense and resilience. A must-read for NATO buffs".

—Iver B. Neumann, *The Fridtj of Nansen Institute, Norway.*

"This book is of immense importance for anyone who wants to understand the development of today's NATO's resilience concept. It closes a significant research gap and gives us some much-needed context for resilience and preparedness planning in Western countries, both historically and today. Breaking new empirical ground, it is a seminal work and a much-needed starting point for other researchers interested in the topic".

—Iben Bjørnsson, *Associate Professor of History, the Swedish Defence University.*

Oscar Larsson

NATO's Approach to the Civil Dimensions of War

From Defense to Resilience

palgrave
macmillan

Oscar Larsson
Political Science
Swedish Defense University
Stockholm, Sweden

ISBN 978-3-032-27870-8 ISBN 978-3-032-27871-5 (eBook)
https://doi.org/10.1007/978-3-032-27871-5

This Palgrave Macmillan imprint is published by the registered company Springer Nature Switzerland AG
The registered company address is: Gewerbestrasse 11, 6330 Cham, Switzerland

Acknowledgments

At the NATO Archives and Library, I would like to thank Lia Largaespada Molina for all the personal services and guidance on accessing the archives. Librarian Katherine McVetty assisted me in finding relevant literature on civil defense in the well-sorted NATO library. Charlotte Desmasures, a fellow NATO researcher, was very helpful in showing some additional ways the archives could be managed. At the Swedish representation, Erika K Nilsson was very helpful in ensuring that all papers were in order before the visits. She did her utmost to assist me in securing interviews and accessing the high spots in the NATO HQ during the visits. Hasit Thankey, the Head of the Enablement and Resilience Section in the Defense Policy and Planning Division at NATO Headquarters, showed great interest in the project and agreed to be interviewed, but also suggested several additional persons to interview and seminars to participate in.

I have presented chapters and drafts on several occasions during the writing process. Chapter 2 was presented at the Research Seminar in Political Science at the Swedish Defense University in 2025. Professor Eva-Karin Gardell served as the main discussant. Still, the seminar at the beginning of the writing process injected a lot of energy into the project, and I wish to thank all who commented and provided valuable feedback. I had the opportunity to present a draft of Chapter 4, "The Politics of Resilience," at Copenhagen Business School in June 2025. I was invited to the Department of Business, Humanities, and

Law by Mitchell Dean and Stina Teilmann-Lock. Josefine Lykkegard was very helpful during the visit and provided some valuable feedback on the chapter. Thanks to all other participants. Jonathan Joseph was kind enough to read parts of the manuscript in the final stages of the writing process. He provided valuable feedback on how resilience, as a national defense concept, could be further analyzed. I presented Chapter 6 to the Department of Political Science in January 2026. The expert on Denmark and Cold War defense efforts, Iben Bjornsson, served as the main discussant and provided nuanced feedback that improved the chapter and the rest of the book.

I received a vital publication grant from the Anna Lindh Library at the Swedish Defense University that enabled open access publication of this book. Frank Olof, working with the library and administration at the Swedish Defence University, was most helpful in the judicial process of signing the OA publication contract. I was fortunate enough to devote my energy to the research and writing the manuscript.

I would like to thank Isobel Cowper Coles at Palgrave Macmillan. We met briefly at the International Study Association conference in San Francisco in 2024, where we discussed the possibility of writing a book on grey zone, hybrid threats, and resilience. Returning from the conference, I started sketching out such a book, but my eyes soon fell on NATO's handling of the current security situation. This spiraled into an interest in vocabulary and historical development. She approved of the new direction and encouraged me to submit a proper book proposal on multiple occasions during the first year of research and writing. I am thankful for her support throughout the project.

I would also like to thank my partner, Josefina Erikson, who is a Political Science Professor at Uppsala University. I suspect she is a bit tired of the answer to the question of how my day was: "I have been working on my book." For the main part of the work, I have kept it within business hours, but on occasions , I traveled to Brussels or went on (short) writing trips, leaving the everyday duties on the "home front" for a few days. In addition, I suspect that she and the rest of the family know more about NATO and civil defense than most people before the publication of this book.

> Modern war is not merely a matter for soldiers, sailors, and airmen. The armed forces are, in fact, only the cutting edge of a mechanism which involves every single national activity. The skill of the Commanders, the valour of the troops, the excellence of their equipment will be of no avail if the home front cracks, Lord Ismay 1952. (SCEPC 1976, 3)

Contents

1	**Introduction**	1
	1.1 Scope and Limitations of the Present Study	7
	1.2 Methodology and Material	8
2	**Security Politics**	13
	2.1 Securitization Theory	15
	2.2 The Balance of Security Politics	20
3	**NATO: A Military Chameleon**	25
	3.1 The Beginning of NATO	25
	3.2 Community and Enlargement	26
	3.3 NATO After the End of the Cold War	30
4	**Political Dimensions of Resilience**	39
	4.1 The Roots of Resilience	41
	4.2 Resilience and Society	42
	4.3 The Political Dimension	45
	4.4 Resilience as Governmentality	47
	4.5 Combining Securitization and Governmentality	49
	4.6 Resilience as Part of National and International Security	51

5 The Early Years 1949–1964 55
5.1 The Unexpected Partnership 56
5.2 Political Dimensions of NATO in the Early Years 61
5.3 The First Guiding Documents 64
5.4 Nuclear Threats and Capabilities 68
5.5 The Role of the Civil Defense 71
5.6 Establishment of SCEPC and the New Assumptions 79
5.7 Difficulties in Coordinating Civil Defense 84
5.8 Conclusions 1949–1964 90

6 Expansion of the (Civil) Security Agenda 1965–1989 93
6.1 A New Military Structure and Strategy 94
6.2 A New Strategic Concept and the Flexible Approach 96
6.3 Détente and the Harmel Report 99
6.4 The Expansion of Civil Tasks 102
6.5 Logistical Support for Military Operations 105
6.6 Nuclear Arms Control 111
6.7 NATO's Committee on the Challenges of Modern Society (CCMS) 113
6.8 Expansion of the Civil Dimensions 116
6.9 Civil Defense Blindness 122
6.10 Conclusions 1965–1989 133

7 Civil Dimensions After the End of the Cold War, 1989–2014 137
7.1 The Fall of the Berlin Wall and the Dismantling of the Warsaw Pact 138
7.2 NATO and the Balkans: The First Out-of-Area Operations 141
7.3 A New Military Model and Expanding Partnerships 143
7.4 The NATO Crisis of 9/11 and the Close Relationship with Russia 148
7.5 A New Strategic Concept 2010 151
7.6 From Civil Emergency Planning to Civil Crisis Management 157
7.7 NATO and the New Disaster Assistance 170
7.8 Conclusions 1989–2014 175

8 The New Concept of Resilience 179
8.1 Resilience as a Key Policy Concept 181
8.2 Formalizing Resilience and Civil Preparedness 187
8.3 Establishing the Resilience Committee (RC) 194
8.4 Resilience and Military Support 200
8.5 Conclusions 2014–2025 205

9 Conclusions and Further Challenges 209
9.1 Theoretical Premises 212
9.2 From Civil Defense to Resilience 214
9.3 Limitations of the Study and Future Research 219
9.4 Theoretical Discussion and Concluding Remarks 220

Literature 223

Index 247

CHAPTER 1

Introduction

The present study aims to conduct a historical investigation into the role and significance that the North Atlantic Treaty Organization (NATO) has attributed to civil defense and civil administration in its member states during its long-standing existence of more than 75 years. This topic has not received much attention in the past, as most academic research has focused primarily on NATO's military dimension, its enlargement process, out-of-area operations and missions, and other forms of external relations. However, recent developments in this area have opened new avenues for a much-needed historical and critical inquiry into the role ascribed to civil defense and civil resources. NATO is perhaps primarily understood as a military defense alliance shaped by Article 5 of the original North Atlantic Treaty of 1949. Article 5 provides that an attack on one of the member states should be considered to be an attack on all member states and that all states will, after a consensus decision, support the attacked state with all means necessary to restore and maintain the security of the North Atlantic area. But what about the rest of society? War and war preparation always involve elements that concern civil administration, civil society, businesses, populations, and even individuals. How have the views and concerns of the civil aspects of war, defense, and deterrence changed over the years for NATO and the member states? What is the current approach, and what does this mean in practice? How far could security and military priorities be stretched in reality? Another way to phrase it might be, what does it mean to be a member state today, and what is NATO currently expecting

O. Larsson, *NATO's Approach to the Civil Dimensions of War*,
https://doi.org/10.1007/978-3-032-27871-5_1

from its member states? What was once a military alliance between 12 countries has evolved into an international organization, with a permanent staff, two headquarters, and 32 member states. However, this also highlights the need to explore how NATO operates beyond its military aspects, Article 5, and its foreign affairs and politics.

As the world grows in technological dependency, more globally interconnected and complex, and with a wide range of actors capable of performing "attacks" that are not military or even physical, NATO, too, has converted its former military orientation to a broader understanding of security in the new security climate and geopolitical situation. However, all security and military efforts come at a monetary cost and involve trade-offs in prioritizing different political goals and values. Such commitments and priorities include serious obligations for member states that go well beyond strict military commitments. The goal of 2% of GDP for military investments for member states was raised to 5% at the Haag NATO summit in 2025, even though most European countries have not met their 2% obligations for a long period of time (Stoltenberg 2025). The extent to which member states should commit to security and military expenditure has varied over the years. Yet the current trend is an expansion of security issues that need to be addressed. As we shall see, NATO is deeply invested in advancing the member states' overall *resilience* to stand fast in the new era of grey zone, hybrid threats, and hybrid wars. This means that the military alliances now operate with a broader understanding of security and ask member states to adjust accordingly. In this book, we can see that the broadening of the security agenda took off already in the late 1960s, several decades before the end of the Cold War. But the current approach to broader security governance is much more explicit and all-encompassing, covering wartime preparation as well as peacetime focus on hybrid threats, disaster relief, and crisis management.

Since 2014, NATO has renewed its strategy to increase the resilience of all member states, which relies on a "whole-of-society" approach. Not only are military attacks on the agenda, but so too are shocks and disruptions that may weaken collective defense.

> Each NATO member country needs to be resilient in order to withstand a major shock such as a natural disaster, failure of critical infrastructure, or a hybrid or armed attack. Resilience is the individual and collective capacity to prepare for, resist, respond to and quickly recover from shocks and

> disruptions, and to ensure the continuity of the Alliance's activities. Civil preparedness is a central pillar of Allies' resilience and a critical enabler for the Alliance's collective defence, and NATO supports Allies in assessing and enhancing their civil preparedness. Rooted in Article 3 of the North Atlantic Treaty, national and collective resilience are an essential basis for credible deterrence and defence, and are therefore vital to NATO's efforts to safeguard its societies, populations and shared values (NATO 2023c)

This approach to national and international security, and the emphasis on resilience and civil preparedness as a "critical enabler for the alliance's collective defense," expands the understanding of national security and the kind of commitment NATO seeks from its member states. Since 2016, there have been specified evaluation charters, biannual reports on each member state's current "resilience status," and, in 2022, a new *Resilience Committee* was established to oversee resilience and its implementation throughout the alliance. In 2022, the number of personnel at NATO Headquarters in Brussels working on civil preparedness exceeded those working on military preparations and operations. Looking back at the history of civil defense within NATO, we can see that this approach is hardly new, but there are important nuances in how NATO has approached civil defense, later civil emergency planning, and, more recently, societal resilience. The main research question and approach of this book are thus:

How has NATO approached the questions of civil defense and the role of the population and other civil dimensions of war and war preparedness throughout history?

NATO is currently working proactively and programmatically to enhance the resilience of its member states. According to NATO, this newfound interest in civil preparedness and a whole-of-society approach to security is motivated by a new security discourse in which *grey zone* and *hybrid threats* are key concepts, which emerged and became familiar following Russia's annexation of the Crimean Peninsula in 2014. This has been identified as an essential element of (Russian) hybrid warfare (Reichborn-Kjennerud and Cullen 2016; Renz 2016, 2018), as well as marking the end of the period in which NATO and Russia were trying to uphold normal diplomatic relations (Pouliot 2010; Eichler 2021). At the same time, it is critical to remember that hybrid threats and attempts to influence the political development, globally or in self-proclaimed "spheres of interests," are hardly new. Such approaches and covert or overt operations have existed since antiquity and have been the modus operandi throughout the Cold War. Why is the old wine in new bottles suddenly so worrying?

NATO proclaims that the organization and its allies now face threats and challenges from both state and non-state actors who use hybrid threats to target political institutions, influence public opinion, and undermine the security of NATO citizens. Hybrid methods that stay just below the threshold of open hostility and warfare include propaganda, deception, cyber or physical sabotage, and other non-military tactics that may have been present all along to destabilize adversaries. However, in recent years, their speed, scale, and intensity, facilitated by rapid technological change and global interconnectivity, have increased and are therefore considered to pose serious security challenges to NATO and its member states. NATO has consequently developed a comprehensive strategy for countering hybrid threats and hybrid warfare (NATO 2023a). NATO motivates its wider understanding of security and concern for member states' ability to withstand all kinds of shocks and disturbances in Article 3 of the North Atlantic Treaty (The North Atlantic Treaty 1949), which states:

> In order more effectively to achieve the objectives of this Treaty, the Parties, separately and jointly, by means of continuous and effective self-help and mutual aid, will maintain and develop their individual and collective capacity to resist armed attack (The North Atlantic Treaty 1949).

This article was part of the original 1949 treaty but has not received the same level of academic attention as the better-known Article 5. NATO now states that "national and collective *resilience* is an essential basis for credible deterrence and defense and is therefore vital to NATO's efforts to safeguard its societies, populations, and shared values." The organization goes even further and notes that "the *principle* of resilience is rooted in Article 3 of the North Atlantic Treaty" (NATO 2023c).

The recent reinterpretation and newfound importance of Article 3 in the original NATO treaty offer an intriguing and complex topic for academic exploration. Specifically, it raises questions about the historical role of civil preparedness within NATO's 75-year existence, from the Cold War era of Mutual Assured Destruction (MAD) to the present-day focus on resilience as a key concept for credible deterrence and defense, calling for an active role of civil administration and civil actors in the member states. One interesting aspect to consider is how the meaning and understanding of civil defense evolved, particularly during the Cold War ideological conflict and the subsequent shift toward international crisis management in the post-Cold War era. Additionally, it is worth examining how *resilience* has emerged as a foundational principle for NATO member states to resist both armed and non-armed attacks, and the implications of the contemporary effort to strengthen NATO's collective resilience. Overall, enquiring into the history of civil defense and civil emergency planning, and the current implementation of civil preparedness and resilience within NATO, offers a broader understanding of the contemporary security discourse and the organization and implementation of security arrangements across member states. There appear to be important aspects to consider in the subtle changes in the vocabulary and terminology surrounding the civil dimensions of war and war preparation. The main aim of the book is to examine how evolving security discourses alter NATO's approach to the civil dimensions of war and war preparedness, with a primary focus on the roles of populations and individuals.

Investigating the evolving nature of NATO's international security and crisis management can thereby inform us about the formation of the current security discourse and its broader implications for member states and their societies. What does it mean to be a member state of NATO today, and how is NATO trying to govern and influence the organization of political resources beyond military capacity?

This background, along with the recent acceleration in interest in war preparedness, motivates a thorough investigation of the role of civil defense and civil administration that NATO has advocated throughout the years. Thus, by tracing the meaning and value NATO has ascribed to civil administration and civil resources throughout its 75-year existence, we can unveil the conceptual development in this political field. It is thus possible to connect specific intellectual innovations with historical events that have shaped the development and interest in civil defense and civil preparedness, and to situate the current key concept of resilience within a longer ideational history. It can also show us the connections and linkages between military preparedness and civil crisis management that today seem closer than before.

To better understand current development, it is interesting to cover a longer period, or, even better, the entire period, as this will provide us with more insights, background information, and context. It will also enable us to observe historical shifts in NATO's perception of its role and identity, its view of national and collective security, and the ways in which civil preparedness complements military efforts and capabilities. This book provides a critical investigation of both historical and contemporary security architecture, as well as the roles of civil defense and preparedness, civil administration, and civil society. Such a study is both timely and significant in sparking a political discussion about the efforts and implications of allowing security politics to dictate and shape the political climate of today's late post-Cold War era, and about the priorities societies should have. The danger, or what we might be wary of, is that excessive emphasis on security creates a narrow view of the future and neglects other social and political issues, as well as alternative routes to national, societal, and human security.

The Cold War is often seen as a period of extreme polarization, marked by an ideological conflict between Capitalism and Communism, and by the division of the world into East and West, Friends and Foes. Neutral and non-allied countries performed advanced balancing acts between the superpowers and their alliances. Both sides invested vast resources in developing weapons and strategic studies to support their nations and allies with the technology and strategies needed to overcome the enemy. It was preparation for total war and complete destruction, where neither side was willing to concede any ground. However, the end of the Cold War temporarily disrupted this geopolitical order until Russia annexed Crimea in 2014. The phenomenon discussed in this text has significant implications for the current global order and deserves further scholarly attention. Since 2014, we have observed a resurgence of traditional binaries in the security discourse worldwide, and they continue to thrive in governments, think tanks, and policy centers. Critically oriented research on NATO may, therefore, face some challenges. Many people view NATO as a guarantor of peace, democracy, and security. This means they may be unwilling to discuss negative aspects or implications, including hidden costs or social and political effects that may arise from a specific security-oriented agenda in politics and international affairs. This can make it difficult to introduce, consider, and discuss alternative perspectives that, in turn, may question NATO's strategies in world politics, its priorities, and its security orientation (Eichler 2021; Hagström 2021; Hellström 2023).

Still, scholars of security politics must pursue research that demonstrates the logic and implications of specific security discourses and the ways in which *security* functions. We need to identify and deconstruct the elements of contemporary security discourses to understand their logic, their rationality, and, not least, their broader implications. Security politics, encompassing national and societal security, constitutes a specific and grave political field that provides instruments for increased social and political control and creeping militarization. This means that we, as social scientists, should conduct studies of security discourses to lay bare the underlying assumptions and the broader implications of security politics, thereby illustrating the political nature of current security discourses and practices. Security and resilience are more than just buzzwords. They are complex political concepts that play a crucial role in shaping the world we live in. Understanding the underlying logic of security politics is essential to grasping the power it holds in enabling and legitimizing political actions. I believe that it is not just a technocratic concept that objectively describes institutional arrangements that protect us from harm, but rather a powerful force that drives change and shapes the course of history. It is thus essential to consider the unique *productive* capacity of this multifaceted concept and how it shapes the decisions of leaders and governments worldwide. I will explain the role and functions of security in greater detail in Chap. 2.

1.1 Scope and Limitations of the Present Study

There has been considerable political and academic interest in NATO, especially since the end of the Cold War, with further articles and books published since 2014 and the return of geopolitics to the European Continent. It is not possible to cover all the events and turns in the eventful years in which NATO existed. In addition, it is impossible to cover all aspects of NATO, including its military capacity and coordination, diplomatic relations with member states, partners, and third parties, and adversaries. Another relevant aspect not addressed in the book is NATO's military operations and its international crisis management. In Chap. 3, I provide a brief historical overview of the key events and operations that have shaped NATO's development into its current form, as well as the security challenges it is addressing. I do this while also relating NATO's development to scientific debates and publications discussing these events or developments. The book's primary focus is the historical development and security discourse that directly addresses the roles and functions of populations, civil defense, civil administration, civil society, and individuals within NATO and its member states. I return to and mention external diplomatic relations, military operations, and specific events when these circumstances produce discursive shifts in the role and function of civil defense. Still, civil defense soon becomes entangled with civil emergency planning, a much broader approach to the civil dimensions of war and war preparedness, including communications, shipping, and critical resources such as oil. Here, I chose to remain focused on the foundations of civil defense and the role of populations, even though civil emergency planning is a much broader approach. It would not have been possible to cover all aspects in a single book. There are thus more grounds to cover regarding civil resources and the dimensions of war and war preparedness.

1.2 Methodology and Material

This section discusses the methodology of constructivism and discourse analysis. This focuses on how particular ideas and interrelated concepts emerge and decisively shape problems, solutions, and actions in the field of civil defense.

This methodology aligns well with the book's historical and archival approach, which examines the adoption and transformation of concepts such as *civil defense, civil emergency planning, civil preparedness, and resilience* within NATO. Michel Foucault also employed a similar approach to illustrate how apparent truths depend on contingencies and power/knowledge in the emergence of the modern state (Foucault 2010). The foundation of a constructivist approach is that it traces how familiar and taken-for-granted frames, forms of knowledge, practices, and norms first come into being and then cement themselves as a governing approach within an organization (Collier and Lakoff 2021; Bartelson 1995). It thus illustrates the contingency and uncertainty of current and historical approaches to specific political problems. In many ways, we can say that for problems to be solved, they need to become knowledge-based and actionable; a similar image of the problem needs to be shared among the actors responsible for solving it (Bacchi 1999). It concerns the proper distribution of tasks among authorities and the ideals or principles that guide the actions of those involved in planning and governance. Therefore: "Government is intrinsically linked to the activities of expertise, whose role is not one of weaving an all-pervasive web of 'social control', but of enacting assorted attempts at the calculated administration of diverse aspects of conduct through countless, often competing, local tactics of education, persuasion, inducement, management, incitement, motivation and encouragement" (Rose and Miller 2010).

The method and design of this study aim to recover the styles of reasoning and the intellectual techniques that actors use to make the problem thinkable and practicable. In this way, civil defense poses a specific problem for NATO: it is central to the doctrine of total war. Questions of civil administration, populations, and member states' societies cannot be ignored in the planning of total war and the risk of total annihilation that has been apparent after the introduction of nuclear weapons and missiles. At the same time, this was codified as a competence and responsibility of the member states. The problem of civil defense and support for the military effort was not only a practical concern for NATO and its planners but also a governance issue. How could NATO govern member states and their respective civil administrations in the desired direction?

A constructivist methodology that investigates security politics would treat security not simply as a given, objective problem but as something embedded in historical struggles over truth, knowledge, authority, expertise, and power. In line with the theory of securitization (see Chap. 2), the analysis of the security discourse in NATO operates as a historical formation, constituting both its subjects, actors involved in the formation, and the role given in planning and execution, and the object itself, how security is understood at a specific time (Buzan et al. 1998).

The roles of civil and market actors emerge as central in shaping security narratives across critical junctures and developmental phases. This examination not only offers a nuanced understanding of historical security frameworks but also highlights the ongoing relevance of civil society in contemporary security discussions. By interrogating the intersections of military strategy and the civil dimensions of war, we can better understand the complex fabric of security discourse and its implications for policy and practice in today's global landscape.

Material was collected, including official NATO reports and documents, such as Strategic Concepts and other planning papers, as well as NATO communications and other primary materials. NATO is relatively transparent for an international defense organization and shares some of its communications and documents online. For instance, it has an online archive that makes available declassified historical documents systematically archived by committee and subject. The online database covers the years 1949 to 1967. Historical documents are searchable online, and I have used this function extensively in all the empirical chapters. But not all documents have been declassified or uploaded to the online archives. Some only exist in the physical (but digital) archive at NATO headquarters in Brussels. I have therefore made two research trips to visit NATO's physical library and digital archives in Brussels. My first trip was conducted from April 22 to 27, 2025—the second from 6 to 10 October. I had the privilege of accessing the NATO Archives at NATO HQ in Brussels and of having a desk in the library. The most essential committee series for my current research was AC 23, Civil Defense Committee, and AC 98, Senior Civil Emergency Planning Committee. It is important to note that although the Senior Committee was replaced in 2022 by the Resilience Committee, the declassification of the documents stopped in 1992. The archive also allowed keyword searches. For instance, "civil defense" received 9556 hits or "documents," and "civil emergency planning" generated 6496 documents. Half of these are duplicates, as all reports are provided in both French and English. I have only looked at the English documents. Searching for keywords helped identify documents outside the committee series A23 and AC 98. Sometimes, the issue of civil defense or civil emergency planning is discussed in the North Atlantic Council or in various military committees.

Many documents are corrections and revisions (often indicated by letters in the file name) and thus do not add new information. NATO policy requires that documents be 30 years old before they are declassified and made available to the public, with some minor exceptions. This means that, since 1992, approximately 20 documents have been published per year, most of which provide general information readily available on the website. Thus, researching the period from 1992 until 2014 provided a specific challenge. Here, I relied on open sources, such as strategic concepts and handbooks, press releases, and public communications outlets. One important source of information was the interviews I conducted with former NATO international staff members who had worked on these issues (see below). In addition, the NATO digital archive is not a prioritized task at present, and the evolving security environment since 2022 also makes it less viable for NATO to maintain an open-source policy. Another issue was that NATO decided to redo its website in late 2025. This made it difficult to obtain information at the time, and previously available sites were either modified or no longer accessible. I also conducted interviews with NATO headquarters staff on civil defense, emergency planning, and resilience, as well as with some experts in the field.

CHAPTER 2

Security Politics

This book primarily follows the premises of the Copenhagen School approach to security politics. In this tradition, it is commonly understood that security is not a neutral or fixed concept; instead, it is created through policy, and the language of the speech act of calling out security issues carries real-world implications. It aligns with the constructivist approach specified in the previous chapter, in that it seeks to map how issues are framed as "security" and what follows. Understanding the foundations of the concept and theory of security is essential to grasping the power it holds to enable and legitimize political actions, as well as the unique *productive* capacity of this multifaceted concept. The idea is that security, the concept, related concepts, and practices are shaped by a specific logic that can significantly impact the social and political world. To demonstrate this, I will explore the foundational ideas of the Copenhagen School of Security and incorporate insights from other scholars on the study of security politics.

Throughout history, the state has been regarded as the primary institution responsible for ensuring security. The state has also been considered the primary object requiring protection against both internal and external threats. To achieve this goal, governing techniques such as sovereign power, hierarchical structures, and command and control have been viewed as fundamental governance instruments for managing security (Wilson and Bakker 2016; Rådestad and Larsson 2020). The legitimacy of state power and violence is central to the liberal political tradition,

O. Larsson, *NATO's Approach to the Civil Dimensions of War*,
https://doi.org/10.1007/978-3-032-27871-5_2

which emphasizes the importance that such strong instruments of power must also be aligned with the rule of law and the protection of individual rights. In the modern world order, the sovereign state is the principal security agent tasked with installing and preserving the rule of law (Rae 2019). This model of domestic authority includes a normative dimension in which sovereignty is vested solely in the state, making it a necessary condition for the outward agency of states and a central part of the responsibility to protect their citizens. However, this raises important philosophical questions about the relationship between the individual and the state and the extent to which violence or other oppressive measures can be justified in pursuit of the common good. Ultimately, the legitimacy of state violence, along with social and political control, lies at the heart of debates about the nature of political power, the role of the state, and the limits of human freedom (Bartelson 1995, 2001; Walker 2010; Dean 2007).

It is with the emergence of the liberal tradition and the notion of autonomous individuals that old hierarchical systems and authorities, the feudal system, and God had to be replaced by a new way of thinking. The idea of a social contract could thus better explain the relationship between the state and the individual that would sustain the authority of the state (and the King) while also making sense of why free subjects would accept the authority of the state (Bartelson 1995, 2001). Here, we find an essential tension and binary relationship between liberty and security, and we will return to this with more nuance shortly. Despite considerable critique of the Hobbesian notion of state security and the image of the state as a Leviathan that protects people, this image remains central to the ideas of security today and may still serve as the foundation for the logic of security.

The discussion above delves into an important matter that has been a subject of debate and concern among political theorists and thinkers: the relationship between democracy and security. While it is evident that democratic states require a certain degree of security management and organization to ensure the survival of the state and the safety of their citizens, the very concept and practices of security pose a threat to democracy itself (Rae 2019). When problems are framed as security issues, the logic of security supports a rhetoric that can be exploited to justify the implementation of exceptional, undemocratic measures; we are awakening the Leviathan. In the face of an attack or a threat, democratic states may feel compelled to take emergency measures beyond normal politics and the rule of law, potentially leading to the erosion of civil liberties and the perversion of democracy into a permanent state of exception. This perilous path can ultimately lead to the emergence of autocratic rule (Bigo 2012).

Therefore, we must tread carefully when discussing the relationship between democracy and security and consider the possibility that measures to protect our safety may diminish fundamental democratic values and principles. I here follow Jeff Huysmans primary warning that "when security issues, institutions, and practices take a prominent role in the organization of social, political, cultural and economic issues, inequalities, exclusions, violence and other limits to democratic politics become more pronounced" (Huysmans 2014). Andreas Behnke has also found the relationship between democracy and security fragile, as the latter risks suspending the usual democratic process (Behnke 2000). For this reason, there can indeed be too much security. I would phrase it as security *crowds out* other values and priorities. The logic of security, the urge to be safe, also crowds out the possibility and desirability of uncertainties, opposition, and debate as it strives toward swift action and resolute decisions. Security politics becomes "a political practice that is defined through its tensions with the democratic organization of political life" (Huysmans 2014).

2.1 Securitization Theory

In today's world, security has become a ubiquitous concept, with its scope expanding across more sectors and issues than ever before. The politics of security is a phenomenon that requires careful examination. The question arises: how can we understand this expansion of security and the framing of more sectors and issues like security problems? This is where the *theory of securitization* provides essential insights. By analyzing how specific issues are elevated to the security realm, securitization theory offers a lens through which we can understand the power dynamics and discursive processes that contribute to the proliferation of security practices. This section will explore securitization theory in more detail, examining its key concepts and usefulness in understanding the contemporary security landscape.

While the notion of security had previously been exclusively associated with the threat, use, and control of military force, after the end of the Cold War, it came to include a host of other issues, including terrorism, global warming, natural disasters, global pandemics, refugees, energy, failed states, domestic vital systems, and a variety of public health problems. Securitization theory is based on the premise that security issues do not exist in themselves but are a product of contextual meaning-making insofar as security agents frame, argue for, and potentially gain acceptance for their specific views regarding a given issue, which they present as of great urgency and with high-stakes implications. Speaking security "is the move that takes politics beyond the established rules of the [political] game and frames the issue as either a special kind of politics or [even] as above politics" (Buzan et al. 1998).

In its most extreme form, security becomes a matter of life and death concerning our survival as individuals or a collective. Risks of annihilation, or even existential threats in specific contexts, would then purportedly justify the use of extraordinary measures to address them, given that both threats and countermeasures are deemed credible. In fact, "by labeling it as security, an agent claims a need for and the right to treat it by extraordinary means" (Buzan et al. 1998), therefore: "[T]he exact definition and criteria for securitization is constituted by the intersubjective establishment of an existential threat with a saliency sufficient to have substantial political effects" (Buzan et al. 1998).

The process of securitization is completed when the acceptance of breaking established rules emerges, but as we shall see, the audience is not always important. Or rather, the audience need not be the general public but could be bureaucrats, experts, and political elite involved in an entirely internal process of an organization such as NATO or the EU.

The view that security issues can be above politics and democracy, and that we may deploy extraordinary means to address this urgent and dangerous problem, has strong similarities with Carl Schmitt's (1888–1985) thought. Carl Schmitt was a German jurist and political theorist, but he was also a prominent and active member of the Nazi Party in Germany. For this reason, many find his writings fraudulent. Still, his work has been very influential among political theorists because he identified the weakness of liberal constitutionalism and the relationship between political power and legal systems. It is in this capacity that we may borrow some of his writings, because by understanding this paradox, it also becomes clear exactly how powerful the logic of security is and how the sense of urgency during a crisis indeed enables the emergence of executive and sovereign power (Vinx 2025). This is perhaps most explicitly captured in Carl Schmitt's discussion of how liberal constitutionalism has been weakened by the politics of exception. Schmitt argues that declaring a security occasion triggers an exception to the accepted rules and procedures, enables us to identify who holds sovereign power.

> The precise details of an emergency cannot be anticipated, nor can one spell out what may take place in such a case, especially when it is truly a matter of an extreme emergency and how it is to be eliminated (Schmitt 2005, 7).

Michael Williams maintains that such situations neither result simply from exercising the authority to declare a security incident nor as a diversion from normal procedures but are rather rooted in a sense of fear and danger that legitimizes the implementation of solutions that violate a given political constitution (Williams 2011, 218).

The Copenhagen School of Security and the theory of securitization currently comprise one of the more promising attempts to identify and understand the dynamics of security issues. It has primarily been successful in understanding the broader security agenda that arose after the end of the Cold War (Buzan et al. 1998). This highly influential theory (see for instance Baele and Jalea 2023) as well as (Salter 2019) is, of course, not without critical engagements. Some wish to raise the point that it is more than "speaking security" as there is also the need to attach the speech act to the material reality (Balzacq et al. 2016; Balzacq 2011, 2019). Others point out the relatively weak role of the audience and question the need for public acceptance (Côté 2016). Others still have suggested that we also need to understand why securitization attempts fail when they really should succeed (Salter 2010). Despite these critical reflections, it stands clear that the theory holds substantial value for understanding how security problems emerge and how the logic of security functions. However, the strength of the securitization theory is that it provides an analytical framework for anyone who wishes to study security politics. The theory provides an analytical framework for determining how different issues are constructed as security issues through the speech acts or other means of communication (images, cinema, podcasts, etc.) of the securitizing actors. It is thus possible to identify the different components of the securitizing process.

Referent objects are things seen to be existentially threatened and have a legitimate claim to survival. Here, we may add that "things" can also be securitized because of their function in a larger security system. Weaknesses and vulnerabilities can be securitized because their remediation may be deemed important for other security goals.

Securitizing actors securitize issues by declaring that something, a referent object, is existentially threatened. If one looks at an organization such as NATO, it is sometimes the securitizing actor, but it could also be specific experts or bodies within NATO that drive the security agenda.

Functional actors: actors who affect the dynamics of a sector. Without the referent object or the actor calling for security on behalf of the referent object, this actor significantly influences decisions in the security field. These functional actors then become central agents in addressing the security problem, they are activated as security agents.

In the case of NATO, we may encounter a range of actors with different roles: specialized bodies within NATO, member states, or even administrative bodies within member states. The concept of civil defense and later resilience in different sectors and administrative bodies, such as the Department of Agriculture or the Department of Transportation, could constitute these kinds of functional actors (see also Buzan et al. 1998). Functional actors are thus those identified to perform specific roles and duties to ensure that security objects are secured and protected. Civil administration and civil society may, at different times, be viewed as referent objects, securitizing actors, or functional actors.

This is very similar to what David Baldwin presented in his article "The Concept of Security." When we investigate security claims and security politics, we may consider the following: *Security for whom, security for which values, how much security, from what threats, by what means, at what costs, and during which time period* (David 1997).

This approach to analyzing and indeed deconstructing security politics fits well with the basic idea of this book, as it offers an analysis of how NATO (and, of course, actors within NATO) have considered the role of civil defense and civil administration in member states in relation to specific security problems. It is already clear that this view has shifted over time, concerning particular events and ideas that have become more salient through speech acts that we now can understand as securitization moves, or the speaking of security.

The idea of security as a contested concept and securitization theory are ways in which the researcher can engage with and problematize security politics. While the speech act of security/securitization can easily be thought of as a rational process in which a security frame is presented and accepted by the audience, securitization theory has been criticized for oversimplifying this process. According to securitization theory, the audience's acceptance of a security frame is essential to the success of a securitization move or speech act. However, this view fails to recognize that security is often a matter of concern for politicians and security experts, while the role of the audience is one of silent acceptance (Balzacq et al. 2016; Bigo 2006). In addition, security is closely linked to emotions, particularly fear and a general sense of danger (Kinnvall and Mitzen 2020). As Michael Williams pointed out regarding the emotions of security, the mere framing of political problems as threats is often enough to activate these emotions and legitimize measures that violate routine political procedures. Uncertainty and a sense of urgency further contribute to the audience's acceptance of extraordinary and extra-political measures (M. C. Williams 2003). The act of communication is complex, indecisive, and uncertain; the role of the audience is not necessarily one of granting legitimacy, and security politics itself is riddled with emotions of fear and uncertainty.

The question of what happens when international organizations such as NATO, UN, EU, AU, and others engage in securitization is pertinent. While these organizations tend to prioritize international, collective, and national security, the question of who constitutes the audience for their speech act remains unclear. In addition, it might even be absurd to talk about security as it would be a neat category or a single goal that we all could agree to, and even accept the obvious trade-offs of potential limitation on democracy and freedom. Security for whom and for which values remains utterly political and conflictual.

NATO is an intergovernmental organization with no public arenas or independent channels for scrutiny or communications. In addition, security, especially national and international security, is often shrouded in secrecy. Moreover, the issue of success or failure for moving issues into the arena of security is that this may be an entirely internal process at the international organization and invited experts; it may, after all, not require an audience or the approval of the public or even the elected politicians in the different member states. Still, once issues and identified problems, vulnerabilities, and weaknesses are identified as "security problems," they fall under the spell of that logic of security that this must be solved swiftly and resolutely, and there is no need or time to engage in the political and democratic process to discuss the matter.

2.2 The Balance of Security Politics

The idea that security policies contain elements that may threaten liberty and democratic values has, in fact, been a key concern for critical security scholars. Fleur Johns remarks, for instance, that security and the notion of exceptionalism "rings liberal alarm bells" (Johns 2005). Jef Huysmans observes in the same vein that

> [O]ne of the key characteristics of the jargon of exception is its suppression of the political renditions of the societal. In doing so, it eliminates one of the constituting categories of modern democratic politics, hence producing an impoverished and ultimately illusory understanding of political contestation and domination (Huysmans 2008)

Huysmans further argues that exceptionalism "erases the societal as a realm of multifaceted, historically structured political mediations and mobilizations" because of the specific way in which it frames political problems and solutions. Security and crisis events thereby allegedly constitute moments in which executive powers, to varying degrees, come to take precedence over democratic institutions and principles.

Others have raised concerns that this relationship might not be so drastic, and the fact that democratic institutions regularly handle both domestic and international security issues without declaring any state of emergency or exception could serve as proof (Neal 2019). A too strict adoption of fear of security or the overemphasis on executive decisions and exceptionalism makes us fall into the Hobbesian or Schmittian trap and ignore the fact that many security issues are often debated in political and public debates without the exclamation of a state of exception, martial laws, or even fear for our lives.

Every day, of course, there is news and political debates in parliament about a significant number of security threats; we might even get the sense that we are living in an era of hyper-security. The presence of climate change will most likely make parts of the world uninhabitable in the near future, and the fact that people are dying today due to climate change and climate-induced disasters. Still, no state of exception. The Russian attack on Ukraine and the many hybrid threats are still managed within a heightened security discourse, but not a state of exception, even though exceptional measures and economic aid packages are decided on to assist Ukraine. Securitization theory is essential for pointing out the logic and dynamics of security management. But it seldom results in any visible state of exceptions, more of a *heightened security politics/temperature*. Instead, security management is much more mundane, modest, granular, and incremental. For the most part, according to Bigo and McCluskey and the *Paris School of Security*, security is handled by experts and finds its way into policy and legal adjustments without public debate (Bigo and McCluskey 2018). This is also a crucial point to consider: we might not be willing to say that simply because something is framed as a security issue or more issues are considered in terms of security, the entire democratic system comes tumbling down. However, we may say that the democratic system and the space for political debate and oppositional voices run the risk of being hollowed out. Being too alarmist and searching for events and ideas that would truly violate rules and procedures would hamper our sensitivity to how everyday security management *crowds out* or *takes control* of the political agenda *without* any state of emergency or weakened civil and political rights.

Andrew Neal maintains that securitization theory is "the archetypical expression of security as anti-politics" and, therefore, alarmist to the extent that we often miss the incremental and everyday practices and adjustments to expanding security discourses. In his view, the conception that socially constructed security issues are, by definition and in practice, lifted from their context, detached from the procedures of everyday politics, and then placed into a context of executive decisions and exceptional and extraordinary measures that involve breaking established rules and violating constitutional rights and democratic procedures, is misleading. We should instead consider the fact that most security and crisis management efforts often go unnoticed as technocratic solutions to problems that may appear self-evident, routine, and not at all directly or immediately connected to high politics or life and death. Security politics must not be loud; it can be dead silent. For the most part, in our everyday lives, we are not experiencing security adjustments as a state of exception or the introduction of martial law. This may be especially true regarding societal security as a branch of, or support to, national security. The idea that societies should become more resilient and reduce vulnerability often includes a proactive stance on building or improving existing systems. Likewise, cybersecurity, increased surveillance in public spaces, more or better infrastructure, and other kinds of "improvements" may often go unseen or unfelt. Still, it is in this way that the sphere and logic of security expand. In this specific case, what is more important is that if NATO, as an intergovernmental organization, can "securitize" and dictate the priorities of civil administration and crisis management for the member states, the room for political and democratic influence diminishes further.

The exceptional tendencies of securitization become a dangerous element for democracies to manage, as they open up extraordinary measures and exceptional circumstances to normality. But less gloomy accounts of exceptionalism do exist. Bonnie Honnig, for instance, speaks of the need and possibility to "democratize the exception" and not allow fear and danger to undermine the democratic foundation of all politics, including security politics. In a similar vein, Aradau suggested that "desecuritization becomes an ethical–political choice which refuses to let democratic politics slip into exceptional politics" (Aradau 2004). If the slowness of democratic procedures ensures the possibility of contestation, the speed introduced by security eliminates the possibility of scrutiny and the expression of critical voices. She suggests that this creates tension in the perfect logic and rather strict binary between normal politics and the exception or security issue. Considering the process and possibility of de-securitization would allow us to de-escalate the speed and tensions brought about by securitization. Challenging security politics is not only essential but also aligns with the democratic principles of transparency and public accountability. As was mentioned earlier, the tension between democracy and security is a balancing act.

The main point is that security and securitization enable specific techniques of government, social, and political control to become more present, and with that, exclusions, violence, and other limits to democratic politics become more pronounced. Or, as I would like to put it, security crowds out other ways of thinking and alternative approaches to governance. The logic of security crowds out other values and priorities, aiming to eliminate uncertainties, opposition, and debate as it strives toward swift action and resolute decisions. This is why an excessive focus on security and specific ideas of security should be critically scrutinized, made debatable, and brought into the public and political sphere.

Security risks orient actors and individuals toward a mindset that extends the logic of security throughout society, skewing political debate and public policy priorities toward national security concerns. The current security situation consequently renders it increasingly necessary to investigate the unfolding discourse on the grey zone, hostility, and hybrid threats, and to examine in detail the policy solutions proposed by leading security organizations and experts. It is difficult to see how an expansion of security within its inherent logic could foster a world of freedom, democracy, or emancipation. It is much easier to imagine how security lends itself to visions of perfect order and social and political control, and how such visions take control of human experience and societies, in the name of security.

Speaking of security in neutral euphemisms such as "security management" or "security arrangements" tends to neutralize the political nature of security politics and make political action, opposition, or criticism redundant or even hysterical. This, while security and silence, fosters concession to authority and institutionalized violence and transforms human beings into objects and resources to be administered and governed (Neocleous 2008, 4). The current approach to countering hybrid threats through resilience and the erosion of clear differentiation between different types of threats and disruption runs the risk of reinstating a hegemonic view of security. We are closing in on a hegemonic view of security as "high politics" that mimics strategic studies during the Cold War. With it, the risk is that we return to an intellectual environment that provides little room for critical engagement with security and its efforts.

Throughout history, war has been an ever-present exception to the ideal of peace and to the pursuit of national and international order. Our own time is no different, but due to the increased complexity of society, it may be more challenging to identify precisely how the population is activated in the state's war-making capacity. War, as Jabri phrases it, "is technology of control" (2006), but not only of the enemy but also of the resources of society as well as the population. It can be said that "the defining moment of the modern state is its capacity, ultimately, to monopolize its control over the means of violence and to do so through the successful control of bodies and populations internally" (Jabri 2006, 56). This is precisely why we need a critical analysis of the current security discourse, including the extensive employment of the seemingly neutral notion of resilience. Only by understanding the logic, architecture, and foundations of the present security discourse can we begin to grasp its role for NATO, its member states, and, ultimately, all populations. This would hopefully provide us with enough insights to engage in a critical debate on the current *politics* of security.

CHAPTER 3

NATO: A Military Chameleon

Even though this book concerns NATO's approach to civil defense, it is essential to consider NATO's broader development in its first 75 years. This chapter, of course, cannot do justice to all aspects and complications. Still, it is crucial to understand what kind of organization NATO is and how it has responded to significant shifts in the regional and global geopolitical context. I write this overview while also considering recent books and articles that have analyzed NATO's various responses and changes, not least in its security discourse and overarching agenda. This chapter is a combined historical exposé and review of the most relevant research.

3.1 The Beginning of NATO

The North Atlantic Treaty was founded in 1949, shortly after World War II ended. In Europe, several agreements were signed among European nations to ensure mutual aid and foster future stability in a war-torn Europe. For instance, the Treaty of Dunkirk between France and the United Kingdom, and the Treaty of Brussels, which included France, the UK, and the Benelux countries. The latter formed the Brussels Treaty Organization, which later became known as the Western European Union (WEU). Both these treaties were designed to ensure mutual support and effort against future German and Soviet aggressions. From the

O. Larsson, *NATO's Approach to the Civil Dimensions of War*,
https://doi.org/10.1007/978-3-032-27871-5_3

outset, European countries were interested in involving North American nations in similar treaties, forming a kind of military cooperation and mutual insurance. In the US, the Truman Doctrine was launched in 1947, stating that communist and other authoritarian movements were to be opposed worldwide and that the US should support democratic nations and democratization in the world. The 1948 Czechoslovak coup d'état spurred the need for a broader alliance against Soviet expansion in Europe. Eventually, 12 countries in Europe and across the Atlantic became part of the original North American Treaty.[1] The North American Treaty Organization was founded on April 4, 1949. The original treaty was drafted by the Canadian diplomat Lester B. Pearson (Kaplan 1999). Lord Hastings Lionel Ismay was NATO's first Secretary General, a position he was initially reluctant to accept. By the end of his service, Ismay had changed his mind and became one of the main advocates of the organization, according to NATO's historical account. He stated the rather catchy phrase of the original purpose of NATO: to *"keep the Soviet Union out, the Americans in, and the Germans down"* (NATO 2023).

3.2 Community and Enlargement

Scholars interested in the persistence of NATO have suggested that rather than a strict military alliance between nations, NATO evolved into a "security community" that, in turn, fostered a new identity among the member states and NATO as an organization (Adler 1997; Risse-Kappen 2016). Throughout the years, cooperation, mutual trust, and intense socialization created a bond between member states that helped reshape NATO's purpose after its counterpart, the Warsaw Pact, dissolved in 1991. Michael Williams and Iver B. Neumann have suggested that a vital part of the identity of NATO was that it was forged by democratic states, and this identity was later used to sustain NATO after the end of the Cold War, as its focus turned away from the Soviet Union and reformed into an idea to defend democracy across the globe. The expansion and inclusion of more European countries, especially those from the former Warsaw Pact, were a consequence of the concept of "democratic security communication" (Williams 2007). Since its establishment in 1949, the possibility of expanding the North Atlantic Treaty Organization (NATO)

[1] Belgium, Canada, Denmark, France, Iceland, Italy, Luxembourg, the Netherlands, Norway, Portugal, the United Kingdom, and the United States.

has been a topic of discussion. The Treaty's founding document, specifically Article 10, stated that "The Parties may, by unanimous agreement, invite any other European State in a position to further the principles of this Treaty and to contribute to the security of the North Atlantic area to accede to this Treaty." This provision reflected a practical, pragmatic approach, recognizing that countries that participated in the pre-NATO discussions could join later.

The principle of an open-door policy has been fundamental to NATO's enlargement strategy. As stated on its official website and reiterated in various statements and communiques, "NATO membership is open to any other European state in a position to further the principles of this Treaty and to contribute to the security of the North Atlantic area." This commitment to openness has been a hallmark of NATO's approach to security and cooperation in the Euro-Atlantic region. Nations such as Ireland, Switzerland, and Sweden participated in the initial discussions that led to the formation of NATO, but for various reasons, they decided not to join in 1949. Sweden, for example, wished to continue with its long-standing security policy of non-alignment in peace and neutrality in war, which it had relied on during the two world wars. Nonetheless, the alliance accepted new members as early as 1952, with the admission of Greece and Turkey, followed by West Germany in 1955.

It is worth noting that West Germany's admission to NATO in 1955 prompted the creation of the Warsaw Pact as a direct response. This military alliance was formed by the Soviet Union and its satellite states in Eastern Europe to counterbalance the perceived threat posed by NATO's creation and unity. The creation of the Warsaw Pact complemented the already existing Council for Mutual Economic Assistance, a regional economic organization established by the Soviet Union in January 1949 for the communist states of Central and Eastern Europe. This precursor to the Warsaw Pact was oriented both toward economic cooperation and ideological unity among its members.

Despite the geopolitical challenges and tensions that accompanied the early years of NATO's expansion, the alliance has remained committed to its open-door policy. This policy has enabled NATO to expand its reach and influence across the Euro-Atlantic region, fostering deep cooperation and security commitment among its member states. The expansion of NATO continued in subsequent years, with the organization welcoming new members from Central and Eastern Europe after the fall of the Soviet Union. Overall, the possibility of enlargement was built into NATO's founding document, reflecting the alliance's commitment to promoting security and stability in the North Atlantic region through partnerships with like-minded nations.

Even though NATO maintained that "NATO enlargement has enhanced the security and stability of the entire Euro-Atlantic area" (Warsaw Summit 2016). Tracey German wrote in *International Affairs* that this "assertion is debatable when considered within the context of current tensions between Russia and the West" (German 2017). As noted by Tracey German, NATO has not been willing to allow Georgia or Ukraine membership. Action Plans also show that NATO prioritized its relationship with Russia and does not want to induce more tension along the eastern boundaries (German 2017). It is worth noting that Western leaders assured Gorbachev in 1990 that NATO would not expand eastward and "take advantage" of the dissolution of the Warsaw Pact, but this soon changed. Former members of the Warsaw Pact joined NATO in two waves after 1990 (Eichler 2021, 34). In addition, NATO has not only expanded by the inclusion of new formal member states. The edited volume *NATO—The Power of Partnerships* explores NATO's partnership structures with non-member states. It outlines different types of partnerships and their political and military utilities for NATO. The authors conclude that partnerships are complex and pragmatic, yet likely to provide NATO with both greater security and global influence. These partnerships were seen as a way to strengthen the Alliance during a time of diminishing resources and an internal legitimacy crisis (Edström et al. 2011). This, of course, is something that needs to be considered besides the growth of NATO through formal memberships.

NATO enlargement should perhaps be considered from a more pragmatic outlook. Although the North Atlantic Treaty listed "democracy" as a "founding principle," Portugal, one of the original treaty partners, was under the authoritarian Estado Novo regime when the treaty was signed. Similarly, Turkey and Greece were the first countries to join NATO after its formation and were not suspended from the alliance during periods of democratic backsliding. Cold War necessities could explain these exceptions to the democratic principle. However, there have been significant changes in NATO's approach and outspoken commitment to democracy. According to Poast and Chinchilla (2020), the Strategic Concept of NATO, periodically revised, has increasingly emphasized democracy over time. The 1968 document contained zero uses of the word "democracy" and 28 uses of "deterrence." In contrast, the 1991 document contained

5 mentions of "democracy" and just 6 of "deterrence," and the 1999 document contained 12 mentions of both terms. Furthermore, NATO's expansion in the 1990s was formally motivated by the encouragement and support of democratic reforms. However, it appears that NATO's true concern for democracy emerged only after the end of the Cold War (Poast and Chinchilla 2020).

The end of the Cold War provided NATO with the opportunity to redefine its purpose to promote international security and stability and support democratic development worldwide. However, NATO's membership did not necessarily lead to increased democracy in its new members or states applying for membership. A quantitative analysis conducted by Poast and Chinchilla of the countries that joined NATO in 2004 and control countries found that NATO membership and the prospect of NATO membership were not associated with increased democracy scores. However, being an applicant or becoming a member state of the European Union was associated with higher democracy scores. Therefore, NATO alone cannot account for the significant improvements in democracy scores among prospective members, as most of these states also applied for EU membership. Their findings suggest that interaction between international institutions composed mostly of democracies and less democratic partners on functional areas like security will not necessarily lead to an increase in democracy in partner states (Poast and Chinchilla 2020).

There is no doubt that NATO wishes to be associated with freedom and democracy. The introduction to the NAT 1949 states: "The Parties to this Treaty reaffirm their faith in the purposes and principles of the Charter of the United Nations and their desire to live in peace with all peoples and all governments. They are determined to safeguard the freedom, common heritage, and civilization of their peoples, founded on the principles of democracy, individual liberty, and the rule of law. They seek to promote stability and well-being in the North Atlantic area. They are resolved to unite their efforts for collective defence and for the preservation of peace and security" (NATO 1949). Despite NATO's best intentions to safeguard and promote democracy, it remains a military alliance focused on building the defense institutions of new member and partner states. Historical analysis of NATO expansion indicates that even when the tools of membership incentives and aid are at their strongest, security regimes and international institutions do not necessarily enhance domestic democratic governance. And no country has yet been expelled from the alliance for democratic backsliding.

3.3 NATO After the End of the Cold War

The dissolution of the Soviet Union and the end of the Cold War marked a significant milestone in NATO's history. The Alliance was established with the primary objective of countering Soviet expansionism through military power, ideology, and geography. The fall of the Berlin Wall in November 1989 and the disintegration of communist governments in Poland, Hungary, Czechoslovakia, East Germany, Romania, and Bulgaria set in motion a chain of events that would ultimately lead to the end of the Warsaw Pact. The Pact was officially disbanded on February 25, 1991, and, subsequently, on July 1, 1991, Czechoslovak President Vaclav Havel declared its end.

An important part of understanding the dissolution of both the Warsaw Pact and the Soviet Union was the reforms introduced by Mikhail Gorbachev. The policy of openness (Glasnost) and restructuring (Perestroika), along with other initiatives, triggered popular uprisings that eventually paved the way for the Soviet Union's fall. The dissolution of the Warsaw Pact was followed by the Soviet Union's collapse in December 1991, marking the end of an era of geopolitical tension and ideological conflict. The significance of these events cannot be overstated, as they had far-reaching implications for global politics and international relations. It reshaped the world as we knew it at the time, sent IR as a discipline into a state of crisis, and could have led to the dissolution of NATO. But it didn't. Let us revisit some key events that shaped NATO during the post-Cold War era.

In the beginning, after the end of the Cold War, NATO and Russia sought common ground. They established some areas of cooperation, focusing on developing dialogue and practical cooperation in areas of mutual interest, foremost in disaster and crisis management. As a result, NATO-Russia relations began to take shape, with Russia joining the North Atlantic Cooperation Council in 1991, followed by the Euro-Atlantic Partnership Council in 1997. Practical cooperation between the two entities began after Russia joined the Partnership for Peace program in 1994 and deployed peacekeepers in support of NATO-led peace support operations in the Western Balkans. The NATO-Russia Founding Act of 1997 provided the formal basis for bilateral relations, including the establishment of the NATO-Russia Permanent Joint Council (PJC) as a forum for consultation and cooperation. Dialogue and cooperation between NATO and Russia were further strengthened in 2002, with the PJC being replaced by the NATO-Russia Council (NRC), which serves as a forum for consultation, consensus-building, cooperation, joint decision-making, and joint action. At the same time, conflicts and issues arose and began to seriously deteriorate by the new millennium. For instance, Russia froze its relations with NATO in 1999 over differences regarding the Kosovo crisis, but cooperation activities resumed following the end of NATO's controversial air campaign in Serbia. However, Russia's actions in Georgia in August 2008 became a crisis for the diplomatic relations between NATO and Russia. This halted the NRC's formal meetings and closed the door to further cooperation in international crisis management. In April 2014, NATO suspended all practical civilian and military cooperation with Russia in response to its military intervention and hybrid warfare in Ukraine, as well as its illegal annexation of Crimea. In October 2021, Russia suspended the work of its diplomatic mission to NATO, required NATO to close down the NATO Information Office in Moscow, and suspended the work of the NATO Military Liaison Mission in Moscow (NATO 2023b; Eichler 2021).

NATO's involvement in the Bosnian War and the Kosovo crisis not only disrupted NATO-Russian relations. In fact, this event provides yet another instance in which NATO's double standards were brought to the fore, underscoring that policing international security issues is very difficult. The air campaign and the bombing of strategic sites in Serbia with civilian casualties have been a source of much controversy. In the book, *Security as Practice—Discourse Analysis and the Bosnian War*, Lene Hansen conducts a discourse analysis of the West and NATO's involvement in the civil war of former Yugoslavia. Hansen argues that identity and divergent discourses on how to understand the "other," i.e., the Balkans, shaped NATO's operations. The bombing of Serbia was the first time it operated without the approval of the UN Security Council. The author argues that identity politics and ethnic discourse played a significant role in NATO's decision-making as it sought to navigate two distinct approaches simultaneously.

The Balkans were viewed as separate from the West and seen as "the other"—something or someone different from the West. This led to the development of the "Balkanization discourse," which suggested that the war in Bosnia was a result of ancient hatred and a conflict that the West could not solve. The other discourse present at the time was the "genocide discourse," meaning that the attack on Bosnia was a genocide committed by Serbia military and police forces and that the West and NATO had an ethical obligation to come to Bosnia's aid. The discourse of "balkanization" was more prevalent in America, while the discourse of "genocide" was stronger in Europe. This resulted in ambivalent approaches to the Balkan crisis and contradictory approaches and internal tensions during the operations. Still, NATO was pressed to demonstrate its utility in the post-Cold War world and to adopt a new approach to international crises (Hansen 2013).

This period of normalization is a topic that Vincent Pouliot covers in the book *International Security in Practice—The Politics of NATO-Russia Diplomacy* (Pouliot 2010). This feels like a book from a completely different era, but it also shows how swift the winds of change can sweep across Europe and the globe. Pouliot analyzes in his book the many ways they tried to normalize their diplomatic relations and find common ground for managing international security in Europe and the world. Pouliot suggests that we could adopt a different perspective on international security—one that emphasizes the practices and logic of day-to-day diplomacy. He argues, based on his study of Russia and NATO, that there is great promise for peaceful solutions when "security practitioners engage in the non-violent resolution of disputes as if it were the axiomatic way to go, they come to debate with diplomacy but not about its opportunity" (Pouliot 2010). Yet despite some important pacification between NATO and Russia, they are still caught up in "intense symbolic power struggles" and this, along with the long period of Cold War and ideological conflicts between NATO and Russia, provided a far too fragile common ground to build a joint security community of shared values (Pouliot 2010). Pouliot identifies the deterioration between NATO and Russia that occurred around 2008. NATO cannot simply accept and admit "Moscow's Great Power habitus," and it became obvious that Russia would not merely subsume to the liberal order of international relations or accept NATO's standpoint and influence over Russian interests and worldview. Pouliot suggests that if NATO wants Russia to play by the rules, it should provide it with enough symbolic resources to at least stay in the game. Eventually, it became impossible for Russia to accept NATO-imposed rules for how to manage international and domestic security (Pouliot 2010). Jan Eichler reaches a similar conclusion in his book, arguing that NATO enlargement has pushed Russia into a corner of the world, with its previous sense of national security resting on the "buffer zone" of Eastern European countries that were part of the Warsaw Pact. National sovereignty to decide which alliance you want to belong to is part of being sovereign and of deciding the nation's fate as the population sees fit. This, however, does not change the fact that Russia may feel very pressed and vulnerable and that finds the new geopolitical situation intolerable. So intolerable that it cannot accept the color revolutions in the Caucasus, and force its will on Georgia in 2008, and Ukraine in 2014, and then again in 2022 (Eichler 2021).

Reflecting on the relationship between NATO and Russia after the end of the Cold War, it is crucial to consider not only NATO's actions but also the political developments within Russia during this period. While many had hoped for a period of increasing democratization and liberal reforms, the Russian society has instead regressed toward an autocratic system. Under Putin's leadership, Russia has become a society in which power is highly centralized, corruption is rampant, public institutions are weak, and the rule of law is not grounded in individual rights. This raises important philosophical and political questions about the nature of power, the role of institutions, and the relationship between citizens and their government in Russia (Snegovaya 2023; Sperling 2018).

Andreas Behnke investigates the discursive processes through which NATO reproduced a geopolitical order after the end of the Cold War. As the former constitutive "other" disappears, NATO is striving to sustain its identity as a community that carries essential moral and political values. NATO engages in peace operations and international crisis management. The conflict in the former Yugoslavia constituted a bridging moment, as well as the 9/11 terrorist acts on American soil, which is the only time that Article 5 has been activated in NATO. A new identity emerges, and instead of the West and the East, it becomes "the West and the rest." NATO expands its agenda, and new threats become more imminent, such as terrorism, weapons of mass destruction, cyberattacks, and other "disturbances" that threaten the peaceful liberal international order. Paradoxically, the end of the Cold War did not result in a final victory for the West. Instead, Behnke argues that it opens the possibility of a de-centering of security and the enemy, as it is no longer possible to completely define the identity, purpose, goals, and strategy of the new "other," the Rest instead of the East. Hence, "from this perspective, what is at stake in NATO's post-Cold War discourse is not only the institutional survival of the Alliance ... at stake is the ability of the pre-eminent Western security institution to surveillance, cognize and map the world on its own epistemic terms..." (Behnke 2013). Behnke's contribution is vital, as it illustrates a substantial shift in the security discourse governing NATO, the broader security agenda, and the geographical scope of NATO, moving beyond national security and armed attacks to a global rather than regional focus. I believe that there have been further changes in the security discourse since the annexation of Crimea in 2014. This event did not simply return NATO to the old Cold War dichotomy, but instead led to further shifts in NATO's underlying security discourse. As 10 years have passed since Behnke's book, it is important to analyze NATO through a critical security lens to understand how these shifts have affected the organization.

The resurgence of NATO and the idea of a collective Western alliance gained significant traction following Russia's aggressive actions in Ukraine, which resulted in the occupation of parts of its territory. This condemnable act drew widespread disapproval from the United Nations, the European Union, and NATO, leading to the imposition of sanctions on Russia and influential Russian individuals imposed by various countries and organizations. While it is not the central focus of this book to delve into this episode exhaustively, it is noteworthy for the present study because Russia's violation of international law, use of violence, and employment of hybrid warfare techniques evoked a renewed sense of purpose for NATO and transformed it from its post-Cold War policies and priorities. This episode has also prompted a re-examination of the philosophical and academic underpinnings of collective security and international cooperation in the modern era, as well as a return to strategic studies.

In early 2014, a series of events unfolded in Ukraine, culminating in the Euromaidan protests. These protests led to the ousting of the pro-Russian president, Viktor Yanukovych, and the subsequent Revolution of Dignity. Despite this political transformation, pro-Russian unrest persisted in eastern and southern Ukraine. The situation was further complicated by the unmarked Russian troops' invasion of Ukraine's Crimea, which was coupled with a wide range of hybrid warfare tactics, such as cyber-attacks and sabotage (Renz 2016, 2018; Allison 2014). A controversial and illegal referendum followed the annexation of Crimea by Russia. In April 2014, a group of pro-Russian separatists seized control of government buildings in the Donbas region of Ukraine. It declared the creation of two independent states—the Donetsk People's Republic (DPR) and the Luhansk People's Republic (LPR). This led to the initiation of the pseudo-Donbas War, which was a proxy war supported by Russia. The separatists received significant but secretive support from Russia, and despite Ukraine's attempts to regain control of the separatist-held regions, they were unsuccessful. Russia has consistently denied its involvement in the war, but it is widely believed that Russian troops were involved in the fighting.

In February 2015, Russia and Ukraine signed the Minsk II agreements to end their conflict. However, the implementation of these agreements never came to fruition over the following years. The war in the Donbas region has since become a violent and unchanging conflict between the two countries, with little change in territorial control and only brief periods of ceasefires. The conflict has been marked by naval incidents, cyber-warfare, and heightened political tensions since 2014, but has remained low-intense. In addition, in February 2022, Russia launched a full-scale invasion of Ukraine, which resulted in the occupation of larger portions of the country and further intensified this long-standing conflict. International organizations such as the UN, EU, and NATO have taken this later escalation far more seriously. There has been massive support for Ukraine in the form of sanction packages targeting Russia and Russian leaders, military equipment, and other forms of military support, as well as economic aid sent to Ukraine.

The 2014 attack on Ukraine and later the 2022 full-scale attack have pushed for an updated and modified orientation toward a bipolar world, and cold war logics, and military conflict and capacity became a vivid topic. But more than that, Russia's actions, hybrid warfare, and the emergence of a grey zone in international relations, in which hybrid threats are present, have since 2014 expanded the idea of (national) security to encompass "whole-of-society" responses. It has introduced resilience as a guiding principle for NATO and, consequently, preparations for coping with all kinds of disturbances and disruptions in peacetime, connecting them with national and military capacity, constitute an unprecedented expansion of security that takes us back to notions of total war and total defense.

The literature reviewed in this introduction, which has analyzed NATO throughout the years, illustrates one vital aspect for NATO: *security comes first*. Security is the defining principle and top priority of the North Atlantic Treaty Organization. The main reason for its birth after WWII was the fear of Russian and German aggression in a war-torn Europe. Throughout NATO's history, different threats and security concerns have come and gone, while others have remained. For instance, West Germany joined NATO on May 6, 1955, only one day after its status as an occupied country ended. When Germany's reunification took place on October 3, 1990, Berlin was reinstated as the capital, and the former German Democratic Republic joined the Federal Republic of Germany and became a part of NATO. East Germany had withdrawn from the Warsaw Pact in September 1990, just a few days before German unity. Russia, the Soviet Union, and soon the Warsaw Pact, and then Russia again, have, however, remained as one of the prominent security threats. During this time, however, the understanding of security has changed quite significantly. In the beginning, security was foremost about national and sovereign security, and military attacks on the territory of member states were the main threat to be considered. A similar situation is now unfolding, but the development in the United States during 2025 and 2026, and what seems to be a return to the Monroe Doctrine as it attacked Venezuela, and the way it repeats its claims and threat to annex Greenland from an ally in NATO, may in fact be the most severe political crisis in NATO history. If we continue to focus NATO's efforts on encouraging, influencing, and gaining control over the civil administration and civil dimensions of member states to boost deterrence under Article 3, this cannot be analyzed without recapturing the key concept in our time: *resilience*. The next chapter is devoted to the conceptual and theoretical debate surrounding resilience, to make sense of NATO's development from 2014 onward.

CHAPTER 4

Political Dimensions of Resilience

I first became interested in NATO's investment in civil defense over the years because of its recent adoption of resilience as one of its main strategic concepts. I will provide more details about the empirical development of this concept in Chap. 8. However, for the theoretical discussion on resilience that I want to focus on in this chapter, it is sufficient to note that resilience was included in NATO's vocabulary at the Warsaw Summit in 2016 and included as a Strategic Concept in 2022. The official communique of the Warsaw Summit states that:

> Today we have made a commitment to continue to enhance our resilience and to maintain and further develop our individual and collective capacity to resist any form of armed attack. Civil preparedness is a central pillar of Allies' resilience and a critical enabler for Alliance collective defence. While this remains a national responsibility, NATO can support Allies in assessing and, upon request, enhancing their civil preparedness. We will improve civil preparedness by achieving the NATO Baseline Requirements for National Resilience, which focus on continuity of government, continuity of essential services, security of critical civilian infrastructure, and support to military forces with civilian means. In this context, we welcome the Resilience Guidelines approved by Defence Ministers in June 2016 (NATO 2016c).

As mentioned earlier, after this summit, NATO has increasingly focused on building resilience to counter hybrid threats and enhance

O. Larsson, *NATO's Approach to the Civil Dimensions of War*,
https://doi.org/10.1007/978-3-032-27871-5_4

deterrence. This emphasis on resilience will significantly shape NATO's approach to civil defense and civil administration across member states. The concept has become so crucial that NATO in 2022 renamed its Senior Civil Emergency Planning Committee (SCEPC), established in the 1950s, to the Resilience Committee (RC). Moreover, NATO now considers resilience a guiding principle and the core meaning of Article 3 in the original treaty. NATO is being proactive in this new defense aspect and is closely monitoring the implementation of an extensive resilience program in its member states. This way, NATO expands what it believes is required by member states beyond its traditional military focus and defense capabilities, and it is of great interest to know the extent of this program and how diligently NATO is pursuing its implementation.

Why might resilience be problematic in this context? To fully comprehend the significance of this newly embraced concept, it is essential to revisit the theoretical debate around resilience. My argument is that when resilience becomes a security matter, it enables preemptive management and promotes programmatic approaches in which the whole society, including individuals, is viewed as a function or cog in a Foucauldian security apparatus. Consequently, resilience is imbued with a specific set of priorities and content that is difficult to challenge. This is partly due to the prevailing notion that resilience is simply the desirable capacity of a unit or system to withstand shocks and disturbances and to quickly recover from adverse events and disruptions without clarifying costs and trade-offs.

In this chapter, I aim to discuss the concept of resilience and show that it can also be understood as a highly political concept that enables specific forms of social and political control, thereby shaping the *governmentality* of security throughout NATO and the member states. Resilience is a crucial concept in the emerging security discourse, and we need a proper theoretical comprehension of it. Furthermore, a vast amount of academic literature has examined and analyzed this concept, and it is to this literature that the book aims to connect its findings and contribute new insights into the new application of resilience as a core part of national and international security regimes.

4.1 The Roots of Resilience

Resilience is a rapidly spreading concept across different policy areas in international organizations, nation-states, and local governments. Despite its popularity, many people and policymakers do not clearly understand its meaning. According to David E. Alexander's (2013) etymological inquiry, it is an old Latin word, but its meaning and immediate connotations have substantially shifted over time. Initially, it had a negative connotation of crawling, avoiding, or simply returning. At the end of the nineteenth century, resilience was widely used to describe disaster recovery as returning to normal, crawling back, or doing minor incremental rebuilding (Alexander 2013). In psychology, it is a concept that has been used since the 1950s, the idea of children and adult patients who have been exposed to trauma and risk, but still do not develop any pathological symptoms (Seery et al. 2010). Some even trace it back to the 1940s within psychology and psychiatry and credit Norman Garmezy, Emmy Werner, and Ruth Smith (Manyena 2006).

According to Alexander (2013), the psychiatrist Fredric Flach popularized the concept among the public as a way to describe the attribute of an individual's ability to recover from trauma in the late 1980s. In the 1970s, ecologist Crawford Holling laid the groundwork for the concept of ecosystem resilience. This understanding of resilience as a system-oriented concept is popular in crisis and security management and may explain its extreme hype in recent years (Joseph 2018; Alexander 2013).

Resilience entered the field of crisis management at the end of the twentieth century. Despite its popularity in this field and in policy practices, its exact meaning is difficult to detect, and it can vary extensively depending on the specific policy area in which it is adopted (climate change or cybersecurity), as well as the context, location, geography, and administrative level. For instance, when talking about resilience and disaster preparedness in the global south to cope with climate change and disasters/disaster reductions, or as NATO has started using resilience to boost deterrence and military strength, resilience appears in two completely different political contexts and purposes. A general note, however, is that resilience often receives a positive or even normative meaning, as it has commonly come to mean systems or actors that are able to "proactively adapt to and recover from disturbances" (Comfort et al. 2010).

4.2 Resilience and Society

Within academic circles, the pursuit and application of resilience in response to crises and disruptions has been a topic of considerable interest and investigation. However, scholars have expressed varying levels of enthusiasm regarding its practical implementation. Extensive analyses of resilience's theoretical and philosophical underpinnings have been conducted, and many researchers have devoted significant effort to creating more detailed analytical frameworks. In this literature, resilience is often linked to societal security or crisis management, but few studies have examined resilience as part of national or traditional security. Some of the most critical voices have, however, suggested that resilience enables and produces substantial social and political control, supports a widespread acceptance of future crises, has an inbuilt connection to neoliberalism, and encourages "the art of living dangerously" (Evans and Reid 2014). For these reasons, some even argue that it is time to abandon this concept altogether as it has become deeply problematic. Let us consider some of the current problematizations in this academic debate.

Holling's seminal 1973 article, "Resilience and Stability of Ecological Systems," provides groundbreaking insight into the changes that occur within ecological systems in response to external shocks and disturbances. Instead of returning to their original state, these systems undergo a process of adaptation, resulting in new relationships and a new equilibrium that is (even) more resilient to future disturbances. In this context, resilience is defined as the capacity of a system to undergo change, reorganize, and adapt while still maintaining its fundamental functions. This ability to persist and change is vital to the survival of ecological systems, and Holling's work provides a framework for understanding how these systems can continue to thrive in the face of adversity (Holling 1973). This is later adopted in systemic approaches to crisis management in complex societies (Joseph 2018). Brand and Jax (2007) suggested that while the original and naturalistic ecological dimension of resilience still holds importance, it is foremost the social, political, and institutional aspects of resilience that have sustained its popularity in crisis management (Brand and Jax 2007). In translating resilience from ecology to society, elements of complexity, self-organization, diversity, and heterogeneity are often added to the mix, creating a comprehensive and forgiving approach to crisis management and social security. This is evident in

Bridie McGreavy's work, which analyzes how resilience is implemented in national policy. She applies a Foucauldian archaeological approach and notes that resilience seldom stands on its own but is part of a more expansive complex of discourses and governance regimes that together shape national crisis management systems. Still, resilience has gained prominence and importance in the UK's national crisis management. She notes that such systems can be divided into a cybernetic view, in which humans are in control, and Complex Adjustable Systems (CAS), in which humans either adapt to the system or stand outside it with little immediate control (McGreavy 2016).

To further complicate the understanding of resilience when applied to crisis and security management, it speaks to all three phases of a crisis. It aspires to have the capacity to bridge both prevention (proactivity) and response (reactivity) to crises (Chmutina et al. 2016), but also play a decisive role in the learning phase and adaptation that usually takes place in the post-crisis phase (Aldrich 2012). Another important caveat that researchers have found is that resilience is being adopted in policies worldwide. This, at the same time, makes it difficult to discern if resilience should be understood as a process or a goal. Siambabala Bernard Manyena studied the FN's International Strategy for Disaster Risk Reduction as the organization adopted the Hyogo declaration in 2005. It was at the time seen as a global blueprint for disaster risk reduction efforts but was replaced by the Sendai framework in 2015. Maynyena noted some core problems with the notion of resilience. For instance, it lacked philosophical foundations, a clear definition, and substance; it offered no guidance for implementation. Manyena also noted that it was difficult to understand whether resilience was to be seen as an outcome or a process (Manyena 2006). The need to differentiate resilience as a goal or process was also highlighted by (Chmutina et al. 2016) in their study of how resilience has been incorporated into crisis management in the UK. They also noted that there was tension between various understandings of resilience at different administrative levels. Indeed lack of commonly accepted definitions and models has inevitably led to tensions in decision-making and intense debates in academic literature (Chmutina et al. 2016; Lizarralde et al. 2015).

While resilience in ecology often considers rapid shifts and external shocks that test the system's ability to adapt, societal resilience is much broader and includes such things as pandemics, economic shocks, terrorist threats, climate change, natural disasters (Welsh 2014), and more recently, as a way to cope with new security challenges such as hybrid threats and antagonistic challenges (Rådestad and Larsson 2018; Larsson 2021). Societal resilience refers to the ability to cope with disturbances and disruptions. Resilience is therefore often connected to a normative element; resilience is always good, and the more resilience, the better (Joseph 2018). In addition, a particular branch of resilience research invokes the sub-concept of *community resilience*. This kind of research may involve public administration, law, and formal institutions, but those elements are secondary to the community's adaptive capacity, i.e., local civil society. This research focuses on how communities utilize their social networks, communication, sense of belonging, social learning, and readiness to accept change (Berkes and Ross 2013; Koliou et al. 2015). Community resilience focuses on how people and local organizations work together to survive and to strive during crises, but it is also, albeit to a lesser extent, considered the recovery phase. Sara Bondesson's recent book provides an excellent example of how political struggles, grief, and anger may arise after a crisis (Bondesson 2022). In such situations, various aspects of social capital, cohesion, and heterogeneity are decisive factors in explaining how communities cope during and after major crises (Aldrich and Meyer 2015; Aldrich 2012).

In a more positive vein, it has also been suggested that crises are not only bad per se but offer opportunities for learning, adapting, and renewal (Berkes et al. 2008; Folke et al. 2010; Pike et al. 2010). Resilience can, therefore, at times, include and promote the capacities of the entire system to cope with shocks and disruptions as well as the capacity to learn and adapt (Joseph 2018, 15). This makes resilience very attractive for policymakers and politicians. It can reduce the safety and security responsibilities that public administrations often bear, highlighting the instability of systems and the need to accept disruptions, renewal, and human adaptability. It also shifts the state's responsibility for safety and security and its administrative capacity toward the community, civil society, and individuals (Bergström 2018; Rådestad and Larsson 2020). This is sometimes considered a positive aspect of resilience, enabling governance to become more reflective and adaptive. For instance, Korosteleva and Flockhart argue in the introduction to the special issue on Resilience in *Contemporary Security Policy* that when we allow resilience to be "an analytic of governance, resilience ought to be seen as a form of "self-governance," which emphasizes the "local" and the "person" in inside-out processes of learning and capacity-building to help a self-referential agency to find its own equilibrium" (Korosteleva and Flockhart 2020). In this way, resilience can make use of "ideational, institutional, and material resources" as well as respond to "internal ontological security seeking" (Korosteleva and Flockhart 2020; Flockhart 2016).

Korosteleva and Flockhart note that promoting resilience as a self-reliant system of governance poses one of the biggest challenges of the resilience-building process. Is it indeed possible to deliver good governance to distressed systems while prioritizing "the local" and "working within, not against the community-based system." It is suggested that self-governance should be promoted without making external intervention embarrassing or implausible. That strength and capacities should be based on a "qualified understanding of choice and freedom." The authors here support such a normative position, drawing on Amartya Sen (1985) and closely following a model of local, democratic, and good governance as a sort of fundamental element of resilience. To conflate resilience with all these elements, the community, the local democracy, and good governance, I would argue, runs the risk of making us blind to precisely the things that Korosteleva and Flockhart warn us about, namely "… to stop resilience from becoming a ready-made solution for security-predicated measures in the interests of the established power configurations" (Korosteleva and Flockhart 2020). I share these concerns and think we need to take them seriously. What exactly is promised and contained in the policies of nations and international organizations that promote resilience? Therefore, it is vital to consider the political aspects of resilience and how it can constitute a form of governmentality that governs at a distance. We cannot simply accept the face value of how NATO and others are currently framing resilience. To understand the social and political power of the resilience discourse, we must also consider critical accounts of resilience before turning to its ongoing practices and implementations in the real world.

4.3 The Political Dimension

Many researchers note that resilience fits surprisingly well with a neoliberal or minimal state and the political agenda of network and community governance (Chandler 2013; Evans and Reid 2014; Rådestad and Larsson 2020; Bergström 2018). We can see some of the elements of such an orientation above, especially the idea of r*esponsibilization* of actors other than the state and the activation of societal actors to manage crises without the state. Resilience often includes ideas of decentralization, contextualization, autonomy, and the independence of political institutions and the public bureaucracy (Korosteleva and Flockhart 2020). The latter are seen as facilitators rather than those who should perform the hard work and assume the responsibility (O'Grady and Shaw 2023). Joseph (2013) argues that resilience aligns well with a neoliberal political agenda that emphasizes self-awareness, reflexivity, and accountability. Joseph, therefore, connects resilience with the idea of "active citizenship" (Joseph 2013a). Neoliberal security governance encourages individuals to take responsibility for their own security rather than relying on the state. This approach promotes resilience and self-reliance rather than dependence on the government for security. There is thus an increasing emphasis upon proactive engagement with society by the authorities regarding domestic security management, along with a growing awareness that the key to security programs and social resilience involves the "coping capacities of citizens," that is, their ability to respond and adapt to crises and security threats (Lentzos and Rose 2009; Collier and Lakoff 2008; Chandler 2013). Unsurprisingly, some authors have suggested that resilience becomes "the art of living dangerously" (Evans and Reid 2014), at least for the individual. Therefore, resilience lends itself well to the theory of governmentality; it is, or becomes, a way for authorities to govern at a distance. This understanding contrasts sharply with the idea that resilience should be equated with local and democratic self-governance, as discussed above by other scholars.

As resilience is a term without specific substance and can thus be applied to several policy areas, it has an expanding and creeping logic. The state, civil society actors, market actors, and individuals and their relationships are substantially altered once resilience is adopted to address a broad range of societal security issues, including natural disasters, environmental protection, food security, and cyberattacks. However, this produces an unclear "division of labor" between the state and society, contradicting the Hobbesian contract and the transaction of liberty for security. In our complex world, where it has become far more difficult for the state to "provide" security, new security discourses are emerging that demand the active participation of market actors, civil society organizations, and individuals in collaborating on security issues.

The term resilience has also been included in the language of the United Nations, the European Union, and NATO (Korosteleva and Flockhart 2020; Tocci 2020). This raises concerns about how resilience becomes entangled with other governing discourses and is mobilized and implemented in existing political systems. The fact that resilience has become a complement to existing neoliberal and/or security policies has already been identified as a problematic aspect of its application. Despite such critiques and problematizations, resilience remains a central part of current political discourse and practice (Joseph 2013a, 2018; Reid 2012; Lentzos and Rose 2009; Rådestad and Larsson 2018; Larsson 2021). Once adopted into national and societal security, risks tilt toward national governing structures rather than local, decentralized, and contextualized systems of self-governance with democratic input. Critical voices have also noted the way in which capitalism functions as a driver for disaster and disaster reduction, which are further enforced by resilience, a concept that could imply that change, uncertainty, adaptability, and acceptance for crises and disasters are "naturalized" (MacKinnon and Derickson 2013; Welsh 2014; Porter and Davoudi 2012).

Through the implementation of resilience projects and policies, state powers are encouraging or even mandating communities and societal actors to become increasingly adaptable, flexible, and open to change through disruption (Cote and Nightingale 2012; Joseph 2018; Chandler 2013). Thus, through instruments of advocacy and nudging, states are advancing ideas about individual responsibilities, extending and harvesting community activities, and volunteering. Resilience emphasizes individual or actor-oriented responsibility without necessarily providing the power or the resources needed to fulfill the new role and responsibility. It is suggested that the states withdraw from performing security-related tasks but serve as facilitators, specifying frames and goals for current security management and indirectly governing. Joseph describes such use applications of resilience as creating "a sphere of governance which [the state] oversees from a distance through the use of its powers" (Joseph 2013a).

4.4 Resilience as Governmentality

Given how resilience discourses produce and, in many ways, presuppose a specific subjectivity described above, it has been suggested that resilience becomes a specific version of *governmentality* (Joseph 2013b). Michel Foucault developed the concept and "theory" of governmentality in a series of lectures at the Collége de France in the late 1970s. He suggests that power and governance in late modern and liberal societies have developed more subtle, less dramatic forms of power, beyond the direct coercion commonly associated with the state. Michel Foucault's discussions of power and governance in liberal states further explore the connection between liberalism and its orientation toward security. Foucault noted in his lectures at the Collège de France that "the general economy of power in our societies is becoming a domain of security... a society of security" (Foucault 2007), with the sovereign and political-judicial notions of power *sustaining* the compartmentalization of security and freedom. However, we need additional dimensions of modern governance in liberal societies and contexts. The sovereign and judicial forms of power need to be supplemented by another type of power matrix that theorizes how liberal states care for and manage the population while optimizing productive industrial behavior, biopolitics, or biopower (Foucault et al. 2008).

This would focus on how states engage in monitoring, surveillance, and disciplinary techniques, in which the population is governed according to its role and functionality vis-à-vis the state. The government focuses more on general population patterns and tendencies than on individual deviations. In this way, the state governs at a distance through structures of encouragement, persuasion, facilitation, and incitement. It can "nudge" its citizens into desirable behavior. Governmentality is the exercise of power in terms of the conduct of conduct, governing at a distance (Dean 2009). The governmentality approach to resilience allows for an analysis of how member states and, ultimately, NATO is engaged in a "conduct of conduct." More specifically, it will enable me to dissect how governance is exercised and the specific techniques of government that support indirect governance at a distance.

Orientation toward security in liberal states allows for various forms of interventionist and non-interventionist governance, which can either utilize or disrupt freedoms (Dillon and Neal 2015; Schmitt 2005; Dean 2013). The freedom of the subjects becomes even more critical in the more advanced form of liberalism (Brady 2014). This is what we today commonly refer to as neoliberalism, and its specific ideas emerged after the end of World War II. Contrary to the common misconception that it comprises a reinvention of classic liberalism and laissez-faire, neoliberalism's ordo-version encourages extensive state intervention precisely to *produce* the societal and economic processes and subjects needed to sustain the market and the capitalist system. Both of these are suggested to be the ultimate guarantor of freedom and the antidote to totalitarianism

(Hayek and Caldwell 2014; Foucault et al. 2008). This view contrasts with Adam Schmidt's idea of the market as a natural place and process. In neoliberal governance, the market needs to be produced and safeguarded. This idea of neoliberal governmentality relies on an interventionist state that aims to produce specific subjects and safeguard the continuation of competition and the market. In the same way, striving toward resilience works, and the interventions would want to produce the right subject and the exemplary architecture for producing security in collaboration with actors on all levels. To achieve a resilient society, the state must produce the proper facilitation and the correct subject to inhabit such a society. O'Malley (2010) discusses resilience in terms of the smallest component, the resilient subject, which is shaped by the focus on personal strength, individualism, and self-sufficiency. This is suggested to stem from the psychological tradition of resilience. As resilience focuses on the smallest component of the security apparatus, the individual, it is easy to see how self-help books on prepping and crisis preparedness, as well as consultancies, are further attempts to train individuals how to be more resilient and cope with life's challenges (O'Malley 2010). Hence, when resilience is suggested as the solution to cope with societal and national security, this often includes the idea of the resilient subject, the active and supporting citizens who both need to be "produced" and later governed.

4.5 Combining Securitization and Governmentality

A neoliberal approach to contemporary security and crisis management would consequently generate new instruments and strategies for governing that utilize individual attitudes and behavior to promote both national and societal security (Bergström 2018; Chandler 2013; Davoudi 2018; Evans and Reid 2014). This marks a convergence of crisis and security management that addresses the full spectrum of threats, disturbances, and contingencies facing modern societies (Larsson 2021; Baker and Ludwig 2018; Adey and Anderson 2012; Dillon and Reid 2001).

Furthermore, the securitization of an ever-widening range of threats is coupled with a preemptive approach to crises and risks. Societal security is thereby translated into civil contingency planning and preparation for future events, which emphasizes building societal resilience (Comfort et al. 2010). This would, in a strict sense, require a population consisting of self-reliant and capable citizens who would willingly support the state authorities during crises, but grievances and problems that may arise due to crises are not evenly distributed (Lentzos and Rose 2009; Chandler and Reid 2016). This leads to interventionism, intending to transform individual citizens into "resilient" neoliberal subjects (Bergström 2016, 2017; Chandler 2013; Reid and Chandler 2016; Davoudi 2016). As Flockart and Koseleva put it: "We posit the need to look at how real people feel about and react to change. This brings us to the personal level and the psychological dispositions of humans as the ultimate site for the constitution of resilience. All communities, whether a state, an organization, a social movement, a family, or a professional network, are composed of people with feelings, complex emotional processes, and psychological dispositions" (Korosteleva and Flockhart 2020).

In this vein, Sage et al. (2015) noted that resilience policy and practice comprise a composite of circulatory mechanisms and the inevitable tensions between liberty and security inherent to the resilience discourse. The consequences of societal security, resilience, and neoliberal security mechanisms would need to be further contextualized to grasp the social technologies currently included once resilience is adopted by NATO and heralded as a means to cope with national and international security.

To make sense of the development of civil defense within NATO, it is fruitful to apply a governmentality approach to dismantle the international security apparatus that relies on the activation of the "whole-of-society." What may appear odd is the idea of an international military alliance now engaging in entirely new ways of governing the civil dimension of member states. The various instruments and techniques that NATO now govern extend beyond sovereign power, coercion, and military means. The organization is also concerned with the fabric of societies in member states, the organization of politics, the management of markets, and political priorities.[1] Everything that can be identified as supporting resilience and resilience building is potentially of interest to NATO.

[1] The empirical investigation has revealed that NATO has engaged in indirect governance of civil defense and emergency planning since 1952. It is an area that is out of reach as it is covered by Article 3, and is within the competence of the individual member states.

4.6 Resilience as Part of National and International Security

Resilience normally appears in national and international policies in relation to disaster reduction, crisis management, and societal security (see Joseph 2018, 16). It was acknowledged in the UK that a more traditional Civil Defence approach was poorly suited to deal with the "complex emergencies" and "new security challenges" of the twenty-first century (Smith 2003, 414; Zebrowski 2013). The "resilience agenda" was seen as a proactive response to a "fast-changing and complex world." It has recently been argued that resilience may, in fact, be vital for the discipline of International Relations, as it captures some new approaches to national security and the way states choose to adapt to the new geopolitical environment, grey zone, and hybrid threats (Bourbeau 2015, 2018). Situating resilience as a concept now incorporated into national defense is a necessary step in a constructivist analysis of the role of civil administration and civil society in connection to national and international security.

It is, in fact, just recently that resilience has been adopted as a concept and strategy to assist national or even international security. In Sweden, resilience was implemented as a catch-all phrase and used as a strategy to bridge societal security with national security, a way to rebuild a total defense for all purposes after 2014 (Larsson 2021; Ljungkvist 2024). In Norway and Finland, we see a similar trend of bridging societal security, crisis management, and national security (Wither 2020). Studies of the Baltic countries (Saxi et al. 2020) and Switzerland (Prior and Roth 2014) also identify the adoption of resilience as part of national defense. The way resilience is incorporated into national defense and military strategies appears to contradict previous notions of resilience as decentralized self-governance and a more passive facilitator role for the state. However, Fjäder (2014) noted that resilience also contributes to the state's security goal before the broader shift toward geopolitics. This is even though resilience and security differ in how they address insecurity and risks. Whereas security is "preventive and proactive in nature and should be aiming at protecting the state and the citizens against threats," resilience provides "a combination of proactive and reactive measures aiming at *reducing* the impact but not preventing threats as such" (Fjäder 2014).

O'Grady and Shaw argue that resilience in this sense may be regarded as a reaction to the homogenizing pathology and hierarchy of top-down resource management that characterized much of national defense during the Cold War. Calls for resilience are purportedly driving so-called society-first approaches that seemingly give non-government actors and individuals a degree of self-determination (O'Grady and Shaw 2023). However, this is accompanied by the presumption and demand that the actors involved can adapt to the circumstances created by all kinds of emergencies (Davoudi 2018), even those that are antagonistic. This adaptive capacity is desirable for governments because of the ontological insecurity and uncertainty associated with future emergencies and hybrid threats, which they cannot prepare for or predict. The underlying logic would then serve to sustain the government of societal security and resilience, rendering critique and resistance futile (Brassett and Vaughan-Williams 2015; Chandler 2013; Bourbeau 2013; Brassett et al. 2013). One might say that resilience is a new key concept for "securitization." When something is identified as related to overall "resilience," it is connected to national (and international) security and thus requires attention and resources to be managed under the security logic that was discussed in the previous chapter.

However, this orients actors toward a mindset that extends a logic of security throughout society and skews political discourse and the priorities of public politics toward national security concerns. The current security situation consequently renders it increasingly important to not only investigate the unfolding security discourse concerning the grey zone, hostility, and hybrid threats but also to examine in detail the policy solutions that leading security organizations and experts are currently proposing, not least because it is difficult to see how a logic of security could foster a vision of freedom or emancipation. It is much less complicated to design a vision of order—of how to take control of human experience—in the name of security. This is why we need a critical analysis of the current security discourse, including its extensive employment of the seemingly neutral notion of resilience.

Corry (2014) stated that the main difference between traditional national security and resilience is that the former focuses on a specific threat, whereas the latter attempts to cope with and accept uncertainties. As Corry argues: "[it] makes little sense to "defend" against catastrophic climate change, pandemics, economic meltdowns, or even certain kinds of terrorism" (Corry 2014). This is because of the nature of social security issues that foremost invoke uncertainty, are located in the future, but most importantly, there are no clear adversaries or enemies. This is currently changing through notions of grey zone and hybrid threats. If it was earlier suggested that resilience shifted responsibility away from the state to cope with inevitable risks and vulnerabilities, we are now entering into a new situation in which geopolitical concern and traditional national/international security have re-entered the political agenda. And whereas neoliberal governmentality shaped the deployment of resilience in the past, we may discover new applications and new forms of governmentalities based on the concept of resilience adopted by NATO as a complement to national and international security. In this regard, the current study of NATO adopting resilience as one of its "strategic concepts" could provide valuable insights into the linkages between resilience and security in the twenty-first century. The advancement of resilience in the field of national security is of great interest to this book and the IR discipline in general.

CHAPTER 5

The Early Years 1949–1964

This book focuses on the role of non-military collaboration and the key actors in civil defense across NATO Member States. It aims to analyze the contingent and political developments over NATO's 75-year history, marked by a wide range of security issues and discourses. Throughout this period, significant events in international politics—such as the Korean War, the Berlin Crisis, the construction of the Berlin Wall, and the end of the Cold War—have occurred alongside diplomatic crises involving external actors and substantial internal disputes. The emergence of new security concerns naturally pushes for new security arrangements within the organization and the individual member states. The focus on civil defense within NATO security discourse constitutes an analytical gap that has not yet been addressed and offers a novel perspective on NATO's history. The roles of civil administration, market actors, civil society, the general population, and individuals are of paramount importance. We discussed the dangers of an excessive focus on security and how security-focused governance crowds out other values and concerns in Chap. 2. Civil actors and their roles are continually evolving, and throughout history, NATO has mobilized them for specific security arrangements when necessary. By interrogating the intersections of military strategy and civil agency, we can better understand the complex fabric of evolving security discourse and its implications for policy and practice in today's global landscape. We need to analyze the inner workings of the security politics

O. Larsson, *NATO's Approach to the Civil Dimensions of War*,
https://doi.org/10.1007/978-3-032-27871-5_5

driven by NATO and explore the historical and political dynamics that influence the alliance's approach to security.

5.1 The Unexpected Partnership

The military alliance founded on 4th of April 1949, was not evident from the outset after the end of World War II. Instead, a set of circumstances and distinct concerns of the emerging states converged, and NATO's formation may even be seen as coincidental. In Europe, war-torn countries did their best to pool resources and form military treaties and alliances. France and the United Kingdom signed the Treaty of Dunkirk on March 4, 1947, as a pact of alliance and assurance of mutual assistance in the event of possible attacks by Germany or the Soviet Union. In March 1948, the alliance was expanded by the Treaty of Brussels to include the Benelux countries, forming the Brussels Treaty Organization, commonly known as the Western Union, consisting of France, the United Kingdom, Belgium, the Netherlands, and Luxembourg. From the outset, European countries were interested in involving the North American nations, the US and Canada, in similar treaties and arrangements. Still, the most valuable partner, the United States, was reluctant to enter a formal alliance and to break the long tradition of American isolationism.

Yet, the US feared communist ideology and Soviet expansion. In February 1946, George Kennan sent the famous "Long Telegram" from Moscow, an 8000-word warning to Washington about Soviet thoughts and plans in a post-World War II geopolitical setting in which the potential spread of communism was apparent. The telegram is said to have spurred both the Truman Doctrine and the Marshall Aid program, and thus pushed the development of NATO (Kennan 1944; Kaplan 1999).

The Truman Doctrine arose from a speech President Truman delivered before a joint session of Congress on March 12, 1947. The immediate cause for the speech was a recent announcement by the British Government that it would no longer provide military and economic assistance to the Greek Government in its civil war against the Greek Communist Party. Truman asked Congress to support the Greek Government against the Communists. He also asked Congress to assist Turkey since that nation had previously been dependent on British aid. With the Truman Doctrine, President Harry S. Truman established that the United States would provide political, military, and economic assistance to all democratic nations under threat from external or internal authoritarian forces.

The Truman Doctrine effectively reoriented U.S. foreign policy from isolationism to activism, with President Truman stating, "I believe that it must be the policy of the United States to support free peoples who are resisting attempted subjugation by armed minorities or by outside pressures" (Truman 1947). It is indeed very telling that Greece and Turkey were the first two countries to join NATO in February 1952, only 3 years after the signing of the Washington Treaty.

Even before committing to NATO, the US was concerned about a weak, war-torn Europe that seemed unable to recover on its own. This potentially made European countries susceptible to internal or external communist influence, and the US felt compelled to extend a helping hand to thwart the dangers of a failed Europe.

The Marshall Plan was born in June 1947 when Secretary of State George C. Marshall gave a speech to the graduating class at Harvard University. He suggested that a comprehensive program was needed to rebuild Europe. It was clear that the European countries struggled to recover from the war and to reprogram their industries for normal production. In fact, rather than recovering, European economies experienced a downturn in the winter of 1946–1947. The US feared an economic collapse, communist influence, and further chaos in Europe, and found that economic support could save the situation and expand the market for American exports. Congress passed the Economic Cooperation Act in March 1948 and approved funding that would extend $ 12 billion to support the recovery of Western Europe (Marshall Plan 1948 [2026]). The Marshall Plan provided aid only to Western Europe and excluded aid to the Soviet Union and its satellite states in Eastern Europe. Given Congress's lingering isolationist tendencies, it was unlikely that they would agree to extend assistance to Eastern Europe or the communist Soviet Union, which had grown into a significant competitor for global influence and thus posed a threat to American interests. The recovery of Western Europe, particularly West Germany, intensified suspicions in the Soviet Union and solidified the division between East and West. George C. Marshall, as the only General so far, won the Nobel Peace Prize in 1953 "for proposing and supervising the plan for the economic recovery of Europe" (Nobel Price Committee 2024). The Nobel Committee states that Truman and Marshall "planned the economic support for Europe that was to secure stability and prevent the spread of Communism" (Nobel Price Committee 2024). It was also another brick in the wall that later would be known as the Iron Curtain, as it solidified an East-West divide in Europe.

The 1948 Czechoslovakia coup d'état, performed by the communist party with support from Moscow, further spurred the idea of a broader and more solid cross-Atlantic alliance against Soviet expansion in Europe (Ismay 1955). It was clear that economic aid was not enough, and military cooperation across the Atlantic seemed unavoidable. Eventually, 12 European and Atlantic countries became parties to the original North Atlantic Treaty, although others were considered. Time was of the essence, and potential members could join later.[1] The North American Treaty Organization was founded on April 4, 1949. Its formation owes much to Canadian diplomats, especially Lester B. Pearson, who is often referred to as its founding figure (NATO 2026 Canada Profile, see also Ismay 1955).

Canadian negotiators collaborated closely with their American and European counterparts to craft the 14 articles of the North Atlantic Treaty.[2] Canada stressed that NATO should be more than a military alliance; it should also foster political, economic, and cultural connections among its member countries. This was a specific position that has been serving Canada's membership orientation. Ultimately, Canada has sought to expand the definition of security within NATO, pushing for greater emphasis on civilian aspects of security (NATO 2026b, Canada Profile). It is a treaty that had to please many different actors and agendas in a time of uncertainty. Thus, the treaty itself had to be kept simple and open (Ismay 1955). It is considered the shortest and least detailed founding treaty of an International Organization in world politics, comprising only 14 articles and 5 pages (NATO 1949). This has enabled significant flexibility and adaptability within the organization from its founding years to the present. It has also enabled strong states and influential leaders to shape the organization's security policy and set its direction. It also enabled NATO to develop into an independent international organization, making it more than the sum of its member states and more than a mere alliance. This development will be visible later in the chapter.

[1] Belgium, Canada, Denmark, France, Iceland, Italy, Luxembourg, the Netherlands, Norway, Portugal, the United Kingdom, and the United States.

[2] The North Atlantic Treaty can be found here: https://www.nato.int/cps/en/natohq/official_texts_17120.htm

The specification for NATO's military structure was not included in the treaty itself but emerged later in response to specific external events. Strangely enough, the Korean War of 1950 spurred NATO to develop its military structures in Europe and the Atlantic region (Ismay 1954). This included the formation of the Supreme Headquarters Allied Powers Europe (SHAPE) in 1951. In addition, the Supreme Allied Commander Europe (SACEUR) office was created in 1951. On the 2 of April, 1951, the five-star general in the US Army, General Dwight D. Eisenhower, became the Alliance's first SACEUR. This post, together with that of the Supreme Allied Commander Atlantic (SACLANT), was created at the same time. SACEUR was responsible for safeguarding the area extending from the northern tip of Norway to southern Europe (NATO Information Service 1959). Eisenhower was the Supreme Commander of the Allied Expeditionary Force during World War II and later became the President of the United States. The permanent offices, commanders, and military structures of NATO furthered the standardization of equipment and military doctrine. It also made it possible for foreign military forces, from the US and Canada, to be stationed in European countries (NATO Information Service 1959).

To further specify NATO's focus and direction, additional governing documents, such as the Strategic Concepts and Military Strategic Papers, had to be drafted. Throughout history, some reports and revisions have become iconic for shaping the organization and political focus, such as the report of the "three wise men" (1956) and the Harmel Report (1968), which will be discussed at length below. Both these reports were intended to address political tensions within NATO and to settle the issues and concerns of the smaller member states regarding consultation and influence in NATO's political development and engagements (NATO 1956, 1968). The fact that NATO's organization, political priorities, and policies have been open to revision over the 75 years of NATO's existence may help explain why NATO has survived external and internal shocks and crises, remaining highly adaptable and addressing new security issues. As we shall see, various articles in the Treaty have been used to justify new directions, not least the recent turn to resilience, which was motivated by reference to Article 3. Perhaps the Articles' open nature, more a declaration of intent and willingness to collaborate, has enabled NATO to earn the epithet of "the most powerful alliance in the world" (Rynning 2024) and allegedly the longest-lasting alliance in history.

When speaking at the signing of the North Atlantic Treaty in Washington, D.C, on April 4, 1949, Lester B. Pearson stated: "This Treaty is not a pact for war, but a pledge for peace and progress" (Canadian War Museum 2023). Pearson and Canada believed that NATO should be more than just a military alliance. The Canadian diplomats forcefully advocated for the inclusion of Article 2, a clause that encouraged members to forge stronger political and economic ties rather than focusing solely on the Alliance's military dimensions. Not all the signatory countries strongly supported this Article. Still, as it did not contain specific requirements and arrangements, it was allowed to stay in the Treaty, informally known as "the Canadian Article" (Canadian War Museum 2023).

Lord Hastings Lionel Ismay of Great Britain was NATO's first Secretary General, a position he was reluctant to accept. By the end of his service in 1957, however, Ismay had changed his mind and become one of the organization's main advocates, according to NATO's historical account. He stated that the original purpose of NATO was to "keep the Soviet Union out, the Americans in, and the Germans down". The post of Secretary General emerged after SPACE and SAUCER. Military structures and commands were prioritized. The position of Secretary General was established in February 1952, and Ismay was appointed a month later. His status as a former British military officer adds a specific diplomatic context. After the headquarters relocated from London to Paris, it became necessary from a diplomatic standpoint for the first Secretary General to be a British national, and Winston Churchill proposed Ismay for the role. At first, Ismay tried to decline, but eventually relented, believing the posting would only last 2 years. He took office on April 4, 1952—NATO's third anniversary (NATO Information Service 1959). Another reason for the preference for a candidate from Great Britain was that the British had been eager to take the position of Admiral and control the naval forces, but had lost it to the USA. The position of first Secretary General may be viewed as compensation for being excluded from higher command within the marine forces (Kaplan 1999).

Ismay is credited with developing NATO's administrative side—setting up offices and committees and assembling experienced staff. At the time of his appointment, the North Atlantic Council (NAC) was reorganized into its current format, with permanent representatives at ambassadorial rank from each member country. This format allows NATO to work more smoothly and swiftly, as these representatives are familiar with NATO's procedures (NATO Information Service 1959, 50). Initially, the Secretary General did not chair this session, but this function was developed a few years later as NATO continued to grow (Ismay 1954).

So far, I have covered the historical aspects of how NATO came into being and how it quickly evolved from a military alliance between 12 sovereign countries to take on a life of its own and become an international organization, with committees, permanent staff, procedures, a Secretary General, and develop its unique military organization with SPACE and SAUCER. This is the necessary background for understanding how civil defense and other forms of political, economic, and cultural collaboration subsequently shape the organization and expand the security focus beyond the military.

5.2 Political Dimensions of NATO in the Early Years

From the outset, it was recognized that defense cooperation was the most urgent requirement and core rationale behind NATO. This was, however, not enough; three articles, 2, 3, and 4, concern the desire and ambition to establish other forms of collaboration, such as economic, cultural, educational, and extensive diplomatic consultations (NATO 1949). As noted above, Canada focused on the economic and political aspects of the alliance, which played a crucial role in drafting the treaty and in advocating for Article 2. A more comprehensive approach to the alliance would grow in importance during the 1950s–1960s, including political consultation and economic cooperation (Kaplan 1999).

Article 2
The Parties will contribute toward the further development of peaceful and friendly international relations by strengthening their free institutions, by bringing about a better understanding of the principles upon which these institutions are founded, and by promoting conditions of stability and well-being. They will seek to eliminate conflict in their international economic policies and will encourage economic collaboration between any or all of them

Article 3
In order more effectively to achieve the objectives of this Treaty, the Parties, separately and jointly, by means of continuous and effective self-help and mutual aid, will maintain and develop their individual and collective capacity to resist armed attack

---

(continued)

(continued)

Article 4 The Parties will consult together whenever, in the opinion of any of them, the territorial integrity, political independence or security of any of the Parties is threatened

Implementing Article 2 and specifying the content of Article 4 proved difficult. By the mid-1950s, NATO remained almost exclusively a military organization, and there was not much progress in the economic, cultural, and scientific sectors. The North Atlantic Council asked the Foreign Ministers of Canada, Italy, and Norway[3] to "advise the Council on ways and means to improve and extend NATO cooperation in non-military fields and to develop greater unity within the Atlantic Community." Pearson and his two colleagues further pressed for political consultation, increased dialogue, and extended collaboration in various sectors among members in a report entitled "The Report of the Committee of Three on Non-Military Cooperation in NATO" (NATO 1956). The report suggested strengthening economic partnerships and cultural connections, given the limited progress in these areas. Ultimately, Pearson and his colleagues laid the foundation for NATO's development in the non-military field and, more broadly, for political consultation among members (NATO Information Service 1959, 54). The background for this was that many of the smaller member states felt excluded when security issues were addressed without their knowledge or input (NATO 1956).

As a telling example, during the drafting of the Three Wise Men's report, the Suez crisis emerged, revealing conflicts among the Member states (NATO 2026a). On October 29, 1956, France and the UK, together with Israel, invaded Egypt to secure the Suez Canal without notifying other NATO members. Although a resolution was reached afterward, the crisis highlighted the need for better coordination and consultation among the Allies. The North Atlantic Council accepted the "Committee of Three on non-military cooperation in NATO" report on December 13, 1956. This report highlighted the importance of considering NATO as a *political* organization and not merely a military alliance (NATO 1956).

[3] Pearson, Foreign Minister of Canada, Gaetano Martino, Foreign Minister of Italy, and Halvard Lange, Foreign Minister of Norway.

> *A direct method of bringing home to public opinion the importance of the habit of political consultation within NATO may be summed up in the proposition "NATO is a political as well as a military alliance". The habitual use of this phraseology would be preferable to the current tendency to refer to NATO as a (purely) military alliance. It is also more accurate* Council Memorandum, (North Atlantic Council 1956 C-M 56 -25).

The importance of the consultation procedures is contested. Kaplan suggested that the message could not have been clearer, and that NATO advanced its political role in addition to military and purely strategic affairs (Kaplan 1999). John Milloy concluded in his 2006 book, *The North Atlantic Treaty Organization, 1948–1957: Community or Alliance?*, that the report of the three wise men was a failure and did not push the alliance toward a proper political community (Milloy 2006). Thomas J. Kennedy Jr. investigated the topic in a publication from National Defence University Press, in 1984 and noticed that the US, along with the UK and France, was reluctant to reduce the leeway of their countries and was suspicious of the requirement of consultation (Kennedy Jr 1984). This view is also shared by Sten Rynning (2024), who argues that neither of the big "powers" was represented on the committee, and that they all had colonial possessions and global interests that "caused them to hesitate before committing to an obligation to consult" (Rynning 2024). There is no clear way to settle this controversial issue, but it may suffice for now to conclude that the report of the 'three wise men' at least formally steered NATO toward a political community that included consultation on political issues other than military operations and war, though it is unclear how successful it was.

The report also called for the development of political solidarity and shared values to enhance economic, technological, scientific, and cultural exchanges among NATO member states. Cold War logic and the East-West divide may further explain why NATO was striving to expand its cooperation in political and scientific areas. As noted by the report "Three Wise Men", the Soviet Union invested in education and research that seemed to give it an edge in developing new and more advanced weapons (NATO 1956). The Soviet Union's launch of the world's first artificial satellite on October 4, 1957, came as a major surprise, startling experts and citizens in the United States and NATO countries. This achievement was part of a series of Soviet technological successes that were largely unanticipated by the United States and NATO, intensifying concerns over Soviet advancements, including the successful testing of intercontinental ballistic missiles (ICBMs) that same year. The launch of Sputnik significantly influenced the Cold War logic, prompting U.S. policymakers to accelerate space and military programs due to fears of falling behind ('Milestones in the History of U.S. Foreign Relations—Office of the Historian', Sputnik 2026). Consequently, Sputnik's launch intensified the space race and accelerated the arms race, escalating Cold War tensions as both superpowers sought to enhance their military capabilities (Ibid).

In a NATO publication from 1959, entitled *Know your NATO—Shield of Freedom,* it was clear that Sputnik had made a significant impression on NATO. "Spurred by Sputnik and scientific developments in various parts of the world, 1958 marked the appointment of a Science Advisor to NATO, who immediately undertook the development of a comprehensive program of cooperation in scientific fields among the NATO powers". "This program is concerned with science for peaceful purposes as well as the necessary technical development for defense. A NATO-supported exchange fellowship in the sciences existed as early as the 1950s. NATO also supports certain cooperative advanced science study institutes" (NATO Public Diplomacy Division 1959, 10).

The Sputnik satellite also heightened political tensions within NATO. With the new satellite and the development of ICBMs, it became clear to America that the Soviet Union had the capability to attack the US and major cities in North America. It was the first time since World War II that the US feared for its security. It was no longer clear that the next theater of war would be continental Europe. The US felt pressed to catch up with the Soviet space and missile capabilities (NATO Information Service 1959). European countries, not least West Germany, who had joined NATO in May 1955, feared that this would diminish the commitment of the US to the country during a time when tensions were increasing between West Germany and East Germany, which soon was to erupt in the Berlin Crisis (Kaplan 1999, 73). The role of nuclear weapons played a significant role in the strategic planning and military strategies that were developed soon after the formation of NATO.

5.3 The First Guiding Documents

In September 1949, the Council established the Defence Committee (DC), composed of the Defence Ministers of the member nations. The Defence Committee was tasked with drawing up unified defense plans for the entire North Atlantic area. The Council also created the Military Committee (MC), composed of the Chiefs of Staff of the member nations, along with a three-nation executive body known as the Standing Group (SG), composed of the chiefs of staff of the US, the UK, and France (NATO Information Service 1959). This group had overall responsibility for controlling and approving the military planning process of the five regional planning groups (Pedlow 1997a).

NATO began producing guiding documents for its undertaking as early as October 1949. These documents are essential as they are more detailed than the North Atlantic Treaty, identifying more specific security concerns and current approaches to security challenges. As for the regional documents, they could, in general terms, discuss how to coordinate between member states and branches of the armed forces, and what to prioritize during the planning and operational phases of military campaigns. The "strategic concept" documents are the overarching documents that outline NATO's main security issues and how it intends to address them. It is not a single or even a set of "concepts" but a more policy-oriented document that provides overall guidance for the organization and its political orientation (NATO 2022e). The Strategic Concept sets the Alliance's strategy. It outlines NATO's enduring purpose and nature, its fundamental security tasks, and the challenges and opportunities it faces in a changing security environment. It also specifies the elements of the Alliance's approach to security and provides guidelines for its political and military adaptation (NATO 2022e).

The first NATO strategic concept, "the Strategic concept for the defense of the North Atlantic Area," was accepted by the North Atlantic Council on January 6, 1950 (DC 6/1). The Standing Group first prepared a working document with the same title on October 10, 1949, under the designation SG 1. It was then sent to the Chiefs of Staff for comments. After a few minor editorials, the Standing Group submitted the Strategic Concept to the Military Committee as MC 3 on October 19, 1949. The main difference between MC3 and DC 6/1 was that after Denmark's objection, the term "atomic bomb" was not explicitly mentioned but altered to "[NATO] to carry out strategic bombing promptly by all means possible with all types of weapons, without exception" (NATO Strategic concept 1950 for more details and Context see Pedlow 1997).

DC 6/1 provides an overall strategic concept for NATO but remains fairly general, specifying only the basic premises for how NATO sees the present situation and how it may respond to specific security challenges. The document stated that NATO's primary function was to deter aggression and that NATO forces would be engaged only if that function failed and an attack was launched. Accepting the fact that the member states had different possibilities to contribute military and financially to the alliance, the document suggests that each member's contribution to defense should be in proportion to its capacity—economic, industrial, geographical, and military—and cooperative measures were to be put into place by NATO to ensure optimal use of resources. The document explicitly notes numerical inferiority in relation to the Soviet Union. It does, however, mention that it already, from the outset, places its trust in US nuclear capabilities, as was discussed above (NATO 1950 Strategic concept DC 6/1).

Although DC 6/1 laid down the foundational strategy, yet more precise guidance was needed to develop comprehensive defense plans for the five Regional Planning Groups that existed at the time. At its second meeting on November 29, 1949, the Military Committee suggested that the Standing Group prepare a more detailed "Strategic Guidance for North Atlantic Regional Planning". After a round of revisions and oversight of national comments, the Strategic Guidance paper (SG 13/16) was sent to the Regional Planning Groups on January 6, 1950. Formal approval of the "Strategic Guidance for North Atlantic Regional Planning" was made by the Military Committee on March 28, 1950, and the working document, SG 13/1, was approved as MC 14 (NATO 2022e; Pedlow 1997a). MC 14 enabled Regional Planning Groups to respond to emergencies until July 1954. This date served as a deadline and was a date on which NATO hoped to have a credible traditional defense force in place. Its key objectives were to "convince the USSR that war does not pay, and should war occur, to ensure a successful defence" of the NATO area (NATO 2022e).

In parallel, SG 13/16 was also used by the Regional Planning Groups to develop more comprehensive defense plans that were consolidated into "The North Atlantic Treaty Organization Medium Term Plan" (DC 13). This document was approved by the Defence Committee on April 1, 1950 (NATO 2022e). That meant that just 1 year after the signing of the Washington Treaty, NATO already had three strategic documents guiding its efforts and collaborations.

- DC 6/1, which set forth the overall strategic concept and political orientation.
- MC 14, which provided more specific strategic guidance for military forces and strategies, and
- DC 13, which included both of these aspects as well as considerable detailed regional planning.

It should be noted that the Strategic concept (DC 6/1) does not mention civil defense. It focuses mainly on the military aspects, which depend on each country's geography and economic capabilities. It does, however, mention psychological means and assets and the need for cooperation in planning and carrying out psychological operations.

> The attainment of the objectives of the North Atlantic Treaty requires the integration by the parties to the Treaty of those political, economic, and psychological, as well as purely military means, which are essential to the defense of the North Atlantic area (NATO 1950, DC 6/1, 1).

> Cooperation, insofar as is practicable, in planning for the conduct of psychological and other special operations (NATO 1950, DC 6/1, 7).

The military organization and command structure developed for NATO in 1951, following the Korean War, was discussed above and included SHAPE, SAUCER, and SACLANT. The latter replaced the North Atlantic Ocean Regional Planning Group, leaving the Canada-Us Regional Planning Group as the only remaining regional planning group in 1952 (NATO Information Service 1959).

On February 18, 1952, Greece and Turkey officially joined NATO. Shortly thereafter, a new Strategic Concept was drafted and approved by the North Atlantic Council on December 3, 1952, entitled MC 3/5 final. The new Strategic Concept did not change any of the core premises outlined in DC 6/1 and, in this sense, did not differ fundamentally from this document. The revisions conducted reflect merely the new organizational structure and bodies (NATO 2022e; Pedlow 1997b).

The Strategic Guidance (military orientation) required revision to align with new Alliance members and organizational changes, as well as updated intelligence estimates, and to extend the planning period to 1956, two additional years beyond the original deadline. On December 9, 1952, the Military Committee approved MC 14/1, which replaced both MC

14 and DC 13, and was subsequently approved by the North Atlantic Council in Paris on December 15–18, 1952. MC 14/1 was more detailed than its predecessor, incorporating topics from DC 13, including assumptions of enemy capabilities. It emphasized NATO's strategic aim to defend the area and undermine the Soviet Union's ability to wage war, primarily through aerial offensives, while also planning ground and sea operations. The document also noted that the existing NATO forces were insufficient, necessitating continued expansion during 1953–54 (NATO Military Committee 1952 MC 14/1; NATO 2022e; Pedlow 1997a).

It is interesting to note that neither the strategic concept nor the strategic documents mention "civil" (defense) nor "society", and that MC 14/1 only mentions "populations" twice. This indicates a clear division of military and civil defense planning, along with a blind spot toward the rest of society in the event of war and overall war capacity.

5.4 Nuclear Threats and Capabilities

In the 1950s, one of the main issues for NATO and the US was how to make use of nuclear weapons. NATO continued to experience difficulties in reaching an equilibrium with the Soviet Union and the Warsaw Pact in conventional weapons. In the United States, even under the former SAUCER and now President, Eisenhower began to realize that the military budget could no longer be sustained and that even more emphasis on nuclear weapons seemed to offer a more cost-effective approach. As a result, U.S. defense policy shifted in 1953 to the "New Look", which placed greater emphasis on the use of nuclear weapons and a slimmer military organization. This was also reflected in NATO and the different strategic documents and military investigations conducted during the 1950s. This did, however, eventually reach a conceptual overload in the sense that NATO and the US could not threaten to use nuclear weapons for any threat or actions carried out by the Soviet Union (Pedlow 1997a; Kaplan 1999).

NATO pursued a "Forward Strategy" during the 1950s, meaning it sought to deploy as many troops and as much military strength as far East in Europe as possible. This also accelerated West Germany's membership in 1955, which eventually led to the Berlin Crisis of 1958–1962 and the construction of the Berlin Wall in August 1961. The forward strategy also included the potential use of nuclear weapons, as many key strategic and military documents and reports include. However, eventually, the idea of retaliating with nuclear weapons only made sense for the most serious political crisis and direct military confrontation with the Soviet Union. Therefore, NATO had to continue building up its troops and conventional military supplies to handle infiltrations, incursions, provocations, local threats, and outbursts of violence, without relying exclusively on nuclear weapons. In this period, NATO also considered the possibility of engaging in political and military disputes outside the territory of Member states (NATO Information Service 1959; NATO 2022e).

Amid the turmoil and revisions to strategic documents and planning during the 1950s, NATO eventually crafted a third Strategic Concept over an 8-year period. This pace of revision of the Strategic Concept will not last. After considerable debate and rounds of revisions, the document "Overall Strategic Concept for the Defense of the NATO Area" (MC 14/2) was approved on May 9, 1957 (NATO, North Atlantic Council 1957). This was coupled with "Measures to Implement the Strategic Concept" (MC 48/2), agreed on the same day, which was more of a military instruction (NATO 2022e). MC 14/2 was the Alliance's first Strategic Concept that advocated "massive retaliation" as a key element of NATO's new strategy. It also marks a shift in the length and details covered in the document of Strategic Concept. While the first two were only 7 pages each, the third was 38 pages. This is partly explained by the fact that strategic concepts and strategic guidance were merged; (see above in Chart 5.1). The first two strategic concepts only mentioned the Soviet Union a few times, whereas the third strategic concept mentioned "Soviet" 34 times and "Soviets" 22 times (NATO, North Atlantic Council 1957).

The third strategic concept explicitly mentions the role of civil support for the war efforts of the member states: "It is a responsibility of national authorities to develop plans and measures which will ensure the continuity of governmental control following a sudden outbreak of hostilities and will also ensure the maintenance of civilian morale coupled with the ability to prosecute the war to a successful conclusion" (NATO, North Atlantic Council 1957). Yet it also indicates that the responsibility for maintaining civilian morale rests with national authorities. Thus, it is unclear to what extent the population is seen as a resource or a liability that could fail the government by caving under the pressure and hardships of war. The

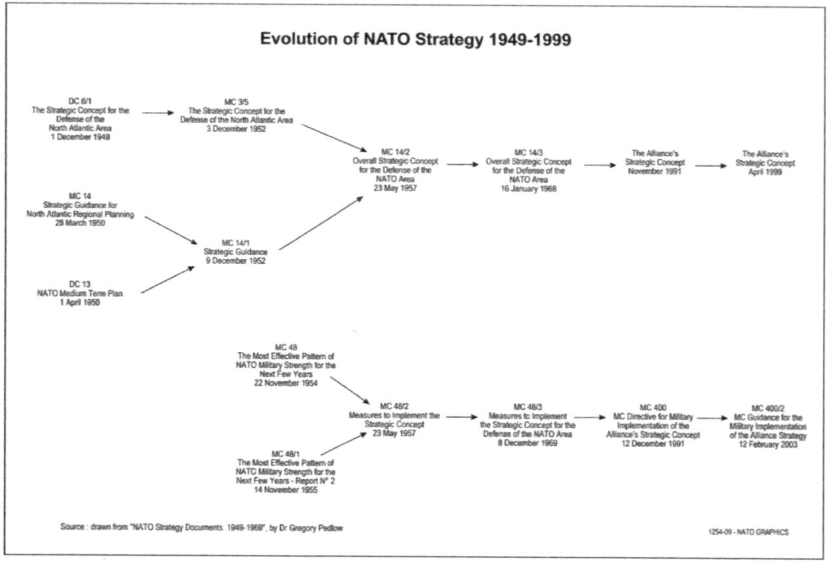

Chart 5.1 Evolution of NATO strategy 1949–1999. Source: Drawn from *NATO Strategy Documents, 1949–1969*, by Dr Gregory Pedlow (1997b)

third strategic concept does not mention "society," but it does identify population centers as potential targets for the enemy. At the same time, the minimal role given to society, civil defense, and populations in this 1957 document is rather strange, as these aspects received much attention in NATO and various reports at the time (NATO, North Atlantic Council 1957). In fact, the "new assumption" (Civil Defense Committee 1955b, 1955c) has already been circulated, which must be understood against the background of the growing arsenals of nuclear weapons:

> "Thus, instead of the gradually increasing rate of destruction prevalent in recent wars of prolonged mobilization and attrition, maximum destruction would occur within the first few days as both sides strove to exploit their nuclear stock-piles to gain nuclear superiority…The destruction resulting from large-scale use of nuclear weapons by both sides would seriously impede subsequent mobilization, troop movement, communications and logistical support" (NATO, North Atlantic Council 1957) (MC 14/2).

The fact that both the USA and the Soviet Union had nuclear weapons and soon developed missiles that enabled a massive attack to be launched from a distance substantially shaped the way the next major war was imagined and how NATO should best organize its joint forces to adhere to the new premises of modern warfare and nuclear arms. This also reshaped the ideas that governed the role and organization of Civil Defense. It was precisely because nuclear war was conceived as the most probable orientation for future war that civil defense became a major concern for NATO and the member states.

5.5 The Role of the Civil Defense

The Treaty does not specify the precise content of NATO's or the Member States' military organization and commitment. Furthermore, it does not specify the exact organization of NATO nor what is expected by the member states under articles 2, 3, and 4. It does, however, specify the leading role of the Council in Article 9, allowing it "to set up such subsidiary bodies as may be necessary", and the need for a Defence Committee for the "implementation of Articles 3 and 5". The wording of "implementation" suggests that NATO is intended to act as an authority above the member states. Perhaps this phrasing will later create tensions around Article 3 and NATO's efforts to influence member states to follow suit.

Article 9
The parties hereby establish a council, on which each of them shall be represented, to consider matters concerning the implementation of this treaty. The council shall be so organised as to be able to meet promptly at any time. The council shall set up such subsidiary bodies as may be necessary; in particular it shall establish immediately a defence committee which shall recommend measures for the implementation of articles 3 and 5

As noted above, Lord Ismay crafted the Council in the early years, establishing a clear structure, diplomatic representation, and a professional NATO staff, and identifying the need for several committees to operate under the Council. Civil defense, however, was mainly seen as the responsibility of the member states. Still, as we shall see below, civil defense and Article 3 were too vital issues for NATO to leave to the member states. NATO has, therefore, in different ways, actively sought to guide and steer the organization of civil defense.

When Lord Ismay delivered a speech on NATO and its development to a NATO audience on Friday, November 5, 1954, civil defense was one of the main topics brought to the speaker's and audience's attention.

> Now let me turn to another aspect of the work of NATO. All the members are, as I have said, pledged to maintain and develop their individual and collective capacity to resist aggression. To redeem that pledge, they must, in addition to building up their armed forces, take all possible steps to ensure that in the event of aggression, the home fronts will stand the strain. One of the most obvious of these steps is Civil Defence, and the Council is working hard at this problem. Civil Defence is, of course, a national responsibility, but the Council can do a good deal by way of stimulation, suggestion, co-ordination, and exchange of information and experience (Ismay 1955).

This quote illustrated that civil defense and the "home front" were vital concerns for NATO and that the Atlantic Council should stimulate, coordinate, instruct, and identify good examples. But it was also a matter of unity and solidarity. The populations of all 14 countries (soon to be 15, with West Germany accepted in May 1955) at the time should feel that sacrifices were evenly spread across the alliance and that those sacrifices were understandable and reasonable. Lord Ismay, secretary general, informs the audience that NATO is "working hard at it" but "a lot more money would be required" (Ismay 1954). This money could be spent on NATO information campaigns about what NATO is doing and how civil defense and the populations of member states could support such efforts.

The importance and concern for civil defense are also shared by parts of the audience. Major R.G Hogg asks Lord Ismay if there is an existing organization that coordinates and builds up civil defense. He adds that in view of "the tremendous and increasing importance of civil defense"… "if the civil population collapse at the explosion of an atom bomb, it would be disastrous" (Ismay 1955, Major Hogg statement). The response from Lord Ismay is that there has been an interchange of literature and publicity, sharing experience between countries, and that a technical adviser, Sir John Hodsoll,[4] is working on this issue. In addition, civil defense experts from all member countries are meeting in Paris for a 3-day conference later that year (1954). He also expresses frustration with the slow work in this area, not least on the part of national governments (Ismay 1955). As we shall see below, NATO's concern for civil defense grew vast in the early years even though it was deemed to be the competence and task of national governments.

The additional NATO organization engaged in civil defense was extensive but less well-known or documented than the "main" organization and its committees (see above). The Committee on Civil Organization in Time of War was the first of its kind, active between 1952 and 1955. In a memorandum dated June 6, 1952, the Secretary General invited the Council to plan for the organization of the civilian population and to counter Soviet infiltration and handle any enemy collaborators in the NATO countries in the event of war. The committee started as a Working group in June 1952 but was renamed (and reorganized as) the Committee on Civil Organization in Time of War after November 1952 (The North Atlantic Council 1952, Ac 23 - D17). The committee was established to deliberate and report to the Council on the civil organization of NATO countries in times of war, as well as on how future studies could be conducted. The committee comprised a representative nominated by each Member State and chaired by Sir Hoyer Millar, who was nominated by the

[4] Sir (Eric) John Hodsoll is often referred to as the "Father of Civil Defence," according to an interview with Colin Harmsworth at the Civil Defence Association in the UK (Colin Harmsworth, "Head of Civil Defence in the UK, Joint Civil Aid Corps", February 1, 2025).

Secretary General (The North Atlantic Council 1952b). The chairman of the two subcommittees, the Civil Defense Committee and the Committee on Refugees and Evacuations (both of these were created in 1952), the representative of the Standing Group Liaison Office in London and then in Paris, and a SHAPE representative also attended the meetings. The Committee on Civil Organization in Time of War held its last meeting on December 2, 1954. On November 9, 1955, the Council approved the creation of the Senior Civil Emergency Planning Committee (SCEPC) and decided to dissolve the Committee on Civil Organization in Time of War. This was to avoid duplication of effort in NATO coordination and between member states. At the same time, the status of SCEPC was higher than that of the previous committee. The Civil Defense Committee became a subcommittee of SCEPC in April 1956 (NATO 2026b). The Senior Civil Emergency Planning Committee took over the work of the Committee on Civil Organization in Time of War and then took the lead and controlled all subcommittees and working groups that worked on civil defense, civil aspects of war, and war preparation, and similar issues of protection of populations.

A memorandum from the Secretary General in 1954 was posted to the Committee on Civil Organization in Time of War, the Civil Defence Committee, the Committee on Refugees and Evacuees, the Committee on Wartime Commodity Problems, the Petroleum Planning Committee, the Food and Agriculture Planning Committee, the Coal and Steel Planning Committee, the Industrial Raw Materials Planning Committee, the PBEIST, the PBOS, the Defence Production Committee, and the Infrastructure Committee illustrates well the broad set of subcommittees engaged in civil defense and the intersections between civil, economic, and military aspects of industry. NATO was well aware of "the important part which Civil Defence must play in the emergency planning sphere of NATO" (The North Atlantic Council 1954). The North Atlantic Council appointed Sir John Hodsoll as Senior Civil Defence Adviser in June 1954. Sir John Hodsoll was a well-established figure in the British Civil Defense Organization, with extensive experience from World War II (Colin Harmsworth, "Head of Civil Defence in the UK, Joint Civil Aid Corps", February 1, 2025). Along with his assistant, Mr Rudler Sir Johnson, Hodsoll immediately started producing a number of reports based on information collected by delegations and reports, dealing with such matters as: "the order of priority to be attached to civil defence measures…aid to the civil population in wartime; mobile columns" (The

North Atlantic Council 1954). The Secretary General believed that "these basic papers should prove of great value to member governments and to those Committees of the Council dealing with the various aspects of Emergency Planning" (The North Atlantic Council 1954).

Apart from the reports, the executive secretary also informs the other committees that "he [Hodsoll] is available—and indeed anxious—to help the many committees of NATO wherever civil defence problems arise in the course of their work" (The North Atlantic Council 1954). Sir John Hodsoll's position as technical adviser was later turned into a special office for civil defense with the help of Lord Ismay.

At the first meeting of the Civil Defense Committee in February 1953, Lord Ismay stated that while civil defense is a national task, cooperation between member states and NATO was crucial because all member states had agreed to build up a collective defense for total war. Civil defense was vital to the collective effort to prepare for and engage in total war. The Supreme Headquarters Allied Powers Europe (SHAPE) representative corresponded and emphasized that the results of this committee would be of great importance to SHAPE, who was "anxious to assist the Committee in its task by every means possible" (Civil Defense Committee 1953, AC/23 R/5). Civil Defense proved challenging because member states held different understandings of the issue, priorities, and concerns. It was also overwhelmed by the fact that civil defense could include any protection issue and societal preparation for war.

Despite these intentions and support from both the Secretary General and SHAPE, the Civil Defense Committee (CDC) was overwhelmed by the numerous tasks and issues that could be incorporated into civil defense efforts. More problematic is that it was close to impossible to determine how much coordination was satisfactory or even possible. In July 1953, the chair of the Committee on Civil Organization in Time of War, Sir Frederick Hoyer Millar, noted that the Civil Defence Committee was struggling to provide any clear policy recommendations. The CDC Chairman, André Pelabon (France), noted that the task was difficult, as information must be gathered from all member states, synthesized, and only then formulated into proposals. The work also suffered from difficulties in identifying common terminology. However, initial discussions had been productive, and the sharing of experience among member states and the opportunity to discuss these issues was valuable in itself (NATO, Committee on Civil Organization in Time of War 1953).

In the autumn of 1953, Christopher Steel from the UK replaced Millar and showed less enthusiasm for common initiatives. In a report to the Council, he highlighted the "wide differences" in countries' preparedness levels and indicated that the Civil Defence Committee was evaluating how the collected information could serve as guidance for all members. The more tempered position, often held by UK representatives, was that the discussion among member states was important but given the national differences, not least in the organization of the state, along with different experiences and priorities it might be difficult to achieve any substantial coordination among the member states (The North Atlantic Council 1953).

The Civil Defense Committee met at the Palais de Chaillot in Paris from November 14 to 15, 1954. One of the main issues discussed was the role of nuclear weapons and how to calculate the implications of a nuclear bomb, as well as the possibility of a hydrogen bomb, which potentially carries up to 1000 times more explosive power. National civil defense organizations were unable to make adequate plans because they still did not have enough precise information about the effects of the hydrogen bombs. The most challenging part was calculating the radiological effects. The US military had preliminary information on blast and heat radiation effects and on radiological impacts, but this information was classified and could not be shared in civilian channels. The way forward on this pressing issue was for the civil defense technical adviser, Sir John Hodsoll, to gather as much information as possible after contacting the US and other NATO committees. It was clear that general guidelines for organizing civil defense considering nuclear, thermo-nuclear, and hydrogen bombs were pressing, to enable the design of the "new look" for civil defense organizations (Civil Defense Committee 1954b). Another issue was how to ensure the continued operation of industrial, commercial, and other establishments and to protect vital systems. It was concluded that if nuclear weapons were deployed, no planning or structure would save any of the vital productions and functions, but certain "blast walls" for key industries had been used during World War II and had been shown to be useful for powerful conventional weapons. In addition, industries themselves should plan for potential attacks and ensure the safety of production and personnel; the Netherlands had a limit of 30 or more, the UK 200 or more, whereas other countries had a 500-person limit. There was also a suggestion to provide a handbook to industries in the NATO region that should provide information and guidance on self-protection measures (Civil Defense Committee 1954b).

Collier and Lakoff have investigated developments in the US during the same time. They noted how the protection of population, industry, and vital systems and infrastructure became a top priority in urban and national planning in the US after the knowledge that the Soviet Union may, in fact, reach US soil with nuclear weapons (Collier and Lakoff 2021). Similar understandings and concerns also shaped NATO's planning and preparations for war.

However, the meeting records also include other, more mundane issues, such as rescuing trapped people, firefighting, and the benefits of standardizing stretchers in NATO countries. This illustrates the vast scope of civil defense during war and in planning for future wars, as well as the extensive efforts at coordination within NATO regarding civil defense (Civil Defense Committee 1954b).

This was not just lofty ideas being discussed in NATO meetings. Sir John Hodsoll, the technical adviser and civil defense expert, informed the committee that 1,950,000 Francs "were set aside in the NATO budget for the activities of the NATO Civil Defense experts" (Civil Defense Committee 1954b). This would potentially make possible:

(a) A library of films and film strips should be built, and handbooks and periodicals should be published, which might be loaned to other countries.
(b) Commentaries in other languages might be added to certain films supplied by countries.
(c) The possibility of issuing a NATO civil defense handbook embodying some of the information collected by the experts.
(d) A glossary of civil defense terms in French and English.
(e) A paper on the maintenance of public utilities.

It was, however, clear that the final decision on the implementation and the willingness to use such material rested with national governments. For instance, the representative from the Netherlands expressed some reservations regarding c, d, and e, as he believed that the public interests of what is being done in other countries would be very limited and that publicity that NATO was engaged in such activities might even "prove disadvantageous in some countries"[5] (Civil Defense Committee 1954b). In a later meeting on the Civil Defense Committee, it was:

> agreed that national authorities should be fully consulted in each case and should be given full opportunity to decide whether any publicity material that was proposed by NATO to issue was suitable for publication in their countries (Civil Defense Committee 1954a).

This indicates a potential conflict between ambition and cultural differences regarding the best way to implement NATO incentives across member states.

The Civil Defense Committee submitted its report to the North Atlantic Council at the beginning of 1955 to raise awareness of the civil defense aspects of a strategic and military nature and to obtain the Council's approval of the list of priorities. It included a wide range of concerns, suggesting that, although civil defense is the competence of member states and national authorities, the efforts and capabilities of different member states directly affect other member states and NATO's overall defense posture and military strength. Here, we see that the priority of civil defense was the protection of populations and individuals not engaged in combat.

> While the civil population will be in the front line and must, therefore, be prepared to fight it out; it is important to remove from probable target areas, or parts of these areas, young children, school children, mothers with young children, people in hospital, aged and infirm persons and others - who for a variety of good reasons ought not to be exposed to more danger than can be avoided; even though in total war there must always be some risk (NATO 1955b).

[5] An interesting side note is that a German Delegation was present at the meeting despite the fact that West Germany only joined NATO in May 1955. The idea that West Germany would join NATO was already widespread in 1954.

5.6 Establishment of SCEPC and the New Assumptions

However, it didn't prove easy to advance and ensure that member states and other committees took civil defense seriously. In November 1955, the Senior Civil Emergency Planning Committee (SCEPC), also known as the Senior Committee, was established by a resolution of the North Atlantic Council (North Atlantic Council 1955 C/M 100). The resolution and the need for a Senior Committee emerged from concerns raised by several member states, not least the US, about the lack of coordination among NATO's various planning committees and gaps in their structures and coverage. The NAC had therefore proposed a working group following a proposal of the United States to review the organization of civil defense efforts in NATO and the need to give these issues extra weight and authority (NATO 1955a AC/95-D/1).

The Chairman of the Senior Committee was the Secretary General of NATO, while the Deputy Chairman was the Executive Secretary. Both the first Secretary General, Lord Ismay, and the Executive Secretary, Lord Coleridge, were enthusiastic supporters of civil defense planning and preparedness. Each nation was to be represented by the senior official responsible for national coordination, with the Secretary General serving as chair. Military authorities and Chairs of relevant committees were also invited to meetings when necessary (NATO 1980, AC/25-N/260). When the SCEPC was established, it took over the role and tasks previously held by the Committee on Civil Organization in Time of War and the Committee on Wartime Commodity Problem (North Atlantic Council 1955, C-M 55/100).

The Executive Secretary was also responsible for the Civil Emergency Planning Office within the International Staff/Secretariat. In 1959, this office had only three officers, one of whom was the long-standing technical adviser on civil defense, Sir John Hodsoll.[6] Later in time, by 1965, the SCEPC had successfully urged the North Atlantic Council to include technical advisors and experts in various fields, such as civil aviation, inland transport, communications, emergency exercises, medical issues, and refugee matters. The SCEPC was pursuing a broader agenda and found it odd that only civil defense experts were in the office. Again,

[6] Sir John Hodsoll retired in 1961 and was replaced by Mr. Aldo Cippico as head of the Civil Emergency Planning Office.

the role of NATO staff at the headquarters furthers the impression of an emerging international organization beyond the alliance.

The SCEPC was initially tasked with advising the North Atlantic Council on civil emergency planning matters, coordinating the activities of related boards and committees, and reviewing country-specific progress in civil emergency planning. There was an apparent need for "a comprehensive" survey of civil emergency planning and for the coordination of plans drawn up for various special sectors of civilian activity. There was also an expressed concern that there was a lack of implementation in the member states, especially regarding "the whole field of problems relating to civil emergency planning for an atomic war." Finally, improvement of implementation was only seen as possible "by the establishment of a committee capable of exercising wide authority" (North Atlantic Council 1955 C-M 55/100). The potential improvement of a senior, more authoritative body was the more immediate coordination of civil emergency planning among the member states, as the committee was instructed to take the necessary steps to ensure the continuity of its actions and efforts in civil emergency planning. For this purpose, it should also periodically review the progress made "…by countries in their civil emergency planning and report to the Council accordingly" (ibid).

The implications of this organizational restructuring are that NATO was concerned about civil defense and that insufficient effort could impair the organization and its defense and military capacity. Even though NATO could not force member states to implement, the periodic review indicates that a form of "naming and shaming" of member states could improve the situation (see also Bjørnsson 2023). This indirect governance approach would become the standard for NATO's efforts to implement the Articles of the Treaty beyond its immediate control.

The first meeting of the Civil Defense Committee following the creation of the Senior Civil Emergency Planning Committee illustrates the various ambitions and concerns regarding the scope of civil defense. Sir John Hodsoll admitted that some of the topics dealt with in the draft report were only distantly related to civil defense. Still, if they are not considered by the committee, they might be overlooked, for instance, public utilities of water, gas, electricity, and sewers that were not covered by any other body within NATO. It seemed "advisable to bring them to the attention of the Senior Committee while making it clear that the Civil Defence Committee only wished to ensure that these important issues were not being neglected." The UK representative remarked that these were indeed vital issues for civil defense in that "the correct maintenance in good working order of the public water supplies was of paramount importance for fire-fighting". These issues were, however, later formally resubmitted to the CDC for consideration. The US representative went even further on why there were really no limits on what to be considered under the pretext of civil defense and said that "during an attack and immediately afterward, everything which was essential to the life of the community was of concern to Civil Defence. Consequently, it was for the Civil Defence Services to look after the basic needs of the population in terms of food, transport, and heating. It was as much the duty of the Civil Defence Services to clothe the homeless and the evacuated as to provide them with shelter and pocket money. Preparations would, therefore, have to be made to build up reserves to meet these elementary requirements" (Civil Defense Committee 1955c).

The first meeting of the Senior Civil Emergency Planning Committee took place at the Palais de Chaillot, Paris, on January 26 and 27, 1956. Lord Ismay gave the opening remarks and noted that the task before them would not be easy. "It was difficult enough to work out plans for the emergency on a national scale, it was far more difficult to attempt this kind of planning in respect to 15 nations. Patience, perseverance, and above all, flexibility would be needed if they were to succeed in the work"…"they were to a large extent working in the dark and would have to learn by experience, any attempt to be dogmatic would be fatal" (SCEPC 1956 AC/98 - R 1). Lord Ismay also pointed out that the role of the international NATO staff would be essential as "a secretarial one… It would be for the governments to provide the ideas and material on which the international staff would work". The continuity of effort on civil defense had somehow to be managed even when the committee was not in session (SCEPC 1956 AC 98 - R 1). This again illustrates the foundational role that NATO and its permanent staff played in sustaining the organization's capacity to address complex issues.

The first meeting of the Senior Committee must have been overwhelming for the participants. Civil defense and emergencies could affect all aspects of full-scale war, not just the military ones. Most issues and reports submitted by subcommittees and working groups were mainly acknowledged and briefly commented on, with little substantial or detailed discussion. Manpower, coal, steel, petroleum, and the production of a range of other materials were among the problems. In addition, food and agriculture, stockpiling, as well as medicine and health care were also discussed. The Civil Defense Committee was not the only subcommittee to raise concerns. Ultimately, the Senior Committee invited the Civil Defense Committee to study problems related to public utilities during wartime and to do so in coordination with other emergency planning committees (SCEPC 1956 AC 98 - R 1). It was dire work for the senior Committee and all the subcommittees to synthesize the elements of civil emergency planning.

The alert reader may have noted the slight shift in terminology that the reorganization created. Instead of discussing civil defense, war, and war preparation, the new terminology of emergency planning also implied a new focus on emergencies affecting populations and civil administration. This was a central part of the *new assumptions* that believed that any future war with the Soviet Union would entail a massive use of thermo-nuclear weapons that would create substantial and grave implications for the populations in the initial phase. In some sense, the problems of warfare and endurance had been reversed between the military and the civil administration, society, and populations. Whereas the military frontlines had been key during earlier wars, they now appeared to be secondary to the "home front" that indeed would suffer the first and most severe attack and dangers (Civil Defense Committee 1955a) (see also Civil Defense Committee 1955b).

In fact, ensuring the population's survival and securing the continuation of national governments and control after the first nuclear strike and initial phase of the war was considered the key for states to later be able to engage in conventional warfare and military operations. This gave the Committee of Civil Defense an accentuated role in that it was to consider how to plan for surviving the first critical phase that would enable the return to conventional warfare for the surviving states and populations.

As the Senior Committee continued its work in 1956, it aimed to focus on two basic assumptions: "our planning for the opening phase of a war should be directed towards:- (a) ensuring the survival of the populations; (b) ensuring the maintenance of governmental and other controls…Planning for the second phase—after the first 30 days of heavy thermo-nuclear attack—is clearly less 'urgent but should not be neglected" (SCEPC 1956a). Civil defense is now explicitly included when discussing the implementation of the strategic concept: "…the disruption and disorganization of communications, transportation, medical services, utilities, and food supplies in countries or regions singled out for nuclear attack would endanger civilian morale and seriously impede the ability of nations to sustain and reinforce their fighting forces. The burden of responsibility for the resuscitation of stricken areas rests upon national civil defence organizations which must be established and trained in peacetime. However, it must be recognized that there is a probability that national military units other than M-Day and first echelon units might be called upon temporarily to assist in this task" (SCEPC 1957b).

The Senior Civil Emergency Planning Committee guided the work of its subordinate boards and committees, including those in the civil emergency planning sector, which had been established at the beginning of 1950. SCEPC also worked closely with the Standing Group and coordinated their views on the best possible way to secure the home front. This continuous work was based on an appreciation of the scale and types of attack that could be expected, of the most important and, therefore, most likely targets, and of the general effects that modern weapons may be expected to have. The most fundamental assumption on which civil emergency planning was based was that the critical period of any future thermo-nuclear war would be the first month, of which the first 3 or 4 days were likely to be of special importance. In fact, a 1958 Military Committee report, The Military Progress of NATO (Report No. 11), explicitly links civil defense efforts to NATO's overall military progress and capacity (Military Committee 1958). It notes that the reports from the Senior Civil Emergency Planning Committee from February 1958 and from the 22 subcommittees, gathered into one general report in September 1958, bring to light "the lack of civil preparedness of the European NATO nations in the event of nuclear war" (Military Committee 1958). In addition, a recent SHAPE study, made available in June 1958, on the lack of civilian preparedness for war outlines the military consequences of these deficiencies. The Standing Group approved the conclusion contained therein that "the present lack of civilian preparedness for war could have grave consequences on the entire NATO defense effort and suggested that action be undertaken to urge the nations to increase the civil defense coverage in the syllabuses of their respective national defense and staff colleges" (Military Committee 1958, 17–18).

The Secretary General also incorporated a section on civil emergency planning into his semi-annual progress report for the NATO organization. This section summarized the activities of each of the specialized boards and committees working in this area and provided the Secretary General with an opportunity to give his views on overall progress and those topics that need further attention. This also included explaining the activities of the Civil Emergency Planning Office and its director in more detail (NATO 1980).

5.7 Difficulties in Coordinating Civil Defense

Throughout the period 1958 to 1965, the Senior Committee and its subordinate committees concentrated on the minimum requirements that would enable the civil population to survive this short period in which thermo-nuclear weapons would be used extensively. Each year, the specialized boards and committees submitted progress reports to the senior committee. These reports were consolidated by the Civil Emergency Planning Yearly Review Sub-Committee, which was renamed the Civil Emergency Planning Co-Ordinating Committee in 1961 and, at the same time, given the additional task of gathering and summarizing the development of civil defense in each of the member states (North Atlantic Council 1959; NATO 1980).

But all efforts to make civil defense effective and manageable seemed in vain. There were too many aspects and details to cover. The fact that the member states ultimately decided what should be done and handed in a self-evaluation country report led to increased confusion as well as scattered and overly optimistic views of the progress. The sheer amount of information on all aspects of civil defense quickly became unmanageable.

One of the first reports on the progress and coordination of the member states from 1956 identifies some key issues in this regard. This is the first report given to SCEPC from the country delegations on the civil defense status of the member states, and each delegation tries to respond to questions relating to the continuity of government control, possible transfer of the government, legislative, and constitutional provisions, arrangements for decentralizing essential public administrative services, the possibility of decentralizing power, the liaison between civil and military authorities.[7] It is clear that the main approach of military strategy and the threat of nuclear war drove NATO and the security discourse in this specific direction. At the same time, NATO indirectly raises problems and the need for constitutional and administrative arrangements to address pressing issues (SCEPC 1956d). We can see that even though NATO does

[7] It should be noted that the reports are not streamlined and the different countries responds to these and other issue freely with some variations.

not force the implementation of measures, it has a clear agenda-setting function by raising specific issues and problems in which the apparent solutions are given, for instance, it is implied that there should be a close liaison between civil and military authorities. The individual countries try to provide answers but are different in constitutional and administrative terms, the length of their reply, and the efforts and concern placed on civil defense in their home countries. The delegations of Denmark, the Netherlands, and Portugal informed the committee that the reports were not yet ready since the issue of maintaining governmental control was still under study in their countries (SCEPC 1956d).

Belgium raises the issue that if there is a lack of detailed information on the implications of a nuclear bomb, and only general information is available, it is difficult to make any advanced and costly preparations. In addition, "peacetime preparations carried beyond a certain stage could not fail to become apparent [for the population] and might cause psychological and political reactions which must be very carefully weighed up in advance" (SCEPC 1956d). A central problem related to the possibility of the continuity of governmental and political control is the population. On the one hand, member states raise issues of providing protection. France, for instance, discusses the possibility of building shelters but understands that the protection of the population can only be provisional. However, it is not only the protection of the population that poses significant problems given the "new assumptions." Another pressing issue is the maintenance of law and order and having 'control' over the population. France, for instance, suggests that "For the maintenance of law and order and the checking of subversive activities, the French Government, ever since 1950, has directed its attention to strengthening the links between the civil and the military authorities". Turkey provides a relatively short reply in this regard: "Arrangements for maintaining law and order, preventing confusion and panic, and keeping up public morale are covered by legislations on civil defence" (SCEPC 1956d). The home front and the population are regarded as both targets and resources that must be protected. At the same time, the population can also be a problem if chaos breaks out; law and order and public morale become major concerns for NATO and the member states.

It should be noted that the United States Delegation had, before the first meeting of the Senior Committee, sent a statement of certain problems of governmental control during crisis and war (SCEPC 1956b) and could thus be seen as shaping the agenda for this issue.

The report from 1956 also considers "administrative and organizational problems in public administration as well as in industrial, agricultural and commercial concerns, connected with the continuing supply of commodities and services, especially those essential to survival in the first phase of a nuclear war" (SCEPC 1956d). Most member states report having established arrangements between the state and market actors in the central sectors that deal with this problem. The report concludes that: "The magnitude of the problems created by thermo-nuclear warfare is such that it is difficult for the civilian authorities to study, or even to visualise them all simultaneously" (SCEPC 1956d).

The following year, 1957, the Civil Defense Committee tried to provide a more coherent report to SCEPC. It focuses on two main issues and uses seven different criteria to track the national progress or lack of progress, broken down in respect of each member nation, toward the seven objectives of civil defense, and to account for the state of planning and physical measures, as well as the financial commitments undertaken by governments. It also aimed to track the progress or lack of progress achieved toward planning and physical preparations with respect to international wartime agencies (SCEPC 1957a).[8] The first part of the report contains a summary of the Civil Defense Committee. In contrast, the second part contains an evaluation conducted by the SCEPC, along with comments and recommendations about how each country should best proceed. It is evident in the first part that no country has met all the criteria. One of the most severe fallbacks is the lack of shelters provided for the population: "Although it is generally agreed that the provision of shelters is of the highest importance, plans to protect populations against blast, heat and radiation would involve immense sums which no country is prepared to spend at the present time. Countries have therefore been led to adopt less ambitious plans" (SCEPC 1957a). The second part is interesting in that regard that SCEPC provides evaluation and that the Civil Defense Committee recommends Belgium to (1) accelerate as far as possible the completion of the radio and wire communications network for air-raid warnings, (2) obtain early government approval to plans for fallout warnings and consequent allocation of funds for implementation,

[8] Seven criteria are (1) warning arrangements including fallout, (2) development of civil defense services, (3) planning for evacuation and dispersal, (4) planning for transit and reception of refugees, (5) shelters + shelters for fallout, (6) planning for maintenance of public utilities, (7) control of population under attack including fallout.

(3) to obtain early legislation for the full organization of all Civil defense services, (4) to remedy the serious billeting situation with regard to evacuees (SCEPC 1957a). This is only an illustration of how precise the "naming and shaming procedure could work, and that NATO indeed provided specific recommendations for how each country should improve civil defense and civil emergency planning efforts. Comments could be very specific, such as the Icelandic case: "That the Icelandic Government should renew their contribution to the municipality of Reykjavik to enable plans now made to be implemented and further stock-piles to be created. If funds are provided, then with the plans already made and the stock-piling which has already been accomplished, further good progress could be achieved" (SCEPC 1957a). Other countries received no comments, which meant an acceptable level, and still other countries had one or two comments on how to proceed. Also, the United States is recommended to address the issue so that "instruction facilities should be brought up to a satisfactory level" (ibid). Still, it is difficult to see any clear evaluation criteria or absolute requirements for evaluation and recommendations. In any case, this report shows how naming and shaming could allow NATO to "govern" at a distance and exert influence over the national competence of civil defense, in accordance with Article 3 of the North Atlantic Treaty. It appears that NATO is indeed following the principles for *implementing* NATO policy.

The problems associated with civil defense and civil emergency planning and how this potentially hampers NATO's ability to stop and wage war are seen as a problem throughout the organization. The Military committee notes that:

> the results of the 1959 Yearly Review of Civil Emergency Planning, brings to light the continuing lack of adequate civil preparedness of the European NATO nations in the event of nuclear war. During the past year, marked progress has been made in the 21 various fields of civil emergency planning, but the existing deficiencies continue to give concern to the NATO military authorities. Continued emphasis on national efforts to overcome these deficiencies is considered important despite the political, economic and psychological problems associated with civil emergency planning (Military Committee 1959; see also 1963).

At the same time, as many committees sought to improve civil defense and civil emergency planning and to streamline and coordinate them, there were also complaints about the frequency and volume of reports on these issues.

Complaints regarding the density of the annual review of civil defense progress in NATO prompted changes to the format for the 1960 annual review. The questionnaire, which had been used to gather the progress of member state efforts since 1958, was thus streamlined and simplified. The International Staff prepared a condensed report highlighting the most significant points. The more detailed report was made available to council members and national delegations upon request, but it is not available in the NATO archives. At the Ministerial Council Meeting in Oslo in 1961, it was further agreed that the annual reviews of civil defense needed to be more focused on clear and standardized evaluation goals (Public Diplomacy Division 1961). In this way, the complete picture of civil defense should be made more manageable. Beginning in 1962, the annual report to the council aimed to avoid presenting an overly optimistic view, thereby revealing both existing gaps and progress made. Subsequent reports were designed to present a more accurate picture of NATO's current state across central areas of national planning under broad yet precise categories: *Government Control, Civil Defense, Communications, Food, Oil, Coal Supplies, Medical, Inland Surface Transport, Manpower, Industry, Ocean Shipping, and Civil Aviation.*

The 1962 annual review reflected the revised requirement, and this version was used until 1965. Over these 3 years, the reports included sections on individual countries that presented the status of civil emergency planning across all aspects, with specific recommendations issued to each country. However, beginning with the 1964 Annual Review of Civil Defense, the country reports were considered as a mere "background" to the more concise report (Civil Defense Committee 1962).

At this time, the North Atlantic Council found it necessary to further reduce the burden of all civil emergency planning issues and reports that it was forced to handle. The solution was the creation of the Coordination Committee, which was to examine the work processes for all issues handled by NATO, including civil emergency planning, and to identify how to streamline them to improve efficiency. In this spirit, a review of the work conducted by the Senior Committee by the North Atlantic Council in 1965 allowed the SCEPC to meet annually in plenary sessions but also more frequently in "permanent sessions" for ongoing work to ease the burden for NAC regarding civil emergency planning. The SCEPC was also authorized to review new studies for compliance with its objectives and to approve the formation of subcommittees and working groups in civil defense planning (NATO 2026e).

The records show that NATO's efforts regarding civil defense and, later, broader civil emergency planning were extensive and coordinated with military planning. This is even though it was the competence and responsibility of the member states. The question of formal responsibility was repeatedly raised in reports and decisions. Civil defense played only a minor role in NATO's first 5 years, but it became a prioritized area once the "new assumption" and the reversed relationship between the home front and military operations emerged. The threat of atomic warfare meant the protection of societies, industries, and populations, and, not least, the continuation of political control in member states was seen as crucial for the ability to engage in conventional warfare and military campaigns after surviving the first waves of attacks.

From the outset of civil emergency planning, it was acknowledged that while the Senior Committee could coordinate planning for an emergency with guidance from military authorities, the actual implementation of those plans would depend on efforts by national authorities. Annual questionnaires sent to member nations and the compiled national responses constituted the most significant knowledge of progress reflected in the Senior Committee's annual reports to the Council. Based on these self-evaluation reports, conclusions were drawn, forming the basis for any recommendations for additional efforts or modifications.

Preparing questionnaires and analyzing responses from member states, along with the numerous detailed reports from the Boards and Committees involved in civil defense and emergency planning, required considerable effort, time, and attention—resources the members of the Senior Committee could not spare. Consequently, much of this work was carried out by the Yearly Review Sub-Committee, the Office for Civil Defense, and international staff. In that sense, we can also see that the issue of civil defense is managed primarily by international bureaucratic staff within NATO. They set out to provide a review of actual national progress since last year and how member states are implementing the most vital measures needed for survival in light of the goals established by NATO. They summarize the work carried out during the year by the Planning Boards and Committees as they prepared reports for SCEPC (NATO 1980). This illustrates the importance of international staff and the bureaucratization of the alliance, and the way NATO grows into an international organization.

This further indicates the extent to which NATO worked to implement civil defense and how such reports could serve as valuable tools for screening and enhancing control and governance over member states. It also illustrates how NATO's permanent international staff could assert its role in evaluating progress and recommending reforms for individual member states. Although NATO had no formal authority in this area, it is clear that this method of distant governance—name-and-shame—could still be highly effective.

5.8 Conclusions 1949–1964

This chapter has covered the first 16 years of NATO and traces its development from a military alliance among 12 countries to an international organization representing the interests of the now 15 member states, with a permanent international staff and permanent representatives. NATO has become more than the sum of its parts, evolving from an alliance into an international organization. It has expanded the military dimension and established a unique military command structure comprising SHAPE, SAUCER, and SACLANT. Beyond its military dimensions, the North Atlantic Council has assumed a more political and permanent role, and the General Secretary has been appointed Chair of the Council. More interestingly, the chapter noted that although civil defense was identified as a core competence of the member states, this issue remains a high priority for NATO. The North Atlantic Council and the Secretary General were highly interested in this issue and established several committees and subcommittees to investigate and coordinate civil defense in the Alliance. NATO also created a specific post to support this work: a technical adviser, Sir John Hodsoll, a British pioneer and founding father of civil defense in the UK. He and his co-workers, who worked outside the committees, wrote reports and provided advice to numerous committees and member states that were interested in these issues. He was later granted an office and two more permanent staff to further support this work. In the first 3 years of NATO, little attention was given to civil defense issues, but that changed dramatically when it became known that the Soviet Union possessed both nuclear weapons and the capability to strike in both Europe and North America. Following the "new assumptions," the relationship was reversed, and the home front, governments, society, and populations, along with the importance of political control of population and public morale, became a top priority. It was also during the mid-1950s that civil defense became part of the much broader approach proposed by the Americans: *civil emergency planning*. New issues and aspects beyond the protection of the civilian population were incorporated into the new concept, and the Senior Civil Emergency Planning Committee was installed in 1955, with its first meeting in 1956.

It was vital for NATO member states to survive the first strike and the initial 30-day period, during which they could recover and transition to conventional weapons to continue the general war against the adversary. Despite ambitious plans and the intense interest in civil defense and, later, civil emergency planning as a central component of NATO's total defense and war capacity, it remained nearly impossible to address these issues satisfactorily. Too many issues and highly divergent political systems among the member states would make it difficult for NATO to govern them indirectly. Still, member states addressed specific issues identified in the annual review of civil emergency planning, which had been established through the questionnaire and summarized in reports by the international staff. Civil defense and civil emergency planning, although identified as national competencies and regulated by Article 3, were of great importance to NATO and to the conduct of war. In the next chapter, we shall see how even more issues are included in these policy areas as the security agenda expands between the years 1965 and 1989.

CHAPTER 6

Expansion of the (Civil) Security Agenda 1965–1989

The early 1960s were turbulent for NATO. The Cuban Missile Crisis in October 1962 was a direct and dangerous confrontation between the US and the Soviet Union that lasted 13 days and illustrated the fragile construct of the massive retaliation policy and how quickly small mistakes or miscommunication could potentially trigger the use of nuclear weapons. The Berlin Wall was erected on August 13, 1961, further intensifying tensions between the East and the West. In addition to external pressure, NATO experienced significant internal turmoil. Sten Rynning refers to the period 1966–1989 as a retreat to pragmatism, which NATO muddled through (Rynning 2024). Ian Hope notes in his chapter that the organization suffered from internal divisions over issues of "Europe-based nuclear weapons, arms control and arms reduction, defence expenditures and the demands of a large and active peace movements and public opinions on the issue of arms race and nuclear threats" (Hope 2024, 41).

Even as NATO maintained a firm political position toward the Soviet Union, it did so with a new, flexible, and more pragmatic approach to its main rivalry than it had articulated during the 1950s and early 1960s. At the same time, NATO had to navigate substantial internal crises among member states that risked its collapse. France's withdrawal from the military structure in 1966 is one such "internal" crisis discussed in detail below. When examining the civil dimensions of NATO's integration, however, a different picture emerges. Between 1965 and 1989, despite

O. Larsson, *NATO's Approach to the Civil Dimensions of War*,
https://doi.org/10.1007/978-3-032-27871-5_6

external and internal turmoil, the role of civil defense and civil emergency planning expanded to include logistical support for the military, civil-military collaboration, dual-use capabilities, and the concept of an all-hazards approach covering crises, disasters, and war, which became more prominent. The fact that this expansion of the security agenda occurred prior to the end of the Cold War is a surprising finding of this chapter and contradicts the more widespread idea that it was only possible after the end of the Cold War, with the demise of conventional war and the imminent nuclear threat. This chapter examines the expansion of the civil security agenda within NATO, while maintaining a focus on efforts toward civil defense and civil emergency planning.

6.1 A New Military Structure and Strategy

In 1964, the US escalated its involvement in the Vietnam War, which put the former colonial power, France, in a more inactive position. Other issues also added to the tension between the US and France at the beginning of the 1960s. The USA insisted on full control over nuclear weapons and assets in NATO. Charles de Gaulle was reluctant to place France's armed forces under the control of NATO and US commanders (NATO 2025b). It is unclear how this position was caused by the fact that France did not have a more active role in NATO's nuclear weapons program. In March 1966, France withdrew from NATO's integrated military command structure at the same time as it wished to remain a political member. France offered to keep the Allied headquarters in French territory, but NATO found it more appropriate to seek a new permanent and stable home (NATO 2025b). NATO was first headquartered in London before relocating to Paris in 1952, where, under Lord Ismay's leadership, it soon transformed into an international organization (see previous chapter). After the breakup with France, a new SHAPE Headquarters was established in Casteau, Belgium, in March 1967. In addition, a new NATO Headquarters was established in Brussels, and the official move was conducted in October 1967. The new building hosted both military and civil authorities under the same roof for the first time (NATO 2016a). Significantly, France remained in the alliance and emphasized its intention to stand united with NATO in the event of hostilities. Still, the timing of France's withdrawal highlighted the rather unusual Article 13 of the North Atlantic Treaty. This article stated that any party may leave the treaty after 20 years, which would have been in 1969. Thus, when

France decided to step back from its military commitments in 1966, the future of NATO became highly uncertain.

Article 13
After the treaty has been in force for 20 years, any party may cease to be a party 1 year after its notice of denunciation has been given to the government of the United States of America, which will inform the governments of the other parties of the deposit of each notice of denunciation

France played a significant role in NATO, as one of the three countries in the Standing Group and one of the European nuclear powers, helping to balance the US's heavy influence in NATO. When France withdrew from its military commitment to NATO, it could no longer participate in the Military Committee that prepared military strategies. In addition, the Standing Group, comprising senior officers from France, the UK, and the US, was dissolved following France's withdrawal. The latter was replaced by the International Military Staff (IMS). IMS was established in 1967 to support work exclusively in the collective and international capacities, in the interest of NATO, the Military Committee, and its chairman. The International Military Staff (IMS) is still (2025) the executive body of the Military Committee and NATO's senior military authority (NATO 2024a). IMS has remained central to collaboration between NATO organs, member states, and civil-military coordination.

In 1963, another body within the military structure was created. The Defence Planning Committee (DPC) was a senior decision-making body for matters relating to the Alliance's integrated military structure. It was later dispersed following a major committee review in June 2010, and the North Atlantic Council absorbed its responsibilities. During its active years, the DPC held significant influence within the NATO structure, and when France withdrew, it assumed the North Atlantic Council's military responsibilities to ensure France could remain in the NAC. The DPC had the same level of authority as the North Atlantic Council and the Nuclear Planning Group (see below). It was, in fact, the highest authority on all questions related to NATO's integrated military structure. The DPC made its first report to the Council in December 1965, covering the coming 5-year period. That same month, the Council decided to base its defense planning on a 5-year cycle, complemented by yearly reviews. When France withdrew from NATO's integrated military structure a year later, in 1966, the Council extended the DPC's mandate beyond strictly military planning to include all integrated matters (NATO 2022a). In this way, the DPC became an engine for military integration within NATO.

In addition, the Nuclear Planning Group (NPG) was established in December 1966, following the Defence Planning Committee's acceptance of a recommendation from the special committee of Defence Ministers, chaired by Robert McNamara of the U.S. (NATO 1967b). The main point was actually to create a consultative process on nuclear issues within NATO, and it was deemed necessary as NATO and the US wanted to move away from massive retaliation to a more flexible approach (NATO 2022c; Rynning 2024). Two bodies were suggested: the Nuclear Defence Affairs Committee (NDAC), open to all NATO members, and the NPG, restricted to NATO's integrated military nations for in-depth nuclear design. Initially, seven countries participated, with the permanent members being the U.S., the UK, Italy, and West Germany. The other three seats rotated annually among eligible nations. Until 1973, the NDAC met yearly to review NPG proposals. Since then, although not formally abolished, the NDAC's duties have been assumed by the NPG, which has become the sole NATO body for nuclear matters.

As shown above, despite France's withdrawal from NATO's military structures, NATO pursued further and deeper cooperation and coordination. In contrast to pragmatism and muddling through, it could be argued that NATO continued down the path of formalization and the cementation of an international organization. This all came to influence the role of civil defense and emergency planning and the new routes proposed in this period.

6.2 A New Strategic Concept and the Flexible Approach

NATO's third *Strategic Concept* emphasized zero tolerance for Soviet aggression and suggested a strategy of massive retaliation, a full strike with nuclear weapons. This strategy relied heavily on the United States' nuclear capability, which initially was greater than that of the Soviet Union, and its willingness to defend Europe in the case of a Soviet nuclear attack. In the meantime, the Soviet Union had developed its nuclear weapons as well as intercontinental ballistic missile capabilities. The world faced a massive standoff, with its entire population at risk. "Mutually Assured Destruction" or "MAD" has been used to describe this situation. In addition, there were a few occasions when the idea of massive retaliation proved less effective. The outbreak of the second Berlin Crisis (1958–1962) made it clear that the Soviet Union was not intimidated enough to avoid conflict (nor were the US and NATO). Upon taking office in 1961, US President John F. Kennedy witnessed the end of the Berlin Crisis, the erection of the Berlin Wall, and the Cuban Missile Crisis in October 1962. It became clear that nuclear war could emerge due to accidents, miscommunication, or "rational" miscalculation. The United States initiated investigations that could advance a non-nuclear posture for NATO and searched for a reliable strategy of "flexible response," which meant a wider toolbox and tempered responses dependent on the posed threat (NATO 2022e). At the same time, NATO Secretary General Dirk Stikker delivered a special report on NATO Defence Policy (The North Atlantic Council 1962, CM 62 48) on April 17, 1962, addressing the political oversight of nuclear arms. This report, referred to as the Athens guidelines, essentially marked NATO's initial effort to moderate its policy of massive retaliation by proposing that the deployment of nuclear weapons be subject to consultation depending on different scenarios (ibid).

Other attempts to introduce greater flexibility followed, but they encountered resistance from several member countries, foremost France. However, when France withdrew from NATO's military arm, it became possible to pursue a new overall strategy, and NATO's fourth *strategic concept* was developed. It was entitled "Overall Strategic Concept for the Defense of the North Atlantic Treaty Organization Area" (MC 14/3). It was adopted by the Defence Planning Committee (DPC) on 12 December 1967 (NATO 1967a). The final version was issued on January 16, 1968. This is the only strategic concept in NATO's history that the North Atlantic Council did not decide on. The reason for this is simple: France was still part of the NAC but not of the DPC (NATO Strategic Concept 2022).

The introductory paragraph states that: "The overall defensive concept of the North Atlantic Treaty Organisation is to preserve peace and to provide for the security of the North Atlantic Treaty area primarily by a credible deterrence, effected by confronting any possible, threatened or actual aggression, ranging from covert operations to all-out nuclear war, with adequate NATO forces" (NATO 1967a)…"In this context, the Soviets will try to exploit any weaknesses to their own advantage, within as well as outside the NATO area, in order to strengthen their position as a world power" (NATO 1967a). The conflict with the Soviets is not only phrased in military means, as NATO identifies that the enemy may use economic means, political means, propaganda, and subversion—including the spreading of the Communist ideology and the exportation of arms and other material, and finally military power (ibid). This is very similar to the way in which grey zone and hybrid threats have been discussed since 2014. To address the complex image of the enemy's potential influence and power, it was suggested that NATO should rely on "flexibility" and "escalation."

Flexibility is understood as "A flexibility which will prevent the potential aggressor from predicting with confidence NATO's specific response to aggression, and which will lead him to conclude that an unacceptable degree of risk would be involved regardless of the nature of his attack" (NATO 1967a). Escalation meant that any aggression or action should be met proportionally, but with the possibility of "Deliberate Escalation." "Deliberate escalation seeks to defend aggression by deliberately raising but, where possible, controlling the scope and intensity of combat…" (NATO 1967a, 14). This meant that nuclear weapons were not excluded, but that each threat and aggression should be met in proportion, and that nuclear weapons would be used if deemed necessary. The document also reveals that the East-West conflict is not restricted to geographical areas and territories of member states. Rather, flexibility could also be used for "Operations Outside the NATO Area" because "The forces of certain NATO nations may need to retain the flexibility required to permit action to meet limited military situations outside the NATO area, especially in peripheral areas. This flexibility should be harmonised with the requirement to protect NATO" (NATO 1967b, 22). It is evident that the east-west conflict expanded during this period and became a vital part of the worldwide decolonization processes, as both camps sought to establish influence and control in new countries.

Again, in the document specifying the strategic concept, the terms "civil" or "civil defense" do not appear, and "population/s" is used only three times. The word "society" is used only in reference to Soviet society. It shows that strategy and the military focus remain functionally separated from civil defense, civil emergency planning, and the home front, which are frequently mentioned in other NATO documents and committees. The 1967 strategic concept, with its flexible approach, escalation options, and the political position of détente, was so open-ended and functional to the current situation that it survived until the end of the Cold War.

6.3 Détente and the Harmel Report

In 1966, Belgium's foreign minister, Pierre Harmel, proposed exploring NATO's future tasks to strengthen the alliance internally and externally. It was against the background of recent developments in the international environment and the fact that the smaller countries in NATO still felt that they could have little or no input when "big" issues were resolved that another political report and investigation were requested (NATO, Harmel Report 1968). In addition, NATO was approaching its 20-year anniversary, which meant countries could renegotiate their membership under the North Atlantic Treaty. France's decision to step back from its NATO military involvement further accelerated the debate over the alliance's future. NATO expert Lawrence S. Kaplan has suggested that the "Harmel Report" or the "Report of the Council on the Future Tasks of the Alliance," which was adopted by NATO in December 1967, has had just as much impact on the development of NATO as the Korean War and the end of the Cold War (Kaplan 2007).

I believe that at least three critical implications of the report are worth mentioning. First, it altered NATO's overall position toward the Soviet Union and the Warsaw Pact. Earlier, it might have been considered possible that war would break out, and NATO would have to devote all its efforts to defense and deterrence. With the Harmel report, NATO now, in effect, accepted the presence and power of the Soviet Union and its allies in the Warsaw Pact. The 1968 report to the North Atlantic Council emphasized the need for both *defense* and *détente*.

> *Military security and a policy of détente are not contradictory. Collective defence is a stabilising factor in world politics. It is the necessary condition for effective policies directed towards a greater relaxation of tensions. The way to peace and stability in Europe rests in particular on the use of the Alliance constructively in the interest of détente. The participation of the USSR and the USA will be necessary to achieve a settlement of the political problems in Europe* (NATO Harmel Report 1968).

This offered a more pragmatic approach to the Soviet Union. Although NATO was not happy about its existence, it would accept it as a counterpart of the Soviet Union's political strategy at the time: mutual peaceful coexistence. In that sense, it acknowledged the importance of continued military strength and the build-up of forces within the alliance. In addition, it advocated continued political solidarity within NATO to deter aggression and a more stable relationship with the Soviet Union to resolve political issues, particularly regarding Berlin and the future reunification of Germany. The report indicated that Soviet and Eastern European policymakers might benefit from a stable European settlement, with détente as a pathway to it. This also included ideas of diminishing the arms race and control of weapons (NATO 2022e). The report itself suggests that "[t]he Allies are studying disarmament and practical arms control measures, including the possibility of balanced force reductions" (NATO, Harmel report 1968).

Such negotiations began in 1968, and the first important agreement was concluded in April 1970 in Vienna when the US and USSR joined the Strategic Arms Limitation (SALT). A second session was held in Helsinki in November of that year. The interim agreement was signed in Moscow on May 26, 1972. In addition, in September 1971, there was a main agreement on Berlin, as the four parties signed the first stage of the Four Power Agreement on Berlin. The beginning of the 1970s was thus a period characterized by the defrosting of the Cold War and attempts to address some of the most pressing issues, such as Berlin and the nuclear arms race, through negotiations.

However, the report also stressed the importance of internal stability and unity, which is its second implication.

> From the beginning the Atlantic Alliance has been a cooperative grouping of states sharing the same ideals and with a high degree of common interest. Their cohesion and solidarity provide an element of stability within the Atlantic area (NATO Harmel Report 1968).

The report called for deeper, more effective political consultations to enhance stability and cohesion within NATO.

> The Alliance affords an effective forum and clearing house for the exchange of information and views; thus, each Ally can decide its policy in the light of close knowledge of the problems and objectives of the others. To this end the practice of frank and timely consultations needs to be deepened and improved (NATO Harmel Report 1968).

Finally, a third implication of the report is that it raised the issue of third parties, states that are not part of NATO or the Warsaw Pact. It proposes an even more ambitious role for NATO beyond the defense of member states' territories, suggesting that the Alliance could contribute to international peace and stability beyond the Euro-Atlantic area.

> The North Atlantic Treaty area cannot be treated in isolation from the rest of the world. Crises and conflicts arising outside the area may impair its security either directly or by affecting the global balance. Allied countries contribute individually within the United Nations and other international organisations to the maintenance of international peace and security and to the solution of important international problems (NATO Harmal Report 1968).

The Harmel report has been described as a key document in NATO's development even beyond the end of the Cold War. It has been suggested that it continues to play a vital role in NATO's conceptualization of security and stability and still influences NATO's strategy today (NATO 2022b). The Harmel report also addresses the role of non-military actors within the member states, but these aspects warrant a more thorough analysis, as they concern civil defense and civil administration.

However, détente was not an immediate success, quite the opposite. In the *Routledge Handbook of NATO* (2024), the author and NATO expert Ian Hope provides numerous examples of dire crises facing NATO following the report and the policy of détente, which heightened both external and internal tensions. The most obvious one, which nearly led to the immediate revision of the détente policy, occurred the same year. On the night of August 20, 1968, 200,000 Warsaw Pact soldiers entered Czechoslovakia from East Germany, Poland, Ukraine, and Hungary. The border with West Germany had to be strengthened and secured, but little could be done to support the Prague Spring, which was thwarted in a single effective blow by the Soviet Union, according to the author (Hope 2024). Following the ministerial meeting of the North Atlantic Council in Brussels, November 1968, the final communique connects détente with the current situation and finds that the Soviet intervention in Czechoslovakia jeopardized the whole policy, arms reduction, and puts the German Question in a new light:

> A year ago Ministers affirmed in the Report on the Future Tasks of the Alliance that, while maintaining adequate military strength and political solidarity to deter any aggressor, the Alliance should work to promote a policy of détente. The Soviet intervention in Czechoslovakia has seriously set back hopes of settling the outstanding problems which still divide the

> European continent and Germany and of establishing peace and security in Europe, and threatens certain of the results already achieved in the field of détente (NATO, Public Diplomacy Division 2003).

It can thus be concluded that the 1960s were a turbulent period for NATO, which faced both internal and external challenges. It might appear odd that, during this period, a broader understanding of security was unfolding, adding new dimensions and tasks to NATO's civil dimensions.

6.4 The Expansion of Civil Tasks

To follow and analyze the development of NATO's civil defense and emergency planning sectors, it was necessary to visit the NATO archives in Brussels. The NATO online archives cover only the committee series of the Civil Defense Committee and the Senior Emergency Planning Committee for 1952–1966. However, they are available for researchers at the NATO Library and Archive Center (NATO 2008). A first research trip was conducted in April 2025 to recover documents pertaining to these two committees for the period 1967–1992. Since 1992, few documents have been available for public scrutiny and research. In addition, other documents continue to refer to the SCEPC and its subcommittees, as well as to a general discourse and understanding of the role of civil defense in NATO during this period. The general impression is that civil defense and the idea of a home front in a nuclear war were deprioritized during this period. One primary reason for this was that atomic weapons had grown so destructive that it was no longer rational to pursue defense and protection from the nuclear bombs themselves. The utility of civil defense efforts ended with the introduction of the hydrogen bomb and the resulting broader understanding of its capabilities. This nuclear weapon utilizes both atomic fission and nuclear fusion to create an explosion. Combining these two processes releases massive amounts of energy, several hundred or thousands of times more powerful than an atomic bomb. The explosion in the Pacific Marshall Islands on November 1, 1952, produced an equivalent of 10.4 million tons of TNT, which is about 700 times more powerful than the bomb the United States dropped on Hiroshima in 1945 (Schumann 2022).

Even if knowledge of the hydrogen bomb and the US's shift in priority from shelter to evacuation had already reached NATO by 1954, it led to the "new assumptions" covered in the last chapter. The idea of business as usual could not be sustained. Even so, civil defense remained a highly relevant issue at the end of the 1950s and the beginning of the 1960s. Still, it can explain why member states were reluctant to invest too much money in civil defense that was largely in vain. In a 1954 meeting of the Civil Defense Committee, the UK representative General F. Irving stated that "Civil defense policy in the United Kingdom was to plan as far as possible to meet an attack by nuclear weapons but they were not prepared, therefore, to spend money on any measures for protection against high explosive which did not at the same time give protection against the effects of thermonuclear, [hydrogen] weapons" (Civil Defense Committee 1954b). Concrete civil defense practices and exercises were in many countries, therefore geared toward less catastrophic scenarios than full-scale nuclear war with thermo-nuclear weapons. Even if full protection of populations, industry, and public institutions could never have been achieved, civil defense and civil emergency planning policies were refocused to a more limited set of functions that appeared more feasible. In this way, civil defense efforts were never completely abandoned (Cronqvist et al. 2022b). In the anthology *Cold War Civil Defence in Western Europe: Sociotechnical Imaginaries of Survival and Preparedness,* the authors and editors find that national resources remained focused on conventional war, minor nuclear attacks, but also peacetime atomic accidents, natural disasters, and traffic accidents. This, they argue, paves the way for the all-hazard approach to emergency planning within today's broader discourse on societal security.

In addition, it illustrates the discrepancy between the knowledge and imaginaries of the total destruction that would follow from total war and the more concrete, manageable practices and exercises in which national defense organizations were engaged. This was, at times, even ridiculed by the population as a sort of political self-deception (Cronqvist et al. 2022b). A closer reading of the governing documents in the NATO archives reveals that civil defense and civil emergency planning remained prioritized issues, even if perfection was never attainable. However, this chapter notes that, rather than seeking to solidify the core of civil defense and civil emergency planning to protect populations and public institutions, NATO continued to expand the scope and tasks included in these two areas and concepts, adding aspects of logistics support to the military, crisis management, and peacetime disaster relief.

The nuclear threat also fluctuated in importance during this period. At the beginning of the 1960s, the recent experiences of close encounters had shown that neither side was eager to initiate a nuclear war. Following the Cuban Missile Crisis, a "hotline" was installed in Moscow and Washington on June 20, 1963, that would enable direct communication as a means to avoid nuclear war by mistake (NATO, Public Diplomacy Division 1972). This year also saw the first diplomatic talks between the US and the Soviet Union on the regulation and proliferation of nuclear arms and nuclear arms tests. The first was an agreement to ban nuclear tests in the atmosphere, outer space, and underwater (NATO, Public Diplomacy Division 1972). Similar agreements will follow in the coming years. These mutual understandings and limitations across various aspects of nuclear arms would also lead to a new direction for civil defense, particularly alongside the policy of détente. Thus, the de-escalation between NATO and the Soviet Union could also explain why new roles and tasks were added to the civil defense committee and SCEPC, even as NATO did not abandon its interests in traditional civil defense planning and implementation during this period.

In 1966, following France's withdrawal from NATO's military structures, NATO undertook a review and streamlining of its organization. In January 1967, about 250 committees or working groups were in existence. More than 30 of those were directly responsible to the Council. "All too frequently, committees with different names and serving different intermediary bodies contain identical people working in the same subject area or on the same function" (NATO 1967b). There was a suggestion that a "Senior Emergency Planning Group" would replace the functions of the existing Senior Civil Emergency Planning Committee to reduce the number of committees. The change in name (and structure) did not occur; SCEPC continued to exist until 2022, when it changed its name to the Resilience Committee (see Chap. 8). However, a direct result of the reorganization was that the number of subcommittees within civil emergency planning was reduced to eight, and SCEPC could not establish new committees; only the North Atlantic Council could initiate new committees.

After adopting the new strategic concept in 1967, which advocated both flexibility and escalation, the focus on managing a nuclear attack was redirected. It became clear that civil emergency planning should no longer be confined to the post-nuclear-exchange period within the new strategy. Instead, it must embrace the entire spectrum of contingencies, including tensions, political crises, natural hazards, conventional war, and nuclear war; it should also incorporate plans and procedures to be in place before any nuclear exchange (Van Heuven 1970). This idea corresponds well to the finding that Marie Cronqvist, with coauthors, identifies when they look at national civil defense priorities during the Cold War (Cronqvist et al. 2022b). The approach of an even broader role for emergency planning and civil defense within NATO also expands NATO's role in governing national development and continues to encourage national crisis management and the management of significant hazards, or at least identifies certain national tasks in these areas as critical to NATO. Rather than consolidating civil defense and civil emergency planning into a few key areas and priorities, the development is the opposite: new areas and tasks are added to the existing ones.

6.5 Logistical Support for Military Operations

One such task that had not been as visible in the early 1960s but became increasingly prominent after 1965 was the logistical support that civil defense and civil authorities should provide for military operations. In addition to managing the home front and caring for civil defense, NATO's civil emergency planning also included establishing an organization that could be activated in wartime to coordinate member states' efforts in agriculture, industrial production, transportation, and civil defense. SCEPC had eight such committees and boards.

They met periodically to provide reports and solve governance and collaboration problems. They consisted of government officials and experts responsible for emergency planning in their respective countries. They also conducted studies on specific topics within their expertise. In this way, they contributed to planning NATO's organizational structure for civil wartime coordination across NATO countries, including resource allocation, air, sea, rail, and road transport, civil defense, and refugee management. In the event of war, these boards and committees would transform into NATO Civil Wartime Agencies and serve as operational units in civil emergency planning, coordinating resources for NATO (see below Table 6.1) (NATO, Public Diplomacy Division 1982).

Thus, civil emergency planning was primarily occupied with preparing plans for the *international civil wartime agencies*—including their functions, staffing, location, and other organizational and administrative questions (Van Heuven 1970). Again, this links national civil defense

Table 6.1

Peacetime
In the field of supplies:
– The Food and Agriculture Planning Committee;
– The Industrial Planning Committee;
– The Petroleum Planning Committee.
In the field of transport:
– The Planning Board for Ocean Shipping;
– The Planning Board for European Inland Surface Transport;
– The Civil Aviation Planning Committee.
The Civil Communications Planning Committee
The Civil Defense Committee
War time
The Defence Shipping Authority
The Interallied Insurance Organisation
The Agencies for the Coordination of Inland Surface Transport in Central Europe and Transport in the Mediterranean
The NATO Civil Aviation Agency
The Central Supplies Agency
The NATO Wartime Oil Organisation
The NATO Refugee Agency

efforts to NATO's overall capacity to wage war, as highlighted in the previous chapter. To test the effectiveness of plans and actors within the NATO system, a series of exercises was conducted for various purposes.

Paal Sigurd Hilde covers the history of NATO exercises that included civil dimensions and actors in his chapter, "NATO and total defence: A framework for national efforts" (Hilde 2025). He noted that previous research has struggled to determine the exact number and dates of these exercises and that it is difficult to recover all the details of each exercise series. Thus, an overview of the exercise series may suffice to convey the magnitude of the civil-military exercises.

As early as 1960, NATO began conducting international exercises that involved civilian dimensions and actors. The alert system was tested as part of a series of smaller exercises in the fall, referred to as NATO Fall Exercises 1960 (FALLEX 60; see Hilde 2025). The next rehearsal, FALLEX 62, was a single NATO-wide command-post exercise rather than several smaller exercises. A key aim of FALLEX 62 was "to practise the relationships between NATO commands, NATO civil agencies, national commands, and national agencies" (Military Committee 1964).

Two years later, in FALLEX 64, the North Atlantic Council, the Military Committee, and several national authorities participated for the first time. With this, the FALLEX series took its final form and remained in use until it was replaced by a similar series, Winter Exercise (WINTEX), in 1971. The element of civil-military integration in WINTEX was evident. It was later renamed Civilian-Military (CIMEX), forming the WINTEX-CIMEX exercise series. NATO conducted WINTEX(-CIMEX) every odd year from 1971 until the end of the Cold War. In addition to this series, the High Level Exercise (HILEX) was a series of tabletop exercises oriented toward political crisis management and governance. This series has been held every even year since 1974. It supplemented the more practical testing of the NATO Alert System in the FALLEX and WINTEX exercises. In 1992, following the end of the Cold War, the Cold War crisis management exercises were replaced by a new series, simply titled Crisis-Management Exercises (CMX). Essentially, the CMX series combines testing of the WINTEX-CIMEX crisis response system with the consultation and procedural processes of HILEX (Hilde 2025; Van Heuven 1970). All these exercises were in addition to the many military exercises conducted by NATO. Two other civil emergency planning exercises are not included in the series above and warrant specific mention.

In 1965, the first NATO exercise explicitly directed toward civil emergency planning and the supporting role of civil actors in military operations was conducted in CIVLOG 65 and repeated 4 years later in CIVLOG 69. These were large-scale military exercises that aimed to test and improve the planning and execution of how civil resources could support large-scale military operations within logistics in different war scenarios.

CIVLOG 1965 was approved by the Council in 1962, but took 3 years of preparation before it could take place (The North Atlantic Council 1962b). The planning and preparation was mainly conducted by the SCEPC and international staff. CIVLOG 1965 was held from May 16 to 21, 1965, and was essentially a large-scale Command Post Exercise (in which one or several HQ engaged in problem-solving but did not carry out all tasks), involving all the NATO Civilian Wartime Agencies. It aimed to test the Civil Wartime Agencies' operational role of supporting military operations beyond the survival of nations. Approximately 400 individuals and other participants from national capitals participated in the NATO Civil Wartime Agency plan during exercise CIVLOG 1965

(Military Committee 1965). This exercise enabled officials from member states and industry appointees designated by the Council to collaborate in an international context under "wartime conditions" for the first time (Standing Group 1965).

The exercise was conducted by staff representing the NATO highest political and military authorities, including representatives of the Military Committee, with a special focus on liaison elements to the various agencies. This indicates that the exercise was prioritized and conducted at the top level. To ensure that civil-military liaison arrangements were established, specific military scenarios were introduced into the exercise. The two most significant of these, according to the Standing Group, were 1, the mounting of a NATO force of Corps strength for a BALKANS landing about D + 90,[1] and 2, the sea movement of a Canadian Brigade from Canada to Europe to reinforce SACEUR (Standing Group 1965).

The Standing Group[2] memorandum indicates that the exercise did not proceed smoothly. The objective was to exercise and test the civil agencies' operating procedures, with a focus on procedural aspects. In that regard, SG found that: "All agencies found various operating deficiencies which will require further study and correction" (Standing Group 1965). The solution proposed by the Standing Group was "It appears evident that strong military representation must exist on many of the agencies if full consideration of military requirements is to be attained. In almost all instances, civilian and military requirements will be competing" (Standing Group 1965). In addition, "the exercise brought forth significant communications and liaison problems between agencies and with NATO HQ" (Ibid). This included lines of communication (the exercise took place in a single location, Port Dauphine, but HQ was located in another location in Paris). Also, it was difficult to decide at what level decisions should be made; it appears that too many decisions were pushed upward, overburdening the senior officers (Military Committee 1965).

The CIVLOG 1965 exercise led to the 1966 decision that military officers should be present in NATO Civil Wartime Agencies. The Military Committee approved MCM-111-65, as amended by MCM-144-65. This document sets forth the policy on military representation in civil

[1] D+ 90 meant that D—deployment of nuclear weapons, and the number afterward indicate the number of days.

[2] Until 1966, NATO's Standing Group was the key military executive body, composed of France, the UK, and the US.

wartime agencies, including the general terms of reference, responsibilities, and predefined levels of authority (NATO, IMS, Working Group Memorandum 1968). This approach of military presence in Civil Wartime Agencies continued after the 1969 exercise.

Before CIVLOG 1969, extensive planning and a symposium were held on February 14–15, 1969 (NATO Military Committee 1969). The symposium hoped to address the new role of NATO Civil Wartime Agencies in light of recent political-military guidance, to discuss "NATO's role in the co-ordination and management of civil resources in support of political and military objectives of the Alliance under various conditions, including those short of general nuclear attack" and how to improve "... civilian-military co-ordination" (NATO Military Committee 1969). 32 inputs, in the form of reports from the member states and key committees, were divided into four panels at the 2-day symposium.

The Senior Civil Emergency Planning Committee was primarily responsible for planning the 1969 exercise, whereas the Division of Defence Planning and Policy oversaw its execution. This ambitious exercise was conducted simultaneously in Rome, at NATO Headquarters, and at an exercise site in the United States. As in the 1965 exercise, it was conducted under the assumption of a "limited" nuclear exchange, D+90 days. Participation in CIVLOG 69 included the eight NATO Civil Wartime Agencies, national capitals, national delegations to NATO, the International Staff, the International Military Staff, and other NATO Military Authorities. Approximately 295 individuals from NATO participated in this exercise at NATO Headquarters, with around 240 arriving from outside (NATO Secretary General 1969). The Evaluation report from the working group of the International Military Staff found that both main assignments, the shipping of troops and equipment from Orlando, Florida, to Lisbon, Portugal, and the shipping from the UK to Italy, had not worked satisfactorily. Communications between agencies and actors had been less than satisfactory, and despite extensive planning, few of the participants had enough information to play out the scenario, which created substantial delays in the planning (NATO, IMS, Working Group Memorandum 1969).

One of the grievances in a later WINTEX 1971 was a lack of communication and coordination between military authorities and NATO Civil Wartime Agencies (Military Committee 1972). Another one was that civil aspects and foremost civil defense issues (protection of populations) were entirely excluded from the scenario. The Civil Defense Committee remarked, rather gloomily, in 1972 that, "in view of comments by representatives of other countries and in view of the limited civil participation in WINTEX 71, it would not be possible for the SCEPC to attempt to draw any conclusions therefrom" (Civil Defense Committee 1972a). Despite attempts to incorporate civil defense dimensions into WINTEX 1973 and to fully activate NCWAs, these dimensions were not fully integrated into exercise planning and were largely ignored throughout the exercise. HILEX 6 was an exercise focusing on NCWA and their collaboration with military authorities. SCEPC concludes in its report that NCWAs were often run over or ignored by the military authorities that wanted things done in specific ways in this exercise (SCEPC 1974a). There are several examples of how exercises concerning the civil dimensions and civil actors at NATO and the national levels are not prioritized in NATO exercises, even though these should focus foremost on the civil aspects of war and political crises. The general impression is that civil defense and protection of the population are not prioritized in the NATO exercises. In civil emergency planning and in exercises involving the NCWA, they have difficulty cooperating with one another and with military committees. The exercises and the evaluations indicate that the civil dimensions are foremost seen as supportive of military operations, even in exercises that are said to be focusing on civil defense and civil emergency planning.

The fact that NATO was engaged in both civil emergency planning and civil defense and developed Civil Wartime Agencies to support military operations and logistics, and to coordinate vital resources for any war effort, illustrates the importance of civil resources and capabilities that, according to Article 3, were beyond NATO's immediate control. Still, the revised basic assumptions for civil emergency planning, formulated as the "new assumptions" for extremely powerful nuclear weapons did not intensify the civil defense efforts within civil emergency planning. Instead, it seems to have triggered an expansion of other tasks, such as wartime logistics support by civil actors. This is visible in a report from SCEPC to the North Atlantic Council in 1973, when SCEPC summarizes it as one of its main tasks: "to identify areas where civil activity or resources might directly and economically help to improve military preparedness or support military operations" (SCEPC 1973).

During this period, member states and NATO merged their civil defense and emergency planning efforts and began introducing the concept of "dual-use planning," meaning that civilian agencies should plan for civil defense and civil emergency planning while also attending to and supporting military operations (SCEPC 1973). Civil emergency planning must be sufficiently flexible to operate at the lower end of the spectrum, including contingencies, crises, emergencies, and war. This core idea and discourse have been emphasized since 2014. This historical analysis shows that the concepts of dual-use and civil-military cooperation are not new and have been present within NATO for over 50 years. Notably, parallel to this development in NATO, the security agenda also expanded to include civil crisis management and disaster relief, thereby opening the door to an "all-hazards approach." Again, this concept appears relatively new but dates to the early 1970s within NATO. One of the core reasons for this was the defrosting of relations between the USA and the Soviet Union and the Strategic Arms Limitation Talks (SALT), which may require clarification.

6.6 Nuclear Arms Control

In the late 1960s, the U.S. discovered that the Soviet Union was significantly increasing its Intercontinental Ballistic Missile (ICBM) capabilities to match those of the U.S. In January 1967, President Lyndon Johnson announced that the USSR had started building an Anti-Ballistic Missile (ABM) defense system around Moscow. An ABM system could enable a first strike while neutralizing retaliation efforts. Consequently, Johnson proposed Strategic Arms Limitation Talks (SALT), which led to a 1967 meeting with Soviet Premier Alexei Kosygin at Glassboro State College in New Jersey. Johnson emphasized the need to temper their arms race regarding ABM systems. Secretary of Defense Robert McNamara added that the escalation of nuclear capabilities limited political options. While abolishing nuclear weapons was deemed impossible, limiting offensive and defensive systems would stabilize U.S.-Soviet relations and benefit both nations.

Richard Nixon, Johnson's successor, was also a supporter of SALT. On November 17, 1969, formal SALT talks began in Helsinki, Finland. Over the next two and a half years, the nations debated the completion of ABM plans, treaty verification, and U.S. concerns regarding Soviet Submarine-Launched Ballistic Missiles (SLBMs). Nixon and Soviet General Secretary Leonid Brezhnev signed the ABM Treaty and the interim SALT agreement on May 26, 1972, in Moscow. For the first time during the Cold War, the U.S. and the Soviet Union reached a bilateral agreement to limit nuclear missiles. SALT 1 is regarded as a significant achievement of NATO's détente. The ABM Treaty capped strategic missile defenses at 200 interceptors and allowed each side to build two missile defense sites, one for the national capital and one for an ICBM field.

Negotiations for a second round of SALT began in late 1972. Since SALT 1 did not prevent each side from enlarging its forces through the deployment of Multiple Independently Targeted Re-Entry Vehicles (MIRVs) on its ICBMs and SLBMs, SALT II initially focused on limiting, and then ultimately reducing, the number of MIRVs. Negotiations also sought to prevent both sides from making qualitative breakthroughs that would again destabilize the strategic relationship. The negotiations for SALT 2 involved three consecutive administrations: Nixon, Gerald Ford, and Jimmy Carter.

At the November 1974 Vladivostok Summit, Ford and Brezhnev established a SALT II framework. It included a limit of 2400 strategic nuclear delivery vehicles (ICBMs, SLBMs, and heavy bombers) per side; a 1320 limit on MIRV systems; a ban on new land-based ICBM launchers; and restrictions on the deployment of new offensive arms.

Despite these agreements, the nations failed to resolve two issues from SALT I: the number of strategic bombers and the total number of warheads. The Soviet Backfire bomber complicated matters, as U.S. negotiators believed it could reach the U.S., while the Soviets excluded it from negotiations. The Soviets also attempted to limit the deployment of American Air-Launched Cruise Missiles (ALCMs). Verification methods divided the nations, but they ultimately agreed to use National Technical Means (NTM), including telemetry and photo-reconnaissance satellites. On June 17, 1979, Carter and Brezhnev signed the SALT II Treaty in Vienna, limiting both nations' nuclear forces to 2250 delivery vehicles and imposing additional restrictions on strategic forces, including MIRVs (US Historical Archive 2025).

Despite this opening and limited success, it did not lead to lasting results in the international arena. On December 24, 1979, the Soviets invaded Afghanistan, and on January 3, 1980, Carter asked the Senate not to consider SALT II for its advice and consent, and it was never ratified. Despite failing to enter into force, Washington and Moscow pledged to adhere to the agreement's terms. Carter's successor, Ronald Reagan, a passionate critic of SALT II during the 1980 presidential campaign, agreed to abide by SALT II until its expiration on December 31, 1985, while he pursued the Strategic Arms Reduction Treaty (START) and argued that research into the Strategic Defense Initiative (SDI) adhered to the 1972 ABM Treaty. The latter, sometimes referred to as "Star Wars," was soon challenged by the Soviet Union (US Historical Archive 2025; NATO, Public Diplomacy Division 1972).

The fact that the US and the Soviet Union engaged in bilateral negotiations and agreed on several different limitations around nuclear weapons and countermeasures gave way to a more hopeful and relaxed (but never naïve) approach to civil defense against atomic attacks. Instead of dismantling civil defense and emergency planning during this era, new problems and tasks emerged that expanded the role of civil agencies within NATO. Above, we saw the development of a supportive role in military operations by the Senior Civil Emergency Planning Committee, its subcommittees, and civil wartime agencies. However, the scope of tasks would also expand to encompass crisis management, emergency planning, and disaster management—the foundational components of what is now referred to as the "all-hazards approach." This evolution emerged from a growing awareness of environmental degradation and the recognition of how modern lifestyles can adversely affect sustainability and well-being.

6.7 NATO's Committee on the Challenges of Modern Society (CCMS)

The creation of the Committee on the Challenges of Modern Society (CCMS) was proposed by the United States at NATO's 20th anniversary in Washington, D.C., in April 1969, to give the Alliance a new "third dimension" and to incorporate societal aspects. The American President at the time, Mr. Nixon, asked for the creation of "a committee on the challenges of modern society... to explore ways in which the experience and resources of the Western nations could most effectively be marshalled toward improving the quality of life of our peoples" and to help twentieth-century man to learn "how to remain in harmony with his rapidly changing world" (NATO, Public Diplomacy Division 1976).

NATO established the Committee on the Challenges of Modern Society on November 6, 1969. NATO was initially concerned that taking on such a task and a new profile would duplicate or compete with environmental activities and concerns of other international and regional organizations. The idea was to establish an objective for the new research-based committee to address practical problems identified in national research agendas. By combining the existing expertise and technology available in most countries, NATO claimed to contribute to fairly rapid conclusions and solutions (NATO press release on CCMS 1972).

A pamphlet from the public diplomacy division suggests that "the cooperation in NATO towards the improvement of modern society evolved both from the terms of the North Atlantic Treaty and from the experience of the Alliance during its first twenty years" (NATO, Public Diplomacy Division 1976). Accordingly, Article 2 of the Treaty provides that member countries would contribute toward the further development of peaceful and friendly international relations by promoting conditions of stability and well-being. As discussed in the previous chapter, this was previously used to motivate the science and technology collaboration and development within NATO. However, integrating social and environmental dimensions into the scientific approach broke new ground and required new solutions from the organization. These new solutions and tasks were directed at the civil emergency planning committee. CCMS was a collaboration that NATO facilitated and supported (NATO CCMS report 1988; NATO, Public Diplomacy Division 1976).

The Committee would not conduct research; all activities would be decentralized to avoid bureaucracy, NATO staff, and direct funding. NATO aimed to address social and environmental issues with minimal investment and limited commitment. This led to three strategies: (1) pilot studies involving national researchers and volunteers; (2) short-term projects focusing on immediate solutions using existing information and technology; (3) broad dissemination and transparency regarding CCMS activities. CCMS meetings were open to observers from all member states and beyond, including Eastern Europe, the Soviet Union, and international organizations, with study results accessible to all institutions and governments.

Still, the CCMS was ambitious in its collaborative and communicative efforts. As of October 1976, eight CCMS pilot studies had been completed, and ten more were underway. Many of these studies focused on environmental issues, such as coastal water pollution and ocean oil spills; environmental and regional planning; road safety; air pollution; inland water pollution; and urban transportation. Others emphasized the natural sciences and energy production and use, including solar and geothermal energy, as well as the rational use of energy. Several projects included sub-studies and were truly ambitious. This is not the place to detail these projects. Still, for the current purpose, one area of research stands out as central to the continued development of civil emergency planning and the recent shift toward crisis management. Those projects focused on disaster assistance and disaster reduction.

In public communication about CCMS efforts, it was suggested that two common natural disasters affecting humanity are earthquakes and floods. In such events, preventive measures are often insufficient to mitigate potential disasters. Instead, the focus should be on planning and preparedness for such disasters. Adequate preparation would enable faster rescue and post-disaster rehabilitation. It then explains how CCMS undertook a pilot study on disaster assistance, which was piloted by the United States and co-piloted by Italy and Turkey. In addition, CCMS organized two international symposia in 1970 and 1971 on flooding and earthquake-hazard reduction, respectively, resulting in concrete recommendations. These called for increased national and multinational action to address earthquakes and floods through enhanced national preparedness and improved coordination of international efforts. The recommendations called upon countries to (a) enhance their readiness for pre-disaster preparation, (b) take emergency measures during disasters, and (c) take actions to speed post-disaster construction and rehabilitation. This resulted in NATO assuming a new role as a coordinator and facilitator in response to natural hazards and crises, as NATO would engage in delivering relief supplies (NATO, Public Diplomacy Division 1976).

NATO member states were also requested to provide full support for the United Nations' disaster relief activities. Follow-up reports from CCMS have indicated that member countries have taken several measures to implement the disaster assistance recommendations approved by NATO. In addition, NATO organized a communications network to coordinate relief activities. This was partly a result of the 1975 earthquake in Turkey, but was also used in connection with the 1976 earthquake in Italy (and later in 1980).

Responsibility for further action under the Disaster Assistance study was then assigned to SCEPC, adding another dimension to their work. This is also an additional step away from the tasks of civil defense and protection of populations during war.

According to Linda Risso, a researcher who covers the establishment and politics of CCMS, this was a carefully monitored public project that could generate significant goodwill and illustrate NATO's usefulness beyond its role as a guard against communism and the Soviet Union. She notes that NATO's political dimension was diminishing as communism and the Soviet Union lost ground as potential alternatives to democracy and capitalism. Yet it was not without internal conflicts. European countries, not least Great Britain, were not overly enthusiastic to cater to this "American project" (see also Hamblin 2010) and (Hatzivassiliou 2017). Interestingly, the project continued and was often signaled in public communications by the public diplomacy division, as seen above. Risso also notes that this effort laid the foundation for NATO's growing interest in crisis management, disaster relief, and environmental disasters as early as 20 years before the end of the Cold War in 1989 (Risso 2016).

It is worth noting that in 1958, NATO already discussed the possibility of "NATO cooperation for disaster in peacetime." This suggestion was discussed at the NAC, but several countries, especially Norway and the Netherlands, pointed out that the United Nations International Relief and Development Organization already existed, raising the risk that NATO would duplicate it (NATO Secretary General 1958). Despite these objections, NATO prepared to assist member states during disasters by allowing stationed military personnel to assist (if possible), establishing an information center, and compiling an inventory of civil emergency resources that other countries could utilize upon request. Even though no formal committee or agency was created for this purpose, the issue and discussion were raised and incorporated informally into the organization (NATO Secretary General 1958). The governing document and the overall approach to peacetime disaster relief were revised in 1971. Still, neither the military authorities nor the Council found it desirable to set up a specific body or structure to manage disaster relief action within NATO, and in 1977 the Secretary General concluded that:

> In the light of these developments, I have reluctantly concluded that there is no point in pursuing the matter further and suggest that the Council may wish to reaffirm that as far as disaster relief action within NATO is concerned, this should remain with the Civil Emergency Planning Directorate, according to the procedures approved by the Council in C-M(58)102, 1971 edition (NATO Secretary General 1977).

6.8 Expansion of the Civil Dimensions

The analysis of civil defense and related tasks of civil emergency planning, military support, crisis management, and disaster relief indicates that NATO struggled to align these issues with expectations. It may be that such expectations were overly high and unrealistic, given that most of these issues lay beyond NATO's immediate control due to their association with Article 3. NATO could engage only in indirect governance, using member states as intermediaries or bridges between NATO and the country's civil defense actors. In addition, it may appear that the military branches and the North Atlantic Council did not fully recognize the significance of civil defense and emergency planning to the same degree as the specialized boards and committees. Many of the reports and documents analyzed during this period convey a tone of disappointment at the lack of appreciation for the work and effort.

At the beginning of the period covered in this chapter, 1965–1989, the focus is on two main tasks: advancing and standardizing civil defense organizations across the member states and enhancing the capabilities of civil actors to support military operations through supplies, communications, and logistics. In 1965, the Civil Defense Committee provided a progress report to SCEPC on the issue of Civil defense efforts of the member states on (a) national fallout warning organizations, (b) fallout protection, and (c) national operational civil defense organizations (Civil Defense Committee 1965). Civil defense efforts would be centered around these three dimensions, even though the outlines of the reports and questionnaires would be largely altered. The 1965 report covers all countries except Iceland, which did not submit a report to NATO. The general conclusion of the progress report was that: "From the information collected during this survey, it appears that, despite considerable efforts, most of which were made with only modest means, deficiencies are more in evidence than progress when the current level of operational efficiency is considered. Only a minority of NATO countries could give a positive report with respect to priority Civil Defence Goals" (Civil Defense Committee 1965). In addition, the report notes that countries have very different national civil defense organizations. Thus, "In Belgium, France, Germany, the Netherlands, and the United Kingdom, the organization is civil, while in Canada, Denmark, Greece, Italy, Luxembourg, Norway, and the United States, the organization is joint civil/military or even controlled by the military. In Turkey, a military civil defense organization has not yet been established. In Portugal, the system is at the planning stage" (Civil Defense Committee 1965). It must be concluded that countries differ in their organizational structures, capabilities, willingness, and economic opportunities to advance their civil defense programs and align them with NATO's priorities and standards, further impairing the indirect governance possible from NATO HQ.

In 1968, the Civil Defense Committee provided a report based on the earlier review questionnaire from 1967 to SCEP (SCEPC 1967). The report concludes that: "In only a few member countries does it appear that national civil defence organizations are approaching, in varying degrees, a credible capability. For the greater part of the Alliance, there are such large gaps in the civil defence structure that, in the event of hostilities, existing civil defence organizations cannot be expected to cope with the anticipated tasks" (SCEPC 1967). Regarding fallout detection and warning systems, the report finds that most countries have satisfactory levels, except for Iceland, Greece, Turkey, and Portugal. When it comes to actual shelter, the report concludes that most countries either lack an adequate proportion of shelter or are unable to report on this issue (SCEPC 1967). At a meeting held in Brussels on 29th February 1968 to discuss these problems, the newly established "Ad Hoc Study Group" [for civil defense] agreed that the only way to obtain the necessary information would be to circulate a new questionnaire. The new questionnaire comprised 25 items to collect information on securing political leadership and control, as well as on populations, through warning systems, fallout monitoring, shelters, and the general organization of the national civil defense. The new questionnaire focuses more explicitly on any changes or improvements from last year (Civil Defense Committee 1968). This report also notes that the civil defense organizations of member states can vary considerably and, therefore, be difficult to control and govern. Some countries have organized civil defense as part of their public administration, whereas others have relied on voluntary forces and more ad hoc organizations. Still others have had a combination of public and private actors and volunteering individuals working together (Civil Defense Committee 1968).

In 1970, the Civil Defense Committee further expanded its work. It began a study on how to cope with the protection of populations from chemical attacks (Civil Defense Committee 1970b). This required additional conceptual work and specifications, building on prior work on nuclear bombs and fallout protection. There was also the introduction of the "stay-put policy," which should diminish both internal and international refugees in the case of a chemical or nuclear attack. Instead, each country should do its utmost to ensure the safety of its population, maintain public order, and control its borders to avoid mass flight and hysteria, which could affect the armed forces' logistical capabilities. Not all countries were willing to abide by the stay-put policy; Canada, for instance, advocated for its right to continue with evacuation plans, citing its geographical capabilities (SCEPC 1970f).

In March 1970, Turkey was struck by a major Earthquake in Gediz. The Earthquake had a magnitude of 7.2 on the M-scale. It killed around 1000 people, injured another 1000 people, and left 26,000 homeless. Although it was not a NATO operation, NATO assisted Turkey by transferring and coordinating bilateral support for disaster relief. Other NATO members contributed significantly to the disaster relief. Behind this effort were previous relief operations, the CCMS group's current work, and initial discussions with the North Atlantic Council dating back to 1958 and document C/M 58-102 (Secretary-General 1971). The civil defense committee report concluded that "this is a new concept, the implementation of which would be very complex and would call for important facilities which are not at present available to NATO. The CCMS is now investigating what is both feasible and desirable in this respect" [to install formal procedures for NATO disaster relief] (Civil Defense Committee 1970a). This induces discussions that civil defense and civil emergency planning should be organized in such a way as to cope with both crisis disaster relief operations and war (Civil Defense Committee 1970a) (SCEPC 1970d). It seems as if the shift in focus actually impairs the more fundamental work with civil defense: "the current review of the NATO Alert System [but] is now falling behind because of the pressure of other work; peacetime disaster relief: arrangements; which are, likely to devolve eventually on the 'Civil' Emergency Planning Directorate, as well as one or two special studies to which we will almost certainly be committed as a result of 'HILEX=4 and our own review of civil emergency' arrangements and exercises" (SCEPC 1970e).

The USA, Germany, and Denmark initiated work on an all-hazards approach, encompassing peacetime contingencies and crises, as well as extensive wartime civil defense and emergency planning, as early as 1972. This is evident in document AC 23 N 221, which is preparing the Civil Defense Committee for a briefing session on September 13, 1972, devoted to the subject of Civil Defence contribution to peacetime disaster relief. Presentations and examples include:

1. The USA: "The development of the US Civil Defence programme from that of a nuclear-oriented programme to one also involved in day-to-day peacetime emergencies."
2. Germany: Developments within the German Civil Defence aimed at increased assistance in the event of peacetime disasters.
3. Denmark: "Tasks performed by the Danish Civil Defence in peacetime."
4. Belgium: "the organization of first aid and assistance in Belgium in case of natural disasters" (Civil Defense Committee 1972b).

The approach that addressed both crises and war remained salient in the years that followed. A report from SCEPC in 1974 made the following suggestions:

> …because the nature and rate of development of a future crisis or war cannot be foreseen the civil emergency organization arrangement of the alliance must be sufficiently flexible adjust to any contingency; there would be a vital need throughout for fully informed, rapid and efficient processes of decision-taking (SCEPC 1974b).

And:

> normal peacetime organization and arrangements, both national and international, for maintaining production, supply, trade and transport, should continue to be used in crisis and war for so long as they were able to function and meet the defence requirements of the Alliance (SCEPC 1974b).

The CDC's further expansion of its areas of concern is odd, given the annual report provided to the Senior Civil Emergency Planning Committee, which indicates that traditional civil defense efforts are lagging. "There are no significant changes as of 1st April 1970 in the overall preparedness of civil defense compared with the 1969 situation. The most critical factor is the lack of progress in the acquisition of an adequate shelter capability for the civil population, as well as for the protection of certain civil defence control centres, both for their personnel and means of telecommunications" (SCEPC 1970f). The report continues: "…this situation is likely to seriously hamper the operational freedom and the flexibility of the Armed Forces. It will have an important impact on the morale of both the civil population and Armed Forces, and also on the flow of supplies for the latter, which should not be exposed to the risk of interruption. Therefore, from the military point of view alone, it is essential that intensified efforts be made, as a matter of urgency, to achieve balanced improvements in the civil defence preparedness of the Alliance" (SCEPC 1970f).

This is not the only gloomy report on the status of NATO's civil defense efforts at the beginning of the 1970s. The Senior Civil Emergency Planning Committee also identifies several shortcomings, which it later conveys to NAC in its annual report to the Council. When it comes to civilian exercise and the overall management of wartime agencies, the evaluation report states that "…it was noteworthy that the Warsaw Pact Countries attach considerable importance to civil defence training for a very wide section of the population, whereas the NATO countries had perhaps let the pendulum swing too far the other way. NATO Civil Wartime agencies do not even have temporary, protected Headquarters, let alone permanent, protected premises. Everything would have to be improvised—premises, communications, other facilities before these agencies could begin to operate" (SCEPC 1970a). In addition, the civil emergency planning committee is struggling to coordinate cross-border communications, signals, and a common alert language. In addition, reports indicate that although SCEPC is requesting radio communication equipment for this work, there are no available funds, and SCEPC is instructed to wait until next year's budget. This shows that there were limited funds at NATO HQ, and civil defense efforts are potentially not prioritized, not least to the extent that immediate funds are presented (SCEPC 1970b). The issues with communications for NATO's civil wartime agencies soon escalated into a "crisis," as the Civil Communications Planning Committee informed SCEPC that only part of its recommendations for establishing communications within and between member states and NCWAs had been implemented. This made several members of the committee, including the chair, ask what the point was of them performing "paper planning year after year if none of the resulting plans were to be implemented" (SCEPC 1970c).

As demonstrated in the preceding sections, NATO's committees and international staff are diligently working to enhance civil defense and civil emergency planning in order to improve NATO's control, governance, and capabilities. However, member states frequently exhibit reluctance to assume additional responsibilities and undertake new tasks. Simultaneously, although civil collaboration and civil dimensions of security are increasingly advocated, and the Civil Defense Committee and the Senior Committee should include additional activities and joint efforts, fundamental civil defense measures for population security remain notably absent.

6.9 Civil Defense Blindness

The AD 70 Report, commissioned by the Defense Planning Committee in May 1970, aimed to assess NATO's defense tasks for the upcoming decade. Senior government representatives and key NATO commanders, supported by civilian and military international staff, conducted the evaluation. It thoroughly examined relevant political, military, and economic issues and concluded that NATO's security strategy for the next decade will depend on the dual concepts of defense and détente. It focuses on nuclear and conventional forces and compares NATO with the Soviet Union and the Warsaw Pact (NATO, Public Diplomacy Division 1971). Although this report has been suggested to be of similar importance to the Harmel report, it does not include any references to civil defense or civil emergency planning, which aggravated the Senior Civil Emergency Committee (SCEPC 1972) that noted that civil defense was "relegated" from the comprehensive understanding of defense and deterrence. This is remarkable given that SCEPC, with the support of the Defence Planning Policy Division and the Civil Emergency Planning Directorate within NATO, had presented a specific paper to AD 70 report working group advocating the importance of civil defense and civil emergency planning as central elements of defense and deterrence (SCEPC 1970h).

Still, it appears to have sparked renewed energy for SCEPC's civil defense efforts and its efforts to further demonstrate its capabilities. Or rather, SCEPC and CDC hoped to demonstrate to other parts of NATO and member states that civil defense and civil emergency planning were important. As a direct response, SCEPC set up an "informal ad hoc group" which produced an "interim report" that was to guide the SCEPC in its continued work, not only with civil emergency planning as such, but to get it on the highest-level agenda of NATO. This informal report outlined three lines of action. In the short term (1 year), all member states should re-examine their civil arrangements and consider how to make funds available for improvements. Mid-term actions (1–3 years) should include "to complete and implement to the extent necessary in peacetime comprehensive planning arrangements for the relocation of government, the mobilization and wartime use of resources, improvement in civil defense and the protection of and information of the public and so on" (SCEPC 1971c). Long-term actions cover the next 5-year period and are ambitious, suggesting that "attempts should be made to complete all planning arrangements [so far suggested by NATO]" (SCEPC 1971c). This was followed by a second interim report that further specified the route forward for SCEPC to get civil emergency planning back on the NATO agenda (SCEPC 1971a). Given the lack of progress and unwillingness to implement recommendations from NATO by the member states, it is hard to think that such ambitious plans should be "completed" within 5 years. Instead, we shall see that in 1975, a crisis committee was launched to investigate the lack of progress in civil defense arrangements.

It was not only that civil defense and civil emergency planning were largely ignored in the AD 70 report; they were also largely ignored by the member states. In fact, NATO was in a constant crisis because it did not find a way to consolidate its and the member states' efforts in these areas. In a review of "the civil emergency arrangements in time of crisis or war" produced in the 1970s, it is noted that the current approach struggles to cover both crisis and war situations due to a lack of clear instructions, mandate, and funding. Civil emergency planning needs to be apt to act "...in a period of international tension would contribute to effective crisis management: within the Alliance, and to meet civil and military requirements generated by contingency situations short of war"(SCEPC 1970k). It is thus notable that a 1970 report mentions both "crisis and war," as well as "contingencies short of war." These expressions have reappeared since 2014 but were present more than 50 years ago within NATO.

In a 1970 report in December from SCEPC to the North Atlantic Council, from the incomplete information available to NATO, the Senior Committee has identified major shortcomings in national civil preparedness: "Although the situation in the various member nations varies in degree and detail. from one to another, the general position is as follows:" (SCEPC 1970j). It then lists 14 main points and defects that are the most important from a civil emergency planning perspective and follows NATO's approach to the matter. One point concerns specifically the safety of populations:

> preparations to protect the public, to warn them and keep them informed, to control population movements and in general to preserve law and order and ensure stability have not been completed (SCEPC 1970j).

According to SCEPC:

> These [all of the 14 points] shortcomings are so serious as to inhibit both civil and military defence efforts in a time of crisis or war. For example, the operational freedom and flexibility of the armed forces could be seriously hampered. Unless the level of civil preparedness is substantially raised, efforts and expenditure in other areas of defence planning could be wasted in an emergency. The proper functioning of the overall Allied defense effort cannot, therefore, be guaranteed. Deficiencies in the civil field will give rise to doubts as to the credibility of the deterrent and the deference posture of the Alliance (SCEPC 1970j).

In the light of these dire conclusions, SCEPC plenary meeting in November 1970 "...agreed that the 1971 programme of work of all NATO civil emergency planning bodies should consist of identifying what would need to be done in the NATO civil emergency field in times of crisis and war, and of developing the practical arrangements and procedure which would allow these tasks to be properly discharged should the occasion arise" (SCEPC 1970g).

This prompted SCEPC to appoint a special group of experts to review the current work of SCEPC, CDC, and all other civil emergency planning groups, as well as the NCWAs. A 34-page-long report was given to SCEPC in November 1971. One of the more interesting aspects of the report was that it clearly specified NATO's role in civil crisis management and the idea of a prolonged period of increased tensions before any nuclear war would erupt (SCEPC 1971d). The report illustrates NATO's more diversified approach to civil emergency planning and its efforts to address both peacetime crises and its traditional role in war preparedness and wartime operations. This expansion of tasks increased the burden and coordination requirements between NATO and its member states, necessitating greater information sharing and collaboration within the NATO framework.

It is important to note the points raised by Norway: the actual work of advancing civil defense is hindered, both for NATO international staff and for member states, by numerous and extensive investigations and requests for additional information from member states. These investigations generate substantial paperwork related to meetings, which hinders the actual work and implementation of civil defense efforts (SCEPC 1970i):

> One of the main reasons for the slow progress in civil emergency planning is that too many problems are being studied at the same time. This generates a large number of meetings, and much time is required of the member states and international staff to participate in the meetings, prepare agendas and decision sheets, and undertake other merely procedural work. Consequently, there is not sufficient time to work forward and the matter of substance which leads to the waste of time for the committee due to extra meetings (SCEPC 1970i).

To this, Denmark adds that NATO's international staff "must concentrate its efforts on the *international* aspects of civil emergency planning" (SCEPC 1971b).

The above section suggests that during this period, NATO's goals and purposes for civil defense and emergency planning expanded, at least in policy and intent. The critiques raised by Norway and Denmark, and the lack of implementation in most areas of civil defense and civil emergency planning, indicate that NATO has difficulty implementing its policies and efforts. This discrepancy exists between the ambitious policies and plans pursued by NATO's specialized bodies and the member states that are implementing them. The member states' critique and lack of effort and enthusiasm did not appear to slow the committees' efforts within NATO.

In 1971, the Civil Defense Committee (via a Study Group) suggested that the minimal questionnaire initiated in 1968 was so curtailed that it did not allow countries to develop their answers in a way that truly reflected their level of civil defense. For instance, it did not enable countries to report on new technologies or innovations that enhanced their national defense capabilities. It did not include any inductive segment that would allow countries to report on other lessons learned during crises and natural hazards that could be of value for civil defense planning. Thus, a more extensive questionnaire would not only elicit more insightful responses but could also decrease the frequency of the investigation from annually to triennially, commencing in 1972 (Civil Defense Committee 1971c). Still, the conclusion by the study group was that "…there is in

1971 a slight improvement in the state of civil defence national preparedness as compared with the 1970 situation. But this state in most NATO Nations is yet so removed from the objectives to be attained, in particular as regards shelter protection, that the overall state of preparedness of civil defence within the Alliance remains critical" (Civil Defense Committee 1971c). This was later reported to the SCEPC, along with a suggestion for a tri-annual questionnaire cycle that would allow for a more detailed report on the progress in each country, along with a broader approach to crisis and war (Civil Defense Committee 1971b).

Even if it was concluded that some progress had been made in most countries since last year, the report provided little guidance on how NATO should proceed in advancing civil defense. At the same time, the civil defense committee sought to advance NATO cooperation on peacetime emergency disaster assistance. In internal working papers, CDC discusses how it can promote a center for disaster relief rather than addressing such emergencies ad hoc and informally (Civil Defense Committee 1971a).

The stay-put policy previously mentioned was controversial and potentially put human lives at risk for the benefit of military response and logistics. The civil defense committee, however, was instrumental in shaping its approach and in making it a central component of the management of the civilian population. It was suggested in 1972 that for the policy to be effective, it was "essential to exert upon the population a psychological impetus by the broadcasting of appropriate information." National agencies should already "… in peacetime 'inform' and 'indoctrinate' the population about what behavior it should adopt." For this purpose, various forms of information campaigns and pamphlets should be presented to the populations in member states (Civil Defense Committee 1972c).

In June 1975, the Senior Civil Emergency Planning Committee agreed to establish a "Selected Group" comprising members from Denmark, the Federal Republic of Germany, the Netherlands, and the US. The task was to review the Senior Committee's method of work and the procedures for achieving SCEPC's current aims and objectives. The Selected Group should also recommend changes if necessary. Before reviewing the methods and procedures, the Selected Group deemed it necessary to assess the status of civil emergency planning. Otherwise, they would be operating in an administrative vacuum and not fully understand the real status of the alliance's deterrence and defense. They submitted this report to the SCEPC in June 1976 and offered a substantial critique of the status of civil defense efforts within NATO and all member states. Civil emergency planning is not prioritized within NATO, and the result is extensive paper constructions of civil emergency planning and civil defense with little (SCEPC 1976a) (SCEPC 1976b). Their conclusion was that:

> while member nations have expressed their own interest in, and ·the importance of, civil emergency planning activities, their actions have not always reflected their words. There is a great disparity between what is needed and what has been done, and national funds have become increasingly limited for even minimal civil defense and shelter programmes. The Selected Group wishes to reiterate the fact that these are primarily areas of national responsibility; however, the impact of their neglect upon the alliance cannot be ignored (SCEPC 1976b).

The Chairman of the Selected Group sent the General Secretary a report of their findings in September 1975 regarding the current state of civil emergency planning over the Alliance. According to the report: "planners have generally recognised the rather obvious and easily definable relationship between civil and military planning, [still] only minimal progress in the past twenty-five years has been made beyond the mere recognition of the relationship" (NATO Secretary General 1976). The General Secretary concluded that "The position described in this summary is anything but encouraging" and that the Council should discuss this matter further.

The Selected Group wrote in its report that "unless member nations improve their capability in civil emergency planning to create and maintain an environment in which the fundamental national requirements are provided, the result would be reduced national cohesiveness and will to resist an enemy. This would endanger the fundamental purposes of the Alliance" (NATO Secretary General 1976). Even if this remained a national responsibility, the Selected Group believed that "international co-operation in the planning area, including the exchange of ideas, has a potential of making significant mutual contributions to the national planners concerned with these tasks" (NATO Secretary General 1976).

This sent shock waves through the organization and required resolution at the highest levels. In his report on this topic, the General Secretary suggested that "the political will as reflected in the preparedness programmes of the member countries gives substance and meaning to NATO plans. Without the national capabilities, NATO plans in most cases could not be successfully implemented" (NATO Secretary General 1976). General Secretary Joseph Luns[3] wrote to the Council:

> the overall state of civil emergency planning in the Alliance and in its member nations is poor. In almost three decades, SCEPC has neither attained its potential nor met NATO's expectations. While civil authorities generally accept the task of planning for civil support to military operations, both they and military authorities seem to lack an understanding of the need to plan for the totality of national requirements in crisis and war. Finally, within the SCEPC itself, there has been a reluctance to accept and follow Council direction on preparing for crisis management situations (NATO Secretary General 1976).

Nevertheless, the crisis of civil defense and civil emergency planning dissolves quickly. In 1977, the Selected Group was disbanded, and the suggestions for how to proceed were formulated in what could be judged as business as usual (SCEPC 1977). For instance, the major priorities for civil emergency planning would be:

(a) civil support for the rapid reinforcement concept (military priorities);
(b) credible and viable crisis management procedures and wartime arrangements for NATO;
(c) corresponding national arrangements to complement and support these arrangements, including any arrangements necessary before full emergency powers were available;
(d) major supply studies on the critical requirements of the essential industry;
(e) improvements in the readiness of protection of populations and the maintenance of the home front (SCEPC 1977).

In 1978, the revised questionnaire was administered to assess the state of civil preparedness in the member states. It was extensive, covering six different topics: (1) Continuity of government, (2) Readiness of Civil populations, including civil defense measures, (3) Supply (focusing on

[3] Joseph Luns was the longest serving Secretary General NATO has ever had—13 years from 1971 to 1984.

petrol and food/agriculture/industry, (4) Transport including (ocean shipping, air, and land transport), (5) Manpower, (6) Civil emergency preparedness *including crisis management and disaster relief* (my emphasis). Many questions were open-ended, requiring free-text responses and subjective interpretation and evaluation of the reporting country. In total, the questionnaire contained over 100 questions, and although some questions permitted yes/no responses, such answers would not make much sense without extensive explanations and clarifications (SCEPC 1978).

The work on these issues at this time was ambitious but lacked focus, or was overly ambitious, as it attempted to cover too much ground. The questionnaire, along with the analysis of responses, would require significant effort from both respondents and the staff preparing a subsequent report that will conclude information from 15 member states. The summary report of the questionnaire, once again, reached a disappointing conclusion: most member states have not yet presented satisfactory results regarding civil defense and civil protection.

"The weaknesses and deficiencies identified in this report are mainly national in character and are therefore basically a national responsibility. But if the policies of the Alliance are to be effective and coherent, national sovereignty and responsibility must allow for maximum co-operation between capitals and at the NATO level with regard to peacetime planning and implementation in an emergency. The interdependence of effective planning at the national and international levels must be fully recognized. Even in those matters which can be dealt with exclusively within a member country, however, other members must be assured that the Alliance as a whole is not put at risk by major shortcomings in *civil* preparedness in a particular country" (SCEPC 1979a). An interesting finding is that the report's title and text use the phrasing "civil preparedness," a subtle variation from "civil defense" and "civil emergency planning." This suggests that civil crisis management and disaster relief have been incorporated into the tasks considered in this policy sector and thus warrant a new conception.

Full reports for each country are found in a series titled AC 98 WP 144 + country name and are available in the digital archives in Brussels for 1979. The summary report for SCEPC, which was not sent to the North Atlantic Council, is more critical of the country's reports and how to make any conclusions for the current state of civil emergency planning. When it comes to civil defense, or preparedness as it is currently called, the report notes the lack of coherent answers and efforts of the member states as problematic:

> The information provided does not constitute a proper basis for statistical processing or for the development of a NATO-wide assessment. It does, however, indicate a wide variation in the scale of governmental expenditure and points to a regrettable reduction in real terms of the funds allocated to civil preparedness in recent years (SCEPC 1979c).

In 1981, a new report raised serious concerns about the questionnaire and the procedures used to produce reports for SCEPC and NAC. What is suggested is more detailed and streamlined information, as well as more coordination between member states and NATO committees (SCEPC 1981). To address these problems, SCEPC suggests that a revised questionnaire would enable a more objective understanding of each country and facilitate cross-country comparisons. SCEPC also provides a detailed breakdown of the work process for producing the next CEPQ cycle, which also specifies substantial coordination within NATO with better control by the International Staff (SCEPC 1981).

> A comprehensive CEP Questionnaire prepared by the International Staff with contributions from the Planning Boards and Committees will be approved and issued by the SCEPC every four years. The CEPQ will be designed to prompt clear, easily understandable answers. A questionnaire so designed will make it possible to eliminate the need for narrative country chapters (SCEPC 1981) (AC 98 D 1022).

The new questionnaire expanded to 120 pages, with 11 sections, over 200 headline questions, several sub-questions, multiple-choice questions, and free-text answers. From an informed external perspective, while the survey expanded in size and number of questions, many of the answers would still not make much sense without contextualization (SCEPC 1983). This survey illustrates the complexity of civil emergency planning, of which civil defense is one small part. Questions about production rates and food-staple storage, the number of shipping containers and aircraft, etc., show that without specific limitations and clear priorities, civil defense, and civil emergency planning become ungovernable due to sheer size and complexity (SCEPC 1983).

In a later report, following the 1982 assessment of the military implications of the state of civil preparedness, the NATO Military Authorities requested increased coordinated and collective efforts to further improve civil support for the rapid reinforcement plan. The fact that member states display less attention to civil defense budgets is identified as the main reason for limited progress. The NATO Military Authorities emphasize that this tendency undermines the credibility of NATO's strategy. The enemy might even be in doubt "about the resolve and willingness of the Alliance and its population to defend if efforts to improve the population's chances of survival are not made" (NATO Secretary General 1983). There is a discrepancy between NATO's ambitious approach, which includes both military and civilian commitment to alliance goals and policies, and the more reluctant member states that cut their defense budgets, as well as the lack of attention to civilian defense and preparedness.

It was noted in a working paper of the SCEPC that there was simply too little understanding of civil emergency planning. What needed to be done was the careful dissemination of relevant information to the capitals, journalists, and general public, as civil defense and civil emergency planning was the least reported aspect of NATO (SCEPC 1979b).

In 1982, NATO pursued and projected a broad approach to civil defense through public diplomacy, publicly positioning it as a central part of the "total defense" of NATO. Total defense is an uncommon concept in NATO documents and communications. This referred to the core functions of civil defense and emergency planning. In the public communique from the Public Diplomacy Division, it is stated that: "The deterrent value of the strategic concept of flexible response can only be fully realised if military preparedness is complemented by credible civil preparedness" (NATO, Public Diplomacy Division 1982). Under the rubric of civil emergency planning, it is noted that:

> The scope of civil emergency planning is therefore extremely wide. It embraces such matters as the continuity of the machinery of government, the maintenance of law and order, the mobilisation and use to the best advantage of national resources (energy, manpower, transport systems, production capacity, food and agriculture, raw materials, telecommunications, etc.) as well as civil defence measures, including warning, rescue services, and health care aimed at minimizing the consequences of enemy action to civilian populations (NATO, Public Diplomacy Division 1982).

Not only should civil emergency planning cope with its primary aim "to maintain the social and economic life of member nations, and to ensure the survival of their populations in the face of, during and after hostilities…" (NATO, Public Diplomacy Division 1982). A second important aspect of civil emergency planning is the "civil support for the military forces." In fact, "a significant amount of the planning effort should, according to the communique, be "directed towards providing adequate civil support for the reinforcement of allied forces in Europe" (ibid). In addition to these two tasks, civil emergency planning also covers handling crises and hazards. Thus, even in peacetime, NATO member states should collaborate "to further national planning by providing for the exchange of experience and opinions on matters of common interest; and to develop arrangements for dealing with matters which would have to be handled in one way or another, at NATO level during an emergency" (NATO, Public Diplomacy Division 1982). Beyond specifying the broader scope of civil emergency planning, it is unclear what impact this public communication effort had.

In 1986, the Civil Defense Committee sent an extensive report to SCEPC, an attempt to cover all the central aspects of civil defense. The report specifies the threatening image and capacity of the Soviet Union and the Warsaw Pact to launch any kind of attack against NATO countries. It states that the aim of civil defense is to "…mitigate the effects on civilian population of all forms of warfare, including conventional, chemical, and nuclear attack. The measures are essentially passive" (SCEPC 1986).

The report strongly advocates for a dual-use perspective: "Considerable advantage will result from a dual-use purpose organizations, plans, training and resources relevant to both peacetime emergencies and a war crisis. Almost all preparations and measures designed to deal with major accidents and disasters in peace would be of importance and value in war. Such dual role activity is both cost-effective and presentational expedient in assisting civil defense authorities to persuade sceptics of the utility of their work" (SCEPC 1986).

The following year, the SCEPC decided to move forward to align NATO members on disaster relief for natural or man-made disasters. The idea was not to advance a specific body but to align the reporting on damage and need for assistance to streamline the data for coordinated assistance and to build up a bank of knowledge that could be used for evaluation further ahead (SCEPC 1987b).

Two research sidenotes at this point could be helpful. First, NATO archives online suggest that the Civil Defense Committee was active only between 1952 and 1970 and was later renamed the Civil Protection Committee, the timing unclear. Potentially, there is a misunderstanding between the Civil Defense Committee and a potential subcommittee on refugees (NATO Archives Online 2026). At the same time, the AC 23 Series (the Civil Defense Committee series) is not included in the digital archive for 1975 and forward, and fewer documents are available from 1971. Still, the report above from SCEPC names the civil defense committee, and it appears to have been active in 1986 (SCEPC 1986). In the archives, you can see that terminology matters significantly to the countries. Some countries are reluctant to use the term total defense, whereas others, for example, Italy in 1987 argues that civil defense leaves uneasy feelings among its population and would prefer the more neutral concept of civil protection (SCEPC 1987a). In an interview with one of the senior staff working in civil defense issues, the name-shift occurred a few years after 1989, but the civil defense committee was active during the whole time (Euro-Atlantic Disaster Response Coordinator; 1998–2005, "Staff Officer," October 23, 2025, Online interview).

The other methodological and material conundrum is that it is not possible to follow the ongoing work with the Civil emergency planning questionnaire and review cycles after 1983, but it appears to be active until the end of the Cold War, as indicated in other documents and with reference to documents that are currently unavailable from the NATO Archives in Brussels.[4]

6.10 Conclusions 1965–1989

Despite détente and de-escalation, NATO continued to emphasize the importance of civil defense and civil emergency planning throughout the period. There is, however, some confusion regarding terminology, as the terms civil preparedness and civil protection were added to security discourse surrounding the civil dimensions. This was most evident in the late 1970s and the 1980s, with primary use in public communication. In a public communication pamphlet from 1988, NATO stated that: "The ultimate purpose of all defence efforts is the survival of our populations and our way of life. Therefore, civil preparedness constitutes an

[4] If there is an interest in continuing pursuing the CEPQ, these documents are mentioned but are not available as of yet C-M(85)76, C-M 85 (25). C-M 85 (26). CR 85 24 AC/98-DS 210, and 206 AC/98-D/I091 AC/98-N 47S.

essential element of the overall deterrent and defensive policy of NATO by enhancing the ability of NATO nations to cope with crises and the consequences of emergencies, including war" (NATO, Public Diplomacy Division 1988). In fact, we can observe an extensive broadening of terminology and concepts. This is most likely a consequence of the broadening of the security agenda and the tasks added to civil defense and civil emergency planning committees since the 1960s. First was the concept of logistics support for military operations, rehearsed in two major exercises, CIVLOG 65 and CIVLOG 69. With this new approach, or an accentuation of this role, also came the notion of civil-military collaboration and a more supportive role for civil actors and resources. This was a sidestep from a purely civil defense focus. At the end of the 1960s, the security discourse broadened to encompass other hazards that modern societies face, as noted above in writings on the "society of man" and the establishment of CCMS. This, in turn, opened the door to a security discourse that linked civil crisis management capacity to war preparedness. Thus, civil preparedness enables societies to cope with various crises and emergencies, including war. The fact that the vocabulary of "all-hazards approach" and explicit connections of how crises and war are connected via civil crisis management took shape already in the beginning of the 1970s is intriguing. Also, the concept of contingencies dates to the 1970s. All of these concepts and ideas will later be reintroduced into NATO vocabulary around 2014 with the adoption of the resilience concept, but it is notable that many of the subsequent suggestions have been present in NATO vocabulary and organization since the 1970s.

In addition, it is worth considering the idea of dual-use of resources and the lack of a clear distinction among civil crisis management, disaster relief, and war preparations. This is something that is emphasized in a public communication from 1988: "advantage should be taken of the mutually supportive roles of preparedness for war and for other kinds of emergencies, including natural or man-made disasters in peacetime, where possible on a multi-use civil emergency program" (NATO, Public Diplomacy Division 1988).

The expansion of new tasks for civil defense and civil emergency planning, and of all the committees in this area, appears odd, given NATO's difficulty in cementing the core tasks of civil defense and civil emergency planning. Every report and inquiry indicates that NATO is unable to influence its member states to advance civil defense. There is an ongoing crisis due to insufficient preparation throughout this period. This may be explained by NATO and its specialized committees constantly requesting too much. Given their expertise, they recognize that civil defense should be advanced further, but member states and civil actors do not share their concerns. In that sense, we can talk of a "failed securitization" for civil defense. Member states do not feel urgency and are either unable or unwilling to meet NATO's high demands. This might also be explained by the difficulties of governing at a distance. Article three states that civil defense and, later, civil emergency planning are the competence and responsibility of the member states. At the same time, member states face other political challenges, and civil defense is a cost that cannot be prioritized because it is invisible or unclear to their publics. What appears odd in this historical expose is that NATO and the member states did not settle for a few prioritized basics in civil defense. Instead, new tasks, demands, and coordination were added, creating insurmountable civil emergency planning questionnaires and review cycles while in practice little advancement was made on the ground and on the homefront.

CHAPTER 7

Civil Dimensions After the End of the Cold War, 1989–2014

"Now that the Cold War is over, we are faced not with a single all-embracing threat but with a multitude of new risks and challenges."
Javier Solana, prior NATO Secretary General, January 25, 1999

The fall of the Berlin Wall, the collapse of the Soviet Union, and the end of the Warsaw Pact could have signaled NATO's demise. Its primary goal of deterring and uniting against Soviet aggression was diminishing, as this threat was no longer considered credible at that time. Given numerous political issues, controversies, and the costs of alliance membership, it was natural to consider dismantling or significantly scaling back the alliance's ambitions, thereby turning it into a more symbolic expression of Western solidarity. The question posed in *NATO Review* in December 1989 is telling: "Can NATO survive if the Cold War is won?" (NATO Review 1989). Although the Soviet Union no longer posed an immediate threat and there were no other military threats to NATO or its member states, NATO remained. NATO had become a well-established security community that, over time, expanded its focus beyond military threats and operations—this shift had begun even before the end of the Cold War. Issues once seen as secondary became more central to the alliance's agenda and helped justify its ongoing existence. These included regional stability in Europe and other areas worldwide, notably the post-Soviet Caucasus. Ethnic conflicts and international terrorism also emerged as key security concerns requiring ongoing monitoring. Moreover, even though the Soviet Union and the former Warsaw Pact states no longer

O. Larsson, *NATO's Approach to the Civil Dimensions of War*,
https://doi.org/10.1007/978-3-032-27871-5_7

posed a direct threat to NATO members, they remained highly unstable. They were expected to undergo significant democratization and reform processes, which NATO members believed required both surveillance and support from NATO (NATO NAC 1990). This also served as a motivation to sustain the alliance. Many new security concerns were external to member territories. Although terrorism posed a real threat to the alliance's populations, there was less need for civil defense and emergency planning involving the general public and the home front. Instead, NATO shifted focus toward international crisis management, disaster relief, and international aid.

7.1 The Fall of the Berlin Wall and the Dismantling of the Warsaw Pact

Even before the fall of the Berlin Wall, East-West relations were improving due to reforms underway in the Soviet Union and other Eastern European countries. In 1985, when Gorbachev became the leader of the Communist Party, he introduced two critical reforms: perestroika and glasnost. Perestroika meant restructuring and signaled economic reforms, later accompanied by glasnost, meaning greater openness in public relations and increased press freedom. In addition, American President George H.W. Bush and Soviet leader Mikhail Gorbachev met several times to negotiate aspects of nuclear arsenals, achieving positive outcomes and developing a good working relationship.

These changes were recognized by NATO at the summit in March 1989, marking its 40th anniversary:

> In the Soviet Union, important changes are underway. We welcome the current reforms that have already led to greater openness, improved respect for human rights, active participation of the individual, and new attitudes in foreign policy. But much remains to be done. We still look forward to the full implementation of the announced change in priorities in the allocation of economic resources from the military to the civilian sector. If sustained, the reforms will strengthen prospects for fundamental improvements in East-West relations (NATO 1989).

The period immediately after the fall of the Berlin Wall on the night of November 9, 1989, during relatively peaceful demonstrations, was, however, not easy. M.E. Sarotte provides a detailed, rich history of this period in her book, *Not One Inch: America, Russia, and the Making of a Post-Cold War Stalemate*. The rapid pace of events and the hasty, perhaps even misstep, to open the borders were followed by intense diplomatic negotiations about the unification of Germany, including the role of NATO, American troops on European soil, and discussions on the placement of nuclear arms (Sarotte 2021). Several documents posted in 2017 on this topic reveal that multiple national leaders rejected Central and Eastern European membership in NATO in 1990 and throughout 1991. The core issue in the negotiation between the USA, the Soviet Union, and Germany was how to allow German unification and continued German membership in NATO. The negotiations in 1990 were not limited to the status of East German territory. The issue of enlargement and the subsequent Soviet and Russian complaints about being misled about NATO expansion can be recovered in written memos and telecons at the highest levels (National Security Archives 2017).

The negotiations ended with the so-called two-plus-four agreement, in which East Germany and West Germany were united, and the four powers that, according to the Potsdam Agreement, were to control Berlin and Germany, renounced their claims and responsibilities (National Security Archive 2017).

The idea of dismantling NATO immediately after the wall fell would have been too hasty, as developments within the Warsaw Pact and the Soviet Union remained uncertain. At the same time, NATO released a new strategic concept in 1991 that substantially downplayed the threat posed by the Soviet Union (Russia) and the notion that the primary danger to transatlantic security was a military invasion. Instead, it was an open policy that suggested a broader security agenda and a new focus on *international crisis management*.

> All the countries that were formerly adversaries of NATO have dismantled the Warsaw Pact and rejected ideological hostility to the West. They have, in varying degrees, embraced and begun to implement policies aimed at achieving pluralistic democracy, the rule of law, respect for human rights, and a market economy. The political division of Europe that was the source of the military confrontation of the Cold War period has thus been overcome (NATO Strategic Concept 1991).

> The monolithic, massive, and potentially immediate threat which was the principal concern of the Alliance in its first forty years has disappeared. On

> the other hand, a great deal of uncertainty about the future and risks to the security of the Alliance remains (NATO Strategic Concept 1991).

The mention of uncertainty about the future and of risks to the alliance's security indicates uneasiness, despite the end of the Cold War, as discussed above. The 1991 strategic concept was the first Strategic concept released publicly and had a nonconfrontational tone toward other nations. The accompanying document to the 1991 Strategic Concept was classified at the time and remains classified. More internal details of the new strategic concept are covered in "MC Directive for Military Implementation of the Alliance's Strategic Concept" (MC 400), December 12, 1991. This document, however, cannot be analyzed (NATO 2022f).

When talking about security challenges and risks, the latter being a new term in this context, NATO explicitly plays down conventional armed attacks: "The security challenges and *risks* which NATO faces are different in nature from what they were in the past. The threat of a simultaneous, full-scale attack on all of NATO's European fronts has been effectively removed, and thus it no longer provides the focus for Allied strategy. Particularly in Central Europe, the risk of a surprise attack has been substantially reduced" (NATO Strategic Concept 1991). Risks are not viewed as serious as a military or strategic attack, but they are still severe enough to warrant mention and, more importantly, numerous. Most importantly, NATO is entering into a domain of uncertainty of what security challenges and risks it is facing: "the risks to Allied security that remain are multi-faceted in nature and multi-directional, which makes them hard to predict and assess. NATO must be capable of responding to such risks if stability in Europe and the security of Alliance members are to be preserved. These risks can arise in various ways" (NATO Strategic Concept 1991). In what is called "a broad approach to security," NATO rearranges its mission: "Managing the diversity of challenges facing the Alliance requires a broad approach to security. This is reflected in three mutually reinforcing elements of Allied security policy, including dialogue, co-operation, and the maintenance of a collective defence capability" (NATO Strategic Concept 1991).

It is a broad post-Cold War security agenda that seeks to address global security challenges and become more politically oriented than before. The 1991 NATO Strategic Concept established the foundation for the alliance's new operational and out-of-area roles, marking a substantial shift in its focus before and after the Cold War. While the practice of these roles was to be developed later, the document signaled a clear departure from Cold War-era collective defense, emphasizing cooperation with Russia and reducing force size and readiness in Europe. However, it also signaled an important shift in its approach to civil defense by explicitly mentioning international crisis management and the deployment of military force beyond its borders. It remained vague about the types of crises NATO should address or whether military intervention outside its borders was intended. Still, the Strategic Concept acknowledged the need for military forces capable of rapid response to various unforeseen contingencies. Despite initial reluctance among some Allies to act outside the NATO area, the document expanded NATO's strategic scope beyond traditional defense, laying the groundwork for future operational flexibility (Williams 2023, 241).

7.2 NATO and the Balkans: The First Out-of-Area Operations

The summit meeting of the North Atlantic Council in Rome, 1991 (which presented the first open strategic concept), also addressed the situation in Yugoslavia. In a joint statement, NATO leaders expressed that they: "...are deeply concerned by the current crisis in Yugoslavia and the grave danger it poses to stability in the region. We deplore the tragic loss of life, the intimidation of civilian populations and the extensive destruction of property" (NATO 1991). The case of Yugoslavia and the ethnic conflicts within it would become one of NATO's main challenges in the post-Cold War period. It would require a book to do justice to this complex case, which spans multiple periods and numerous internal conflicts within NATO (N. Williams 2023). Still, it would be difficult to understand NATO's development at the beginning of the 1990s without a summary of events in the Balkans and of NATO's role and operations.

Nine months after the NATO Summit in Rome in 1991, NATO's role in international crisis management needed clarification. A 4-year war began in June 1991, involving Bosnia and Herzegovina and marking the breakup of Yugoslavia. This breakup included Bosnia and Herzegovina, Croatia, Montenegro, North Macedonia (then known as the former Yugoslav Republic of Macedonia), Serbia, and Slovenia, resulting from the end of the Cold War. NATO was compelled to take action (NATO 2024d). In June 1992, NATO Foreign Ministers agreed to make NATO resources and expertise available to the Conference on Security and Cooperation in Europe (CSCE), which had developed organizational features in the early 1990s (N. Williams 2023). CSCE was a key part of the détente process in the later Cold War years. It acknowledged the boundaries of post-war Europe and established a mechanism to mitigate political and military tensions between East and West. This had all been formalized in the Helsinki Agreement of 1975. In 1995, CSCE was renamed the Organization for Security and Cooperation in Europe (OSCE).

NATO first decided in July 1992 to deploy a naval force in the Adriatic to monitor compliance with UN arms sanctions on Yugoslavia. The Western European Union (1954–2010) deployed maritime monitoring in the Adriatic at the same time and coordinated its activities with NATO. As the situation in Bosnia and Herzegovina worsened, it was believed that a military presence and peacekeeping force could stop ethnic conflicts. NATO had the capability and credibility to carry out such an operation, and it aligned well with the new focus of NATO on international crisis management. The fact that this occurred in the heart of Europe further pressured NATO to get involved.

In November 1992, the NATO naval force was authorized by the NAC, in accordance with UNSCR 787, to enforce sanctions from the UN Security Council. By the end of the year, NATO declared that it stood ready to support peacekeeping operations under the authority of the United Nations. After the United Nations authorized the enforcement of a no-fly zone over Bosnia and Herzegovina, NATO began Operation Deny Flight in April 1993. On February 28, 1994, four warplanes violating the no-fly zone were shot down by NATO aircraft in the Alliance's first military engagement. In November 1994, NATO carried out a bombing raid against an airfield used by Bosnian Serbs. The following year, between August 30 and September 14, 1995, NATO launched an extensive bombing campaign against Bosnian Serb positions, involving 400 aircraft and 5000 personnel from 15 nations. By the time the Dayton Accords were signed in 1995, NATO had deployed an Implementation Force (IFOR) of over 60,000 peacekeepers to Bosnia, including non-NATO states and former UN forces (NATO 2024d).

According to Nicholas Williams, the experience gained from this initial military operation and subsequent peacekeeping efforts proved "…invaluable and provided an operational template for its intervention in Kosovo four years later" (N. Williams 2023). In effect, the Balkans operation changed NATO from a primarily defensive alliance, designed to deter or repel attacks on its members, into an organization with offensive and interventionist capabilities. This was a significant shift for an organization accustomed to defensive measures against the Warsaw Pact. This also created a far broader role for NATO and laid the foundation for a more proactive NATO engaged in multiple operations and missions worldwide.

7.3 A New Military Model and Expanding Partnerships

In January 1994, the NATO summit was held in Brussels. Although it did not generate a new strategic concept, the meeting introduced substantial policy alterations and presented decisive new ideas and approaches. The previous summits in London and Rome set the stage for a post-Cold War agenda, presenting a broader understanding of security and striving for a peaceful relationship with the Soviet Union and, later, Russia, while also making public the 1991 Fifth Strategic Concept. The 1994 meeting continued the path taken, aiming to develop a more active role and approach for NATO. First, it was decided to endorse the idea and model of Combined Joint Task Forces. This was a step to adapt further "the Alliance's political and military structures to reflect both the full spectrum of its roles and the development of the emerging European security and defence identity" (NATO 1994). This marked a shift from a traditional territorial defense to a multi-purpose force capable of operations beyond Article 5 areas and non-Article 5 assignments, as exemplified by the operation launched in Bosnia and Herzegovina in 1993. The press release document informs further that:

> The concept of Combined Joint Task Forces (CJTF) provides flexible and efficient means to enable the Alliance to generate forces at short notice, providing rapidly deployable, multi-national, multiservice task forces with appropriate command and control arrangements. A CJTF is a deployable multinational, multiservice task force generated and tailored primarily, but not exclusively, for military operations not involving the defence of the Alliance territory, such as humanitarian relief and peacekeeping (NATO Information Service 1994).

This new orientation, with specialized forces operating out of area, would not require the same kind of logistical support from civil actors within the member states, or rather, it would require a different kind of support than had been planned for a large-scale nuclear attack and a prolonged war with an adversary.

The other main thing stated in the press release after the meeting was the "reaffirmation that the Alliance remains open to the membership of other European countries" (NATO 1994). This can be seen as the beginning of the enlargement process, and even if NATO does not explicitly mention countries from Eastern Europe and the Soviet Union, it does not exclude such states. In fact, the first states that joined NATO in 1999 were the Czech Republic, Hungary, and Poland (1999), and then in 2004, Bulgaria, Estonia, Latvia, Lithuania, Romania, Slovakia, and Slovenia. All these states have either been in the Warsaw Pact or part of the Soviet Union.

The summit also decided to launch the initiative Partnership for Peace, "inviting Partners to join us in new political and military efforts to work alongside the Alliance" (NATO 1994). The PfP program was said to "...go beyond dialogue and cooperation to forge a real partnership... Active participation in the Partnership for Peace will play an important role in the evolutionary process of the expansion of NATO" (NATO 1994). During the 1990s, NATO expansion, as well as the PfP program, was well underway under the concept of an open-door policy. At the same time, it was also a brief period during which NATO and Russia engaged in constructive dialogue, normalizing diplomatic relations and even reaching an agreement on potential threats to their mutual security (see for instance Pouliot 2010).

In 1997, NATO and Russia took further action to normalize their relationship. In May 1997, they signed the Founding Act on Mutual Relations, Cooperation and Security between NATO and the Russian Federation, in Paris, France. This document stated that:

> NATO and Russia do not consider each other as adversaries. They share the goal of overcoming the vestiges of earlier confrontation and competition and of strengthening mutual trust and cooperation. The present Act reaffirms the determination of NATO and Russia to give concrete substance to their shared commitment to build a stable, peaceful and undivided Europe, whole and free, to the benefit of all its peoples (NATO 1997a).

The document also specified and confirmed the broader security aim and ambition for NATO:

> NATO has expanded and will continue to expand its political functions, and taken on new missions of peacekeeping and crisis management in support of the United Nations (UN) and the Organisation for Security and Cooperation in Europe (OSCE), such as in Bosnia and Herzegovina, to address new security challenges in close association with other countries and international organisations (NATO 1997a).

The act also contained a paragraph that stated that both NATO and Russia would show: "…respect for sovereignty, independence and territorial integrity of all states and their inherent right to choose the means to ensure their own security, the inviolability of borders and peoples' right of self-determination as enshrined in the Helsinki Final Act and other OSCE documents" (NATO 1997a). Additionally, the act established a joint council called the "NATO-Russia Permanent Joint Council" (NRPJC), which was to serve as a place for consultations, cooperation, and consensus-building.

Later that year (1997), following the NATO summit in Madrid, NATO announced that 12 countries were aspiring to join NATO and that the Czech Republic, Hungary, and Poland had begun accession talks with NATO (1997b). The communique also restated NATO's open-door policy that any country in Europe could ask to join NATO if it fulfilled basic requirements and adhered to the values and principles in the North Atlantic Treaty (NATO 1995).

In 1999, the NATO summit was held in Washington, DC, USA. This was also the celebration of the 50-year anniversary of NATO, and during this event, the three new member states could participate: the Czech Republic, Hungary, and Poland. NATO was still engaged in the conflicts in the former Yugoslavia, and the close relationship with Russia had started to deteriorate that year, following the bombing of the Federal Republic of Yugoslavia. The United Nations Security Council had not sanctioned the air campaign. The 50th anniversary reaffirmed "commitment to the enlargement process of the Alliance and approved a Membership Action Plan for countries wishing to join" (NATO 1999). Under the headline "An Alliance for the 21st century" and with the adoption of a new strategic concept, new members, and a plan for further enlargement, NATO showed no sign of quitting or becoming obsolete. Rather, NATO, as a "new" security community, was striving. In the edited volume, *Evaluating NATO-enlargement—From the Cold War to the Russia-Ukraine War*, editors and chapter authors discuss various aspects of the journey and enlargement process that has taken place since the end of the Cold War, which was brought to an end with Russia's interventions regarding the potential inclusion of Georgia and Ukraine (Goldgeier and Shifrinson 2023). They note that NATO's complex history makes it difficult to explain or evaluate its enlargement. Large-scale and long-lasting policies often have multiple consequences, including unforeseen ones at the time of the policy's creation. The debate of NATO enlargement is intense, where "critics make the case that enlargement has caused the collapse of US-Russian relations, (and is even responsible for provoking the Russian invasion of Ukraine), whereas proponents praise the policy as one of the great success stories of US post-Cold War foreign policy" (Goldgeier and Shifrinson 2023, 12). Thus, the expansion and enlargement policy is likely to remain controversial and debatable for a long time.

In 1999, the same year that NATO celebrated its 50th anniversary, it also adopted the Sixth Strategic Concept. To a large extent, it followed the broader definition of security from the former strategic concept, recognizing the importance of political, economic, social, and environmental factors alongside defense issues. The document identified new risks that had arisen since the Cold War, including terrorism, ethnic conflicts, human rights abuses, political instability, economic fragility, and the proliferation of nuclear, biological, and chemical weapons and their delivery systems (NATO 2022f). The 1999 Strategic Concept was complemented by a strategic guidance document that still remains classified entitled "MC Guidance for the Military Implementation of the Alliance Strategy" (MC 400/2), adopted February 12, 2003 (NATO 2022f).

In this Strategic Concept, Civil and international crisis management was explicitly mentioned. "To stand ready, case-by-case and by consensus, in conformity with Article 7 of the Washington Treaty, to contribute to effective conflict prevention and to engage actively in crisis management, including crisis response operations" (NATO Strategic Concept 1999). This could also include civil crisis management and disaster relief, indicating a continued, but more accentuated focus on civil issues.

The strategic concept also contains statements about the role and efforts NATO has undertaken since the end of the Cold War:

> NATO has played an essential part in strengthening Euro-Atlantic security since the end of the Cold War. Its growing political role; its increased political and military partnership, cooperation and dialogue with other states, including with Russia, Ukraine and Mediterranean Dialogue countries; its continuing openness to the accession of new members; its collaboration with other international organisations; its commitment, exemplified in the Balkans, to conflict prevention and crisis management, including through peace support operations: all reflect its determination to shape its security environment and enhance the peace and stability of the Euro-Atlantic area (NATO Strategic Concept 1999)

NATO also identifies potential security threats outside the NATO area: "However, Alliance security must also take account of the global context. Alliance security interests can be affected by other risks of a wider nature, including acts of terrorism, sabotage and organised crime, and by the disruption of the flow of vital resources. The uncontrolled movement of large numbers of people, particularly as a consequence of armed conflicts, can also pose problems for security and stability affecting the Alliance" (NATO Strategic Concept 1999).

Hence, the military organization "...must also be prepared to contribute to conflict prevention and to conduct non-Article 5 crisis response operations. The Alliance's forces have essential roles in fostering cooperation and understanding with NATO's Partners and other states, particularly in helping Partners to prepare for potential participation in NATO-led PfP operations. Thus, they contribute to the preservation of peace, to the safeguarding of common security interests of Alliance members" (NATO Strategic Concept 1999).

Even if civil defense is not explicitly mentioned, the policy document emphasizes the importance of civil-military relations: "The interaction between Alliance forces and the civil environment (both governmental and non-governmental) in which they operate is crucial to the success of operations. Civil-military cooperation is interdependent: military means are increasingly requested to assist civil authorities; at the same time civil support to military operations is important for logistics, communications, medical support, and public affairs. Cooperation between the Alliance's military and civil bodies will accordingly remain essential" (NATO Strategic Concept 1999).

The relationship with Russia is mentioned with enthusiasm: "Russia plays a unique role in Euro-Atlantic security. Within the framework of the NATO-Russia Founding Act on Mutual Relations, Cooperation and

Security, NATO and Russia have committed themselves to developing their relations on the basis of common interest, reciprocity, and transparency to achieve a lasting and inclusive peace in the Euro-Atlantic area based on the principles of democracy and cooperative security. NATO and Russia have agreed to give concrete substance to their shared commitment to build a stable, peaceful, and undivided Europe. A strong, stable, and enduring partnership between NATO and Russia is essential to achieve lasting stability in the Euro-Atlantic area" (NATO Strategic Concept 1999).

Although it did not age well, this position illustrates the extremely high hopes NATO had for democratic development in Russia. It aimed to establish enduring diplomatic relations and shared national-security interests, grounded in stability and in addressing security threats beyond military conflicts between superpowers and their alliances.

7.4 The NATO Crisis of 9/11 and the Close Relationship with Russia

As shown above, NATO shifted its focus and modus operandi during the 1990s. It expanded the security agenda and geographical scope, including out-of-area operations in the former Yugoslavia, and invited new member states. The disintegration of the Soviet Union made it increasingly difficult to achieve consensus within the alliance and to reconcile different national interests and security agendas. It appears the USA remains in the driver's seat. In addition, the USA and European states viewed the crisis and conflict management in the Balkans and ethnic conflicts differently. The division between the USA and European states accelerated further by the events of 9/11. Strangely enough, this was the first time in history that NATO invoked Article 5, on September 12, 2001. The attacks against Afghanistan and the subsequent US invasion showed that one of the most severe threats against NATO members was coming from outside Europe and was in no sense traditional. It could not be won with conventional military methods. Although European states expressed solidarity with the United States, it was evident that the U.S. preferred to address this issue outside of NATO channels and military structures. In preparation for Operation Enduring Freedom, the United States assembled a "coalition of the willing." This approach allowed Washington to exercise greater control and freedom over the operation, including strategies and tactical decisions, free from NATO bureaucracy. Subsequently,

NATO agreed to assume command of the International Security Assistance Force (ISAF), which by then was characterized as a peacekeeping operation. This was, in fact, the first NATO operation outside Europe (NATO 2004). Academics and experts would still proclaim that 9/11 and the subsequent way in which the USA and European states tried to align their different security agendas and priorities illustrated both "US distrust of Europe and European uneasiness to go along with US policies" (Hallams et al. 2013, 13). Similar divisions had been present in NATO during the Vietnam War and also during the invasion of Iraq in 2003, the Second Gulf War.

Even though 9/11 and the Iraq invasion brought about tensions in NATO, showcasing the different security agendas of the USA and European states, the NATO-Russia relations continued to develop toward negotiation and cooperation. In the 2002 Rome Declaration, NATO and Russia established the NATO-Russia Council. This followed the 1997 Founding Act, formalizing the NATO-Russia relationship and advancing a common security agenda. The text announcing the new council states: "In the framework of the NATO-Russia Council, NATO member states and Russia will work as equal partners in areas of common interest. The NRC replaced the Permanent Joint Council (PJC), a forum for consultation and collaboration created by the 1997 NATO-Russia Founding Act. The individual NATO Allies and Russia met as equal partners in the NRC, which indicates that this was a more profound establishment (NATO 2024b).

The NATO-Russia Council wished to provide a mechanism for consultation, consensus-building, cooperation, joint decision, and joint action for the member states of NATO and Russia on a wide spectrum of security issues in the Euro-Atlantic region" (NATO 2002).

The announcement suggested the following areas for cooperative efforts:

- **Struggle Against Terrorism including** strengthen cooperation through a multifaceted approach, including joint assessments of the terrorist threat to the Euro-Atlantic area, focused on specific threats, for example, to Russian and NATO forces, to civilian aircraft, or to critical infrastructure; an initial step will be a joint assessment of the terrorist threat to NATO, Russia and Partner peacekeeping forces in the Balkans.

- **Crisis Management:** strengthen cooperation, including regular exchanges of views and information on peacekeeping operations, including continuing cooperation and consultations on the situation in the Balkans; promoting interoperability between national peacekeeping contingents, including through joint or coordinated training initiatives; and further development of a generic concept for joint NATO-Russia peacekeeping operations.

Beyond these two, the NATO-Russia Council would also cooperate on Non-Proliferation, Arms Control and Confidence-Building Measures: Theatre Missile Defence, Search and Rescue at Sea, Military-to-Military Cooperation and Defence Reform, Civil Emergencies, and addressing New Threats and Challenges (NATO 2002). However, following Russia's annexation of Crimea in 2014, NATO suspended practical cooperation with Russia. Still, it maintained ambassador-level communication channels through the NRC and the Euro-Atlantic Partnership Council, primarily to discuss the situation in Ukraine. The NRC continued to hold meetings, meeting 11 times between 2014 and 2022, often discussing issues relating to Ukraine, even as late as January 2022. In total, the NRC was summoned over 70 times. Russia's full-scale invasion of Ukraine in February 2022 significantly changed NATO's approach to Russia, leading the Alliance at the Madrid Summit in June 2022 to deem Russia no longer a partner. However, NATO continues to seek dialogue to mitigate risks officially (NATO 2024b).

In 2006, NATO recognized the need to develop further its ability and readiness to conduct out-of-area operations and missions. Rather than drafting a new Strategic concept, it created a new policy to complement the 1999 Strategic concept entitled *Comprehensive Political Guidance* (NATO 2006b). The Comprehensive Political Guidance, endorsed in 2006, was intended to set out the framework and priorities for all NATO's capability issues, planning, and intelligence for the next 10–15 years (NATO 2015). The threats, risks, and challenges faced by the allies in 2006 were very different from those of the Cold War, including regional instability, ethnic and religious-based rivalries, competition for natural resources, the proliferation of weapons of mass destruction, failed states, genocide, mass migration, organized crime, cyber attacks, and terrorism. It was therefore necessary to transform NATO forces and make them ready for the new kind of operations and missions that required "agile and interoperable, well-trained and well-led military forces – forces that are modern, deployable, sustainable and available to undertake demanding operations far from home bases" (NATO 2006b).

The Comprehensive Political Guidance (CPG) outlined NATO's operational and capability requirements, with a focus on expeditionary forces and their deployment and sustainment. The specific methods to achieve these capabilities were left to member nations to determine through NATO's defense planning. To undertake all missions, it was suggested that NATO must have the capability to conduct both large-scale and smaller joint operations for collective defense and crisis response across and beyond its territory. The document itself indicates that NATO's out-of-area operations and international crisis management will continue and increase substantially: "...it is likely that NATO will need to carry out a greater number of smaller demanding and different operations, and the Alliance must retain the capability to conduct large-scale high-intensity operations" (NATO CPG 2006).

The NATO Response Force (established in 2002 and terminated in 2024) was considered the ultimate foundation for this. Still, it required fully operational and deployable land, air, and maritime forces. Political targets included having 40% of the member states' land forces prepared for deployed operations and 8% for sustained operations, with Allies committed to increasing these efforts, considering national priorities (NATO 2015, 2025d). The tendency here bears witness to an entirely new purpose for NATO. During the Cold War, NATO was primarily a defense-oriented alliance. However, within the broader security agenda and the 1999 Strategic Concept, we observe a more active and proactive approach, in which NATO prepares for external force projection, international crisis management, and intervention. This will also have implications for NATO's view of civil defense, as there is no home front for such operations, given that NATO and its member states no longer fear large-scale military attacks.

7.5 A New Strategic Concept 2010

During the NATO Summit held in Lisbon on November 19–20, 2010, a series of pivotal decisions were taken that had substantial implications for NATO's strategic outlook and operational models. Foremost among these was the unveiling of a new *Strategic Concept*, which delineates NATO's core purposes, strategic priorities, and future directions, and will be examined in greater detail subsequently. It was also agreed that NATO should assume full security responsibility for Afghanistan starting in 2011, marking a transition from the "coalition of the willing" to NATO-led efforts. The idea was that Afghanistan would be supported in restoring its "sovereignty" and regaining control of its security in 2014. The Summit therefore underscored the intention to establish a long-term partnership agreement with Afghanistan to foster sustained cooperation and stability. A new facet of this summit was the adoption of a new defense orientation, exemplified by the decision to develop a missile defense system intended to bolster European security and by the deployment of additional military personnel to the region ("NATO Lisbon Summit Declaration" 2010). This did, however, signal a return to a military orientation to complement the extensive international crisis management effort that had been guiding NATO operations since around 2000.

Furthermore, the Summit invited Russia to engage in cooperative security efforts, representing a broader strategy of a "reset" in diplomatic relations. However, significant disagreements had arisen between Russia and NATO before the Lisbon summit. These issues included military operations in the Balkans, Georgia's intentions, and NATO's interest in Georgia's accession to NATO. The same applies to Ukraine's process for joining NATO ("NATO Lisbon Summit Declaration" 2010).

At the same time, NATO adopted and confirmed a comprehensive approach to international crisis management, emphasizing stabilization, reconstruction, and the training of local forces as essential components for conflict resolution and peacekeeping. This is a rather extensive approach to Out-of-Area concerns for a defense alliance, as NATO decided to "enhance NATO's contribution to a comprehensive approach to [international] crisis management as part of the international community's effort and to improve NATO's ability to deliver stabilisation and reconstruction effects" ("NATO Lisbon Summit Declaration" 2010).

The summit's centerpiece was the new Strategic Concept, adopted in 2010, which remained in effect until a new strategic concept was adopted in 2022. The strategic concept from 2010 pointed out, as its second paragraph, that the new policy "...commits the Alliance to prevent crises, manage conflicts and stabilize post-conflict situations, including by working more closely with our international partners, most importantly the United Nations and the European Union" (NATO Strategic Concept 2010a).

In the strategic concept, NATO mentions three core tasks and principles. The first one is **collective defense** in accordance with Article 5 of the Washington treaty: "NATO will deter and defend against any threat of aggression, and against emerging security challenges where they threaten the fundamental security of individual Allies or the Alliance as a whole" (NATO Strategic Concept 2010a).

The second one is **crisis management**. It is suggested that "NATO has a unique and robust set of political and military capabilities to address the full spectrum of crises – before, during and after conflicts." NATO, therefore, wants to be able to "actively employ an appropriate mix of those political and military tools to help manage developing crises that have the potential to affect Alliance security, before they escalate into conflicts; to stop ongoing conflicts where they affect Alliance security; and to help consolidate stability in post-conflict situations where that contributes to Euro-Atlantic security."

This should be improved by "further developing doctrine and military capabilities for expeditionary operations, including counterinsurgency, stabilization, and reconstruction operations" (NATO Strategic Concept 2010a). It is suggested that new forms of "appropriate but modest civilian crisis management capability to interface more effectively with civilian partners" should be developed, but also that civil-military collaboration in out-of-area operations should be improved. For this purpose, NATO also suggests that it should "identify and train civilian specialists from member states, made available for rapid deployment by Allies for selected missions, able to work alongside our military personnel and civilian specialists from partner countries and institutions" as well as "broaden and intensify the political consultations among Allies, and with partners, both regularly and in dealing with all stages of a crisis – before, during and after" (NATO Strategic Concept 2010a). Obviously, this is not as encompassing as the ideas of civil defense and "whole-of-society" responses that would recur after 2014, but it shows that NATO considers civilian resources and dimensions, even "out-of-area operations."

The third core ask is **cooperative security**. NATO argues that "the Alliance is affected by, and can affect, political and security developments beyond its borders. The Alliance will engage actively to enhance international security, through partnership with relevant countries and other international organisations; by contributing actively to arms control, non-proliferation and disarmament; and by keeping the door to membership in the Alliance open to all European democracies that meet NATO's standards" (NATO Strategic Concept 2010a). Both crisis management and the concept of cooperative security further reinforce the notion that

NATO will continue its out-of-area operations and address various political crises and conflicts that may impact Euro-Atlantic security. It is extensive in both geographical reach and scope. This is explicitly stated in the strategic concept: "instability or conflict beyond NATO borders can directly threaten Alliance security, including by fostering extremism, terrorism, and trans-national illegal activities such as trafficking in arms, narcotics, and people" (NATO Strategic Concept 2010a). In 2010, the notion of conventional threats and military attacks remained low: "the Euro-Atlantic area is at peace and the threat of a conventional attack against NATO territory is low." In contrast, more direct concern is placed on international terrorism:

> Terrorism poses a direct threat to the security of the citizens of NATO countries, and to international stability and prosperity more broadly. Extremist groups continue to spread to, and in, areas of strategic importance to the Alliance, and modern technology increases the threat and potential impact of terrorist attacks, in particular if terrorists were to acquire nuclear, chemical, biological or radiological capabilities (NATO Strategic Concept 2010a).

This is a concise, publicly available strategic concept that primarily offers general statements and phrases outlining NATO's approach to securing its member states and their populations. At the same time, it is essential to question "whose security" and "what costs." NATO acts in accordance with the interests of its member states and partners. It is a matter of priority for NATO to determine how and where it will engage in international crisis management. Still, NATO remains a military-based organization, as it defines one of its greatest and unique assets with regard to crisis management by its military capacity:

> Where conflict prevention proves unsuccessful, NATO will be prepared and capable of managing ongoing hostilities. NATO has unique conflict management capacities, including the unparalleled capability to deploy and sustain robust military forces in the field. NATO-led operations have demonstrated the indispensable contribution the Alliance can make to international conflict management efforts (NATO Strategic Concept 2010a).

How can we make sense of the extension of NATO's approach to collective defense and security concerns? Yost (2010) argues that the difference between Cold War collective defense and post-Cold War defense orientation, with a new focus on out-of-area threats and subsequent operations, is overstated. He maintains that NATO has somewhat blurred the distinction between Article 5 (collective defense) and non-Article 5 missions, while preserving the traditional meaning of collective defense. Since the end of the Cold War, NATO has extended security commitments to non-allies that have participated in non-Article 5 missions, such as Afghanistan and Operation Active Endeavour. During this time, NATO has also shifted toward a more proactive, anticipatory approach, grounded in Article 5, yet not threatened by conventional military adversaries. However, it can also be argued that this approach still concerns collective defense and security. Other evolving issues during this time, such as missile defense, cyber-warfare, space operations, WMD threats, and regional political-military dynamics, reflect a similar expanded understanding of "new threats." All these issues could serve as potential grounds for non-Article 5 operations, including collective defense contingencies and crisis management operations (Yost 2010).

Writing in 2023, Nicholas Williams argues that there was an inherent tension between NATO's original and ongoing purpose of defending the territory of its member states and its post-Cold War focus on actively engaging in crisis management beyond its borders. During a brief but intense phase in NATO's history, from 1990 to 1995, NATO "transformed itself from a single-purpose collective defense organization to a multi-purpose security organization, specifically specializing in crisis management interventions beyond its borders" (N. Williams 2023). NATO has carried out operations covering nearly the entire spectrum of military interventions: from peace enforcement in Bosnia and Herzegovina to complex security assistance in Afghanistan. It has participated in maritime operations combating piracy and enforcing embargoes along the coasts of the former Yugoslavia and Libya. Additionally, NATO has been involved in humanitarian aid and disaster relief efforts in Albania and Pakistan. It is crucial to remember that NATO does not possess the broader political and economic tools necessary to influence crisis prevention the way the European Union does. For NATO, "crisis management and prevention are virtually synonymous with military intervention. This stems from the fact that NATO's prime value and competitive advantage as an international organization is its highly developed multi-national, US-led military capability" (N. Williams 2023).

At the 2012 Chicago Summit, the press release was lengthy and addressed various operations and missions, as well as other issues concerning new and future member states. For instance, Kosovo and K-for, along with Afghanistan and ISAF, Libya, Syria, and Iraq, are the most pressing international crises for NATO. In addition, it seeks to continue the membership process with Macedonia, Montenegro, Bosnia and Herzegovina, Georgia, and Ukraine. At the same time, NATO strives to maintain a good relationship with Russia and find common ground on a range of security issues (NATO 2012). In fact, the press release for this meeting was more extensive and covered a broader range of topics than the 2010 strategic concept. The feeling might be that NATO is overstretching its capacity and resources at this point; there are too many international hotspots and crises, and the fact that there are no specific limitations or principles on how NATO should prioritize among all these crises could be causing fatigue within the organization (NATO 2012). In 2012, approximately 140,000 military personnel participated in five ongoing NATO-led missions and operations across three continents: crisis management and peace support in Afghanistan and the Balkans; a counter-terrorism operation in the Mediterranean; a counter-piracy operation off the Horn of Africa and in the Gulf of Aden; and a support mission for the African Union (NATO 2013).

This, along with the open-door policy, which is inclusive of other democratic and European states, but perhaps also stretched to its limits? Still, only 2 years later, in 2014, Russia invaded Ukraine by seizing the Crimean Peninsula in February–March and then supporting pro-Russian paramilitaries in the Donetsk and Luhansk regions of eastern Ukraine, which later escalated to a full-scale invasion in 2022. In 2014, NATO was compelled to return to its core mission of defense, deterrence, and countering Russian aggression. But as always, it takes a long time to turn a battleship around.

Writing in 2023, Williams suggests that NATO's intervention and crisis management operations are likely to decline as NATO shifts its primary focus back to deterrence and collective defense against Russia. It is rediscovering its original purpose and political orientation. Furthermore, most of NATO's crisis management efforts have faced criticism regarding their purpose and operational modes. Williams cites, for example, the chaotic scenes at Kabul airport in August 2021, when NATO concluded its mission in Afghanistan. Former General Secretary Jens Stoltenberg writes in his recent book *On My Watch* (2025) that this was a devastating blow for NATO, marked by numerous broken promises to former Afghan staff members, as well as to the majority of the population. The situation became tense when the US decided to withdraw before the schedule it had communicated to other NATO allies, creating a dangerous, fragile situation edging toward chaos (Stoltenberg 2025). This outcome will probably discourage NATO from assuming responsibility for peace support missions on behalf of the international community or from taking over operations initiated by individual member states (N. Williams 2023). A similar outcome is suggested by ..., which also mentions the operation in Libya as a failure, as NATO was unwilling to deploy troops on the ground for a prolonged period, leaving Libya with an even more chaotic situation after the NATO operation.

7.6 From Civil Emergency Planning to Civil Crisis Management

After the end of the Cold War, the role of traditional civil defense and the protection of civilians in wartime naturally receded into the background. The concept of civil administration and civilian resources used to support military operations and logistics also diminished, but it never fully disappeared. It was initially challenging to determine whether there were differences in ambition and effort among the Senior Civil Emergency Planning Committee, its subcommittees, and working groups, mainly because the NATO archives have not made available documents from after the end of the Cold War (1992). Here, interviews with key personnel who worked at NATO at this time were essential to understanding the shifts within the organization. Still, the organizational units remained, along with many of the routines and practices, though some critical changes also occurred. Thus, Civil defense and civil emergency planning did not fade away after the end of the Cold War but changed in character and focus to fit NATO's new, broader security agenda. For instance, the Civil Emergency Committee continued to play a crucial role even after the introduction of the new strategic concept in 1991, as it shifted its focus to the emerging security agenda. It later became active in anti-terrorism efforts, including terrorism and chemical, biological, radiological, and nuclear (CBRN) incidents (NATO Public diplomacy division 2009). The main reorientation, however, was toward civil crisis management and hazard relief. These aspects had already been introduced within NATO during the 1970s, but a clear shift in priorities warrants exploration.

In the 1988 guidelines for civil emergency planning for the following 4 years, 1989–1993, called the Ministerial Guidance for Civil Emergency Planning, the instructions reversed the priorities between war and crisis. The timing of the shift is thus slightly prior to the end of the Cold War.

> The ultimate purpose of all defense efforts is the survival of our populations and our way of life. Therefore, civil preparedness constitutes an essential element of the overall deterrence and defense policy of NATO by enhancing the ability of NATO nations to cope with crises and the consequences of emergencies, including war (SCEPC 1988)

It continues, "civil preparedness is a very cost-effective contribution to NATO's overall defence. It not only enhances the credibility of deterrence but can also increase the efficiency of peace-time disaster relief" (SCEPC 1988). What is fascinating is the way in which communications, globalization, and technology are identified as the foundation of "vulnerabilities" that were not present one generation ago (SCEPC 1988). This is very similar to our current discussion of hybrid threats and the pursuit of resilience. The document recognizes that: "civil emergency planning remains primarily a national responsibility, but to be effective, the action of the Alliance in this field must be based on maximum co-operation between capitals and the NATO level" (SCEPC 1988).

The road ahead is formed around:

> Effective consultation and coordination for crisis management for all stages of a crisis.
> Effective arrangements for the protection of the population
> Effective planning around industry, food, energy, medical, transport, and telecommunication
> Support of armed forces

In pursuit of these broad goals, countries are encouraged to develop multi-purpose civil emergency programs (SCEPC 1988). It is interesting to observe the similarities between the problem description and the proposed solution for multi-purpose civil emergency and crisis management systems, which have essentially been pursued since the 1970s and later continued under the banner of resilience.

In March 1989, 6 months before the fall of the Berlin Wall, the SCEPC organized a symposium at the Canadian Government Conference Centre in Ottawa, attended by approximately 120 participants from 13 member nations. The central theme for the symposium was “decision-making in crisis management.” A general agreement was that “in the currently changing political, economic, and military environment, there continues to be scope for NATO civil emergency planning involvement.” It was concluded that changes often lead to a crisis. Therefore, there remains a need for crisis management and decision-making. New venues, innovative approaches, and preparatory or anticipatory actions in procedural, technical, and human aspects are likely to increase. In addition, the report also identified additional challenges: “Greater consideration should be given to emerging issues like, for instance, the implications of the single European market… In addition to changing East-West relations, North-South relations and transnational issues, e.g. environment, disasters, drugs and terrorism, need to be considered for increased CEP involvement” (NATO SCEP 1989). Here, we also see the broadening of the security agenda and the role of civil emergency planning and civil crisis management, which were formulated prior to the end of the Cold War. These insights will serve as a foundation for civil emergency planning during the 1990s.

In January 1990, it appears that business is as usual for SCEPC. The committee was tasked with conducting more than 80 tasks over the next 2 years, including reviews of Civil Emergency Planning Questionnaire, which should continue to follow its review cycle. A highly labor-intensive task which seems to be outdated given the new focus on civil crisis management. Other tasks included monitoring and reviewing, preparing and developing, and improving various reports and manuals (NATO SCEPC 1990b). There are thus no immediate signs that NATO is slowing down or downgrading the importance of civil emergency planning in the immediate aftermath of the Cold War. Many of the tasks do in fact remain focused on traditional aspects of military support and logistics, including support for wartime agencies and continued work on civil defense and civil protection.

However, discussions had emerged in NATO concerning the role of civil emergency planning and NATO Civil Wartime Agencies given the new geopolitical situation and the foundational idea that Soviet Union no longer posed a credible or even capable threat to the alliance: In a paper from 1990, it was concluded that: “In view of the growing public expectations in most Allied countries to see early and visible reductions in spending related to defence, it must be for each member country to decide to which extent further civil preparedness programmes should be maintained or curtailed" (NATO SCEPC 1990d). Rather than proposing a dismantling of national and international civil emergency planning for NATO member states, the paper suggests "a need for the Alliance to maintain the ability to co-ordinate the use of civil resources in a broader context" (NATO SCEPC 1990d). The current development and shift in focus for NATO as an international organization could even "...mean enhanced responsibilities for the CEP community in its efforts to continue to support civil and military crisis management arrangements" (NATO SCEPC 1990d).

At the ministerial defense planning meeting later that year, the ministers "confirmed the continuing need for major NATO crisis management exercises and invited the Defense Planning Committee in Permanent Session to undertake a review of the future crisis management exercise programme" (NATO 1990). Ministers also requested further effort for civil-military cooperation and civil support of the military as they "invited the Military Committee, Senior Civil Emergency Planning Committee and the Senior NATO Logisticians Conference to examine possibilities for enhanced military/civil cooperation, including the potential of dual use of technologies, facilities and resources, and invited the Senior Civil Emergency Planning Committee to consider further ways in which civil resources can be used to support the military" (NATO 1990). Later that year, in a working paper, SCEPC was looking forward to the main planning of 1991–1993 it was suggested that SCEPC should aim for three specific tasks:

> to support NATO's overall role as a stabilising, crisis managing and peacekeeping organization by enhancing the ability of member nations, individually and collectively, to cope with the threat [risk] and consequences of tension, crisis and war... to contribute to the Alliance's efforts to establish a new pattern of relations between the countries of the East and West... (and) to promote conditions of stability and well-being by enhancing the ability of member nations to cope with the effects of natural and man-made disasters in peacetime (NATO SCEPC 1990a).

In order to do this, it is suggested that NATO should aim to establish or maintain the national organizations, headquarters, communications and information systems, as well as legislation, training and exercising of staff and any other measures to ensure the functioning of nations in periods of tension, crisis and war as well as during disasters in peace but also that it should "maintain a NATO civil preparedness organization able to support nations as required in peace, tension, crisis and war" (NATO SCEPC 1990a). NATO should be able "...to support the Alliance's military defence and mobilisation efforts" and "contribute to the maintenance life for our nations in crisis and war" (NATO SCEPC 1990a).

It is also suggested that NATO strives to establish and maintain the means necessary to protect the population and to facilitate the recovery from disasters both in peace, crisis, and war. It should also:

> assist Central and Eastern European nations in their efforts to promote stability and well-being for their populations by co-operating in the field of peacetime emergency preparedness"; the paper also pushes for the importance "to ensure that credibility and public support be part of' any civil emergency planning programme" and that it "ensure that all civil emergency planning include, as a fundamental ingredient, the dual use of resources (NATO SCEPC 1990a).

It appears that NATO is attempting to maintain both control and initiative for a broader security agenda (NATO SCEPC 1990c). Rather than reducing the role and capacity of civil defense and civil resources, it appears that these actors and resources within member states are being asked to expand their efforts and NATO-focused activities to support peace, crisis, and war.

This document provides valuable insights from an additional perspective. As a foundational document grounded in NATO's ministerial and political guidance, it exemplifies how NATO, as an organization, influences the security agenda in a specific direction. After the end of the Cold War, NATO was indeed struggling to identify new tasks and to remain "useful." In an interview with a former senior staff member, active 1984–1994, he recalls how Alfred Wörner, the then general secretary, was very pleased with the ideas of how civil defense could be made useful for civil crisis management and disaster relief, precisely because it provided a new and active role for NATO after the end of the Cold War. This policy domain later became the foundation for the Partnership for Peace, as collaboration in this area was seen as highly non-political and self-evident (Former Chair of SCEPC, "Senior International Staff, Chair Person for SCEPC," October 10, 2025, Online interview).

Another indication that civil defense and civil emergency planning were not disbanded after the end of the Cold War was the continued effort to improve the Civil Emergency Planning Questionnaire. At its meeting on January 18, 1989, SCEPC agreed to prioritize the examination of those chapters of the Civil Emergency Planning Questionnaire (CEPQ) that do not fall within the responsibility of any particular Planning Board or Committee. Member states were invited to review the CEPQ "Governmental Readiness and Continuity," which a Canadian expert had drafted. The questionnaire remained extensive, but the revised version aimed to simplify it and permitted broad, nominal-scale responses (NATO SCEPC 1991g).

I have touched on this issue in previous chapters, noting that the CEPQ appeared overly broad and raised numerous questions, leading to idiosyncratic responses from member states. A conclusion that also finds support in NATO's later reviews of these questionnaires (NATO SCEPC 1991g). After the Cold War ended, many committees and working groups opposed continued civil emergency planning, arguing that there was no apparent need for it. The chairperson of SCEPC at the time, Michael Elmquist, decided to counter such attitudes and criticism, which also threatened the ongoing and transformative work on civil emergency planning and the questionnaire. He agrees that there have been issues with the questionnaire in the past, but these concerns are currently being addressed:

> The past questionnaires, unfortunately, seemed to endeavor to unveil all possible aspects of a planning area without clearly determining the need for anybody to know the answer. This resulted in reluctance, on the part of several nations, to provide answers and, consequently, an insufficient base on which to establish a meaningful report on the state of civil preparedness (NATO SCEPC 1991b).

He concludes with two crucial points for the continuation of developing the questionnaire and the civil emergency planning within NATO:

> In toto, the Planning and Review Cycle is the most important means available at the NATO level for bringing the civil emergency planning area to the attention of ministers. Without it, civil emergency planning might not be able to maintain its position in the Organization, and the overall NATO support for the work of Planning Boards and Committees (staff support, training funds) might suffer. The disappearance of the threat from the

> Warsaw Pact does not, in my view, diminish the need for the Planning and Review Cycle. On the contrary, I would argue that the dramatic changes in the political climate make it even more important to monitor the status of readiness in each member country. As the civil side is not subject to integrated NATO planning, the Alliance would have no other way of keeping abreast of the decisions 16 member countries take as to the future of their national civil preparedness (NATO SCEPC 1991b).

At the same time, these were turbulent times, and it was unclear how NATO should sustain its existence. In 1991, there was an immediate concern that NATO could no longer maintain civil defense, civil emergency planning, and the NATO Civil Wartime Agencies due to substantial shifts in the geopolitical situation and threat perceptions. Working papers from the SCEPC indicated that civil emergency planning should focus more on civil crisis management and disaster relief than war preparedness. A rebranding of NATO's civil wartime agencies to the NATO civil emergency agencies was suggested in 1991 (NATO SCEPC 1991a, 1991f).

This did not happen, and the name and organization of NATO Civil Wartime Agencies remained until they were terminated in 2003 (The Head of the Joint Health Issues Group, "International Staff," October 13, 2025, Brussels NATO HQ). The former chair of SCEPC 1984–1994, explained in his interview that the energy and effort devoted to the NCWA were minimal at the beginning of the 1990s and remained so throughout his time in NATO service (Former Chair of SCEPC, "Senior International Staff, Chair Person for SCEPC"). The SCEPC continued to indicate, under the branding of "a helping hand," that they should establish contact with civil emergency agents in central and eastern European states. The French representative, however, stated that although the London Declaration indicated that Western and Eastern countries were no longer immediate adversaries, this did not imply or require that SCEPC proactively seek partnerships with these nations (NATO SCEPC 1991c). The former Chair of SCEPC confirmed this and other similar discussions shortly after the end of the Cold War. The helping hand approach was later mentioned to Alfred Wörner, the secretary general, who endorsed the strategy (Former Chair of SCEPC, "Senior International Staff, Chair Person for SCEPC").

Within the fields of science and development, and in the context of continued work with the Committee on the Challenges of Modern

Society (CCMS), established in 1969, the North Atlantic Council decided in April 1990 that the CCMS should expand its program mechanisms beyond pilot studies and fellowships. This was an expansion of the previously more cautious approach of harvesting and harboring ongoing national projects. It was also decided that CCMS should seek arrangements whereby experts from Central and Eastern Europe and the USSR may be invited to participate in CCMS workshops, conferences, and seminars (NATO Public Diplomacy Division 1991). This was another example of how civil crisis management issues were used in diplomatic efforts to establish collaboration with former Warsaw Pact countries during this time.

In July 1991, the North Atlantic Council directed SCEPC to submit a list of activities for the committee and its subordinate Planning Boards and Committees by mid-October. This list should indicate the expected future relevance of each activity, taking into account the development of the new Strategic Concept from the same year. The Council also instructed SCEPC to prepare an appraisal of the consequences of the new Strategic Concept for each of the recommended civil emergency activities, to be considered after the November 1991 Summit meeting. Activities should be developed, reduced, or deleted according to the recommendations (NATO NAC 1991). The SCEPC did not hesitate to take on this task and produced a 168-page working paper. The overall message was that civil emergency planning must adapt to both the changing security environment and the new strategic concept. The working paper states that SCEPC and the many subcommittees have already initiated a critical review of their individual activities:

> ...out of the 291 specific activities or tasks contained in the current work programs, 109 have been eliminated either because the item had been completed (60) or deleted (49) because it was considered irrelevant in the new situation. Additionally, a further 90 activities under the SCEPC have been modified in light of the progress made, developments within that field of activity, or changes in the security environment (NATO SCEPC 1991d).

The overall message from SCEPC was that civil emergency planning should be modified to focus on contingencies and civil crisis management rather than abandoned.

SCEPC states in this document that the 1991 Strategic Concept will affect most of its activities while also creating opportunities for diversification. The new Strategic Concept is expected to signal a new era of heterogeneous conflicts, but not war, implying increased focus on civil crisis management. Regarding military forces, there will be increased emphasis on transatlantic and intra-European reinforcement, as well as on the flexibility and mobility required to handle a wide range of potential contingencies and international crises. The ability to rapidly build forces will be a crucial part of NATO's strategy and will increasingly depend on the availability and effective use of civilian resources. Although the threat from nuclear and chemical weapons has significantly decreased, some defensive measures will still need to be maintained (NATO SCEPC 1991d).

This working paper was later reduced in length by half as a result of the SCEPC Plenary Session on the September 9 and 10, 1991. This Plenary session examined in detail the working paper and agreed that the report, having been revised in accordance with the instructions of the present meeting, could be forwarded to the Council by October 15, 1991 (NATO SCEPC 1991e).

NATO's Strategic Concept (1991) places great importance on military readiness and argues for the necessary use of civilian resources. Civil emergency planning and continued support from member states remained vital to NATO, even as it expanded into out-of-area operations and missions. We noted above how civil emergency planning shifted from war preparedness and civil defense to civil crisis management and a more societal-oriented focus on security issues and contingencies. This is later reflected in NATO operations manuals and instructions for personnel.

> The aims and activities of national and NATO Civil Emergency Planning (CEP) reflect the new political situation and the Alliance's Strategic Concept...priority will be accorded to those activities in support of NATO's overall crisis prevention and management arrangements, as well as support of, and co-operation with, the military in peace, crisis and war (NATO Public Diplomacy Division 1994).

The new and broader approach to civil emergency planning is further advanced:

> Civil emergency planners, nationally and at NATO level, must be fully prepared to support the military in peace, crisis, and war. The Alliance's Strategic Concept and the new NATO Concept of Reinforcement place *increased* reliance on civil resources in general, and transportation resources in particular, to meet military requirements for strategic and operational mobility, and for the sustainment of operational forces (NATO Public Diplomacy Division 1994, emphasis added).

In 1997, it was noted that the ships, aircraft, and vehicles controlled by NATO's armed forces provided only a fraction of the transport capacity that might be required in a crisis or war. NATO, therefore, proclaims that it is dependent on civilian resources, including fuel, food, medical facilities, and industrial goods, required for military and international crisis operations. NATO's strategy is based on three mutually reinforcing elements: dialogue, cooperation, and the maintenance of a collective defense capability. While civil emergency planning remains a national responsibility, it is argued that it "is essential to the *implementation* of NATO's strategy and the actions of the Alliance must be based upon maximum cooperation between capitals and NATO" (NATO 1997c my emphasize).

When discussing the role of civil support in military logistics and disaster relief, the *NATO Logistic Handbook* (1997) confirms the importance of strong civil support. The extent to which such efforts existed is far more difficult to assess. Still, it certainly indicates that NATO expects strong support from member states' civil actors and resources:

> Civil emergency planners, nationally and at NATO level, must be fully prepared to support the military in peace, crisis, and war. The Alliance's Strategic Concept and the new NATO Concept of Reinforcement place increased reliance on civil resources, in general, and transportation resources, in particular, to meet military requirements for strategic and operational mobility, as well as for sustaining operational forces. It is therefore important that civil emergency planners are brought in at the earliest possible stage in the preparation of plans in support of Alliance strategy (NATO 1997c).

To ensure the fullest possible cooperation in providing civilian support to the military, NATO and national planners should, during peacetime, establish the necessary agreements and arrangements for effective support and collaboration in crises and war. Each nation must review its laws and procedures to facilitate the required support in peacetime. Member States should also carefully monitor the conclusion of general agreements with Major NATO Commands (MNCs) to ensure compatibility. It is also recommended that member states identify and update bilateral support arrangements and continue to enhance cooperation between civil and military authorities in Host Nation Support (HNS) planning and reinforcement planning. These are strong requirements imposed by NATO on its member states, indicating that NATO considers itself to have an agency beyond the member state.

Despite the fact that the Cold War has ended 8 years earlier, The Ministerial Guidance for Civil Emergency Planning from 1997/1998 (a core governing document provided by the Ministers of Defence), suggests that civil emergency planning is still needed to keep track of "the traditional areas of concern, i.e., maintenance of social and economic life and protection of the population" (NATO 1997c). It also emphasized the need for emergency legislation or other measures to enable, during a crisis, the use of civil resources to support NATO operations, as outlined in the New Strategic Concept (1991). Additionally, the document suggested specific recommendations and guidance for CEP activities related to cooperation between civilian and military authorities, as well as the Partnership for Peace (PfP) program (NATO 1997c).

In NATO's civil emergency planning during this period, in addition to the biannual ministerial guidance, NATO continues to use the Civil Emergency Planning Questionnaire, which is sent to member states and follows a 4-year cycle. These two dimensions are held together by the international staff and the specific Civil Emergency Planning Directorate (CEPD) (NATO 1997c; Former Chair of SCEPC, "Senior International Staff, Chair Person for SCEPC").

In fact, CEPD (the division within NATO HQ responsible for CEP) functions as an "engine and facilitator" for civil emergency planning and connects all levels in this area. This administrative body managed the CEPQ and the national responses on issues such as crisis management legislation, arrangements, plans, and procedures; communication arrangements in support of crisis management arrangements; cooperation between civil and military authorities; what kind of training and exercises are conducted in the member states; activities with Partners; the stockpile of specific resources; as well as how the planning and review are conducted. In an interview with a former international staff member working on these issues between 1994 and 2000, he recalls the importance that NATO placed on CEPQ, even after the end of the Cold War. Part of the explanation was that most issues were related to the civil dimensions of cooperation within the PfP-programs (International Staff at NATO 1994–2000, "Responsible for CEPQ and Kosovo reports," November 12, 2025, Stockholm, SEDU).

One crucial task was to oversee all programs and functions of the Planning Board and its committees (PB & C). Nine such bodies existed in 1997. See organizational schedule below. In this schedule, Civil Defense is now referred to as the CPC (Civil Protection Committee) rather than CDC. The name change, according to one interview, occurred a few years after 1989. He stated that the traditional civil defense committee changed its name to the civil protection committee, indicating that civil crisis management, emergencies, and contingencies became priorities and a core concept of population safety. The idea of keeping populations safe and continuing with early warnings and clear lines of communication remained important, of course. However, new aspects of civil crisis management and disaster relief were also addressed in their work (Euro-Atlantic Disaster Response Coordinator; 1998–2005, "Staff Officer").

Civil Emergency Planning Committee Structure

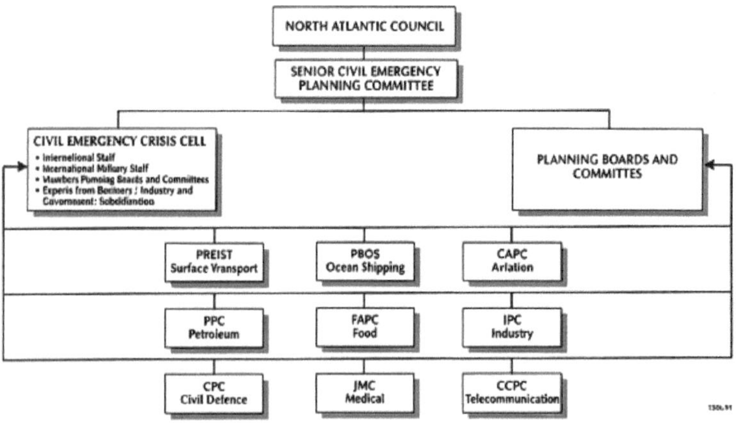

Source NATO (1997c)

This approach to civil emergency planning remains in place at the dawn of the new millennium. In the *NATO Handbook* (2001), it is stated that: "The aim of Civil Emergency Planning in NATO is to coordinate national planning activity to ensure the most effective use of civil resources in collective support of Alliance strategic objectives" (NATO Public Diplomacy Division 2001, 187).[1] The primary roles of the civil emergency planning in NATO reflect "…the fundamental security tasks of the Alliance… civil support for military and crisis response operations, support for national authorities in civil emergencies, and the protection of civilian populations" (NATO Public Diplomacy Division 2001, 187). In addition to these roles, civil emergency planning would also be involved in "managing the availability of civil assets and facilities and the maintenance of normal life during emergencies, such as war, crises, and disasters" (NATO Public Diplomacy Division 2001). The handbook also mentions that "…this work is carried out in close cooperation with Partner countries, who now play an active part in Civil Emergency Planning in NATO" (NATO Public Diplomacy Division 2001). Still, in 2001, the organization remained unchanged from 1997, as shown above, but the handbook notes that Petroleum production and supply (PPC) was inactive.

One development during this time is the collaboration with countries participating in the Partnership for Peace program. The original program began in 1994 and was seen as a potential middle ground for countries that wanted to collaborate with NATO but did not want to, or could not, become members. For some countries, the Partnership for Peace was a way to move closer to NATO membership, a first step toward membership. For others, it seemed natural to cooperate with NATO in areas such as civil emergency planning, as in Sweden, even if there was no political desire to join NATO at this time. Other countries may be non-European

[1] The contact person at NATO Archives told me that the Public Diplomacy Division, active since the mid-1950s, had been terminated in September 2025. The main reason seemed to have been budget cuts. A media team manages the webpage, but it is unclear whether other information channels will be maintained after 2025, e.g., larger publications such as handbooks and information sheets. The archive is also struggling to keep records open and up to date, leading to potential backlogs.

States in the Mediterranean area and therefore ineligible for membership as "non-European" states. Partnership for Peace later evolved into candidate programs for potential candidates.

7.7 NATO and the New Disaster Assistance

On May 9, 1995, the Council approved the NATO Policy on Cooperation for Disaster Assistance in Peacetime, which was extended to the North Atlantic Cooperation Council (NACC) and Partnership for Peace (PfP) countries. This policy states that the standing operating procedures for NATO cooperation in peacetime disaster relief are in effect and include NATO member states and partner countries. If requested by NATO, a Partner, a stricken country, or a relevant international organization, NATO should be prepared to employ these cooperation procedures, even in cases of disasters outside NATO's boundaries. The policy also suggests expanded cooperation among NATO countries, harmonization of member-state systems and policies, and the readiness of NATO Headquarters to ensure the rapid dissemination of official information about major disasters within NATO. It emphasizes the prompt exchange of emergency information among member countries regarding assistance needed by the stricken country, including pharmaceuticals, vaccines, food, clothing, emergency shelter, prefabricated housing, water purification equipment, rescue teams and equipment, medical teams, field emergency hospitals, and disaster experts. These efforts and assistance could be provided bilaterally to a stricken country by governmental and national voluntary organizations, either from member or non-member countries (NATO 1997c). The idea of disaster relief and civil crisis management coordination among member states had been discussed previously within NATO (actually since the 1950s), but has hitherto not been approved and formalized by the North Atlantic Council. After the Cold War, it was codified for member states and later extended to partners outside the alliance. As noted earlier, SCEPC had previously approached the subject of coordination informally, but the 1995 policy formalizes NATO's role in disaster relief and further extends its civil crisis management orientation.

The expansion of civil emergency planning, both in scope and geography, can be seen as a strategic effort to maintain NATO's relevance in the post-Cold War era. Interviews with individuals working in the SCEPC and on the subcommittees indicate that this area has significant potential for improvement within NATO and could serve as a diplomatic bridge to Russia, former Warsaw Pact countries, and other nations and international organizations. The general secretary at the time, Alfred Wörner was also keen to find an adjusted role for NATO (Euro-Atlantic Disaster Response Coordinator; 1998–2005, "Staff Officer"; Former Chair of SCEPC, "Senior International Staff, Chair Person for SCEPC"). In the interviews, interviewees noted that this dimension of NATO is often obscured by the overall image of NATO. Despite being related to security and human safety, it is not really regarded as "high politics," military efforts, or national and international security.

In the PfP program, CEP activities have become the largest non-military component. The CEP program aims to develop emergency planning structures and procedures under civilian and democratic oversight, as well as humanitarian and disaster response arrangements, and civil-military cooperation. The program includes command post and field exercises, workshops, seminars, training sessions, meetings, and team visits. The focus is said to be on practical cooperation, enhancing interoperability, regional collaboration, and fostering good neighborly relations (NATO Public Diplomacy Division 2001).

The Euro-Atlantic Disaster Response Coordination Center (EADRCC) was established in 1998 by the Euro-Atlantic Partnership Council. The center is not exclusively for member states and PfP countries; other partners can also use it, as it is intended to cover both acute responses and preparedness for natural and human-made disasters and other emergencies. Initiating cooperation with partners in emergency response was initially a Russian proposal and an example of the fruitful collaboration NATO and Russia once had in the interest of international security (NATO 2025a). The interviews provide additional historical details. According to at least two interviewees, the international staff within Civil Emergency Planning saw the potential to raise awareness of civil crisis management and disaster relief. They also aimed to promote cooperation with non-NATO countries. They provided a draft for the Russian delegates to review and submit to NATO as an official proposal. This approach would make it harder for some hesitant member states to oppose the push for civil crisis management and disaster relief centers, as it has become a matter of high politics and diplomacy.

The EADRCC is based at NATO Headquarters in Brussels, Belgium. It is operated by a small team but can be significantly expanded during a crisis. One of the first missions was civilian relief during the Kosovo crisis, a complicated and dangerous mission that was not without disruptions and mishaps. Still, the report covering this operation was polished for political purposes (International Staff at NATO 1994–2000, "Responsible for CEPQ and Kosovo reports"). This is the sense of most NATO publications and reports; they are tailored to fit NATO's self-image. The EADRCC also relies on expertise from national civil experts, who can be called upon to provide advice in specific areas during major disasters. Even if tracking the budget each year is difficult, figures from a 2006 information sheet are instructive. It states that the Civil Emergency Planning operational budget at NATO Headquarters is approximately 2.7 million €/year, representing about 1.5% of NATO HQ's total civil budget. In 2006, 8 years after its establishment, the EADRCC had been involved in more than 30 operations worldwide. These included coordinating relief supplies for refugees, aiding victims of flooding, hurricanes, and earthquakes, and fighting forest fires. Notably, large-scale assistance included support during Hurricane Katrina in the US (2005) and aid to Pakistan during the massive earthquake in 2005–2006 are mentioned as prime examples (NATO 2006a).

Much of the documentation and interviews indicate that, after the end of the Cold War, NATO, with the support of international staff, quickly identified new tasks and expanded the civil emergency planning agenda and section, with extensive collaboration within NATO and with external partners. The notion that civil resources are integral to NATO's strategic approach at all levels has been a core tenet since the 1950s. Still, it was not until the 2000s that civil crisis management and disaster relief efforts were truly formalized. In the *NATO handbook* of 2006, it is stated that: "Civil emergency planning has long been one of the mainstream activities of NATO…However, the characteristics of NATO civil emergency planning activities have fundamentally changed since the end of the Cold War. No longer focused primarily on managing civil resources and protecting the population in the context of large-scale war, they are oriented towards providing support for military crisis response operations and dealing with the consequences of natural disasters or terrorist attacks" (NATO Public Diplomacy Division 2006).

In a 2008 public pamphlet, the NATO Public Diplomacy Division explains the historical development of this area:

> The need to support NATO's Military Authorities with a civilian dimension was identified very early in NATO's history. In 1956, the Report on Non-Military Cooperation by the Three Wise Men stated that 'security today is far more than a military matter'. After the end of the Cold War, the increasing importance of civil resources in responding to challenges in the evolving security environment was recognized in the Strategic Concepts developed in 1991 and 1999 (NATO Public diplomacy division 2008).

Thus, "Planning and conducting modern military operations as well as responses to disasters or humanitarian crises is a complex process...Close cooperation and interoperability between military and civilian actors is vital, and NATO plays an important role in facilitating such cooperation" (NATO Public diplomacy division 2008).

NATO recommended "a *comprehensive approach* involving a wide spectrum of civil and military instruments" (NATO Public diplomacy division 2008). It is noted that SCEPC facilitates specific areas when NATO's Military Authorities may require civil support for collective defense operations under Article 5 of NATO, for non-Article 5 operations, and for regular crisis and disaster response operations. These operations and missions, it is said, all require civilian capabilities and tools. Two main instruments should facilitate civil support for NATO operations: the Civil Capabilities Catalog and the Rapid Reaction Team. The Catalog lists 13 areas in which civilian assets can rapidly support NATO during crises, enabling force commanders to access civilian expertise from NATO HQ, national ministries, or commercial organizations. While its usage frequency is unclear, its designation as a mechanism suggests that it is used and desired. The Rapid Reaction Team, established in 2006, quickly assesses civil needs and supports NATO operations by deploying experts within 24 h in areas such as transportation, communications, civil protection, and related fields. It complements the Catalog by offering on-the-ground support tailored to military needs (NATO and Swedish Civil Contingency Agency 2009; NATO Public diplomacy division 2008).

In a 2009 *Handbook on International Civil emergency Planning* (authored by the Swedish Civil Contingency Agency in collaboration with NATO), it is suggested that: "NATO has always placed emphasis on the protection of civilian populations and critical infrastructures against the consequences of armed conflict, natural and technological disasters, and terrorist attacks, including the possible use of CBRN agents" (NATO and

Swedish Civil Contingency Agency 2009). This is, of course, an idealized picture given the controversies noted in previous chapters.

Still, even if NATO has been advancing its engagement in civil emergency planning and disaster relief, it stresses that:

> Civil emergency planning is first and foremost a national responsibility and civil assets remain under national control at all times. NATO's added value lies in sharing best practices, cooperation in training and exercises and, in the event of a large scale emergency, in facilitating coordination and cooperation (NATO and Swedish Civil Contingency Agency 2009).

It also points out the "diplomatic function" of CEP programs.

> NATO/CEP represents an important component of NATO'S partnership programmes. Cooperation on CEP is an important aspect within the various cooperative frameworks: the Euro-Atlantic Partnership Council (EAPC); the NATO-Russia Committee (NRC); NATO-Ukraine Commission (NUC), Mediterranean Dialogue countries, and Istanbul Cooperation Initiative countries. Civil and military representatives from branches of national, regional and local government, international organisations and NGOs take part in NATO CEP activities (NATO and Swedish Civil Contingency Agency 2009).

In the 2010 Strategic Concept, NATO explicitly mentions its engagement in crisis management:

> The lessons learned from NATO operations, in particular in Afghanistan and the Western Balkans, make it clear that a comprehensive political, civilian and military approach is necessary for effective crisis management. The Alliance will engage actively with other international actors before, during, and after crises to encourage collaborative analysis, planning, and conduct of activities on the ground, in order to maximise coherence and effectiveness of the overall international effort (NATO Strategic Concept 2010b).

Still, this mainly refers to international crisis and conflict management rather than civil emergency planning within NATO countries. An idea of potential crises and vulnerabilities is mentioned under the headline of the Security Environment: "All countries are increasingly reliant on the vital communication, transport and transit routes on which international trade, energy security and prosperity depend. They require greater international efforts to ensure their resilience against attack or disruption" (NATO Strategic Concept 2010b).

Since the September 11 attacks and subsequent incidents in Istanbul, Madrid, and London, Civil Emergency Planning has also been asked to focus on improving national and civil preparedness for chemical, biological, radiological, and nuclear (CBRN) threats. Since 2001, the EADRCC also played a role in coordinating nations' responses to terrorist acts involving chemical, biological, or radiological agents, as well as managing consequences. In 2002, a Civil Emergency Action Plan was adopted at the NATO Summit in Prague to protect populations from weapons of mass destruction, leading to the development of an inventory of capabilities like medical aid and radiological detection. Guidelines and standards have also been developed to support planning, training, and response to CBRN incidents, enhancing cooperation among Allies and Partners. In addition, critical infrastructure assets, identified as essential to health, safety, security, and economic stability, are identified as "vulnerable to disasters and terrorism." Protecting these assets ensures societal resilience and involves international cooperation on threat assessment, best practices, and training. NATO's Civil Emergency Planning also includes critical infrastructure protection, recognizing its importance for national and global stability as early as 2006. Contrary to common belief and the adoption of the resilience concept and whole-of-society approach, we can see that critical infrastructure was on the agenda already in 2006 (NATO Public diplomacy division 2008).

7.8 Conclusions 1989–2014

NATO evolved from a military alliance into a comprehensive organization during the 1950s and 1960s, with extensive infrastructure and personnel in Mons and Brussels. The organization adapted its military and political structures post-Cold War to remain relevant, focusing on flexible command, rapid deployment, peacekeeping, WMD counter-proliferation, crisis management, and disaster relief. As a result, NATO has transformed into a political-military organization distinct from its Cold War origins and the initial alliance between 12 countries. NATO lost its immediate rationale but quickly filled that void with a broader understanding of security, turning its focus to civil and international crises, peace operations, terrorism, and disaster relief. In addition to broadening the security agenda, NATO was expanding geographically, growing from 16 countries in 1989 to 28 in 2014. This, despite the promise of "not one inch eastward" given to Mikhail Gorbachev by U.S. Secretary of State James Baker if Germany were "allowed" unification and NATO membership in 1990. However, it later became a policy that states must decide for themselves if they wish to join an alliance such as NATO (the open-door policy), and many of the new member states actually came from Eastern Europe and were former members of the Warsaw Pact (German 2017; Eichler 2021; Edström et al. 2011).

After the end of the Cold War and the implosion of the Warsaw Pact and the Soviet Union, the emphasis on democratic values became even more critical as the foundation for a transatlantic security community, a way to further the value and reason d'être of the alliance (Adler 1997; Risse-Kappen 2016). Andreas Behnke notes that NATO engages in peacekeeping and crisis management, with key moments such as the Yugoslav Wars and 9/11, when Article 5 was activated. In the war against terrorism that followed the shift, it is from "West versus East" to "West and the rest." The Cold War's end did not lead to immediate "security" but de-centered security, threats, and enemies (Behnke 2000). In this way, NATO's post-Cold War security discourse becomes more political, in the sense that it concerns deliberate choices about which issues to tackle, which conflicts and crises to engage with, and who is a worthy enemy. Lene Hansson identifies similar discourses in the first military operations outside NATO territory. Hansen argued that identity and divergent discourses on how to understand the enemy, or the "other," in the Balkans shaped the nature of operations there. She notes that the air bombing of Serbia in 1999 was one of the leading causes of the deterioration of the diplomatic relations between Russia and NATO in the 1990s. This was the first time NATO had operated without the UN Security Council's approval. Hansen showed that identity and discourse played significant roles in NATO's decision-making as it navigated two approaches simultaneously, Balkanization and genocide. The discourse of "balkanization" was more prevalent in America, while the discourse of "genocide" was stronger in Europe. This resulted in ambivalent approaches to the Balkan crisis and domestic war, ethnic conflict, and genocide on the European continent (Hansen 2013).

Other out-of-area operations have sparked similar debates about NATO's mandate and modus operandi in Afghanistan and Libya, both of which have their own controversies. One aspect that appears to have remained politically secure is NATO's civil crisis management and disaster relief. This domain has consistently been viewed as a safe and non-controversial area for international cooperation and policy implementation. This, even though there were initial concerns and hesitation among some member states about allowing this policy expansion. In this policy area, we can see that, after the end of the Cold War, civil crisis management and disaster relief within NATO have been accentuated compared to prior eras, when more traditional civil defense and civil emergency planning focused on efforts during total and nuclear war. This "turn" functioned well with NATO's search for a new role in a security environment in which human security and broader concerns could be considered. In addition, civil crisis management and disaster relief were also areas that worked well to establish new West-East relations, and the willingness to cooperate with Russia and the former Warsaw Pact countries under EACP. The Euro-Atlantic Disaster Response Coordination Center (EADRCC) established in 1998, was a result of Russian proposal crafted with NATO HQ by international staff, In addition, civil crisis management and disaster relief has also functioned well with several programs and collaborations, PfP, as well as the Euro-Atlantic Partnership Council (EAPC); the NATO-Russia Committee (NRC); NATO-Ukraine Commission (NUC), Mediterranean Dialogue countries, and Istanbul Cooperation Initiative countries. Obviously, the NRC has been halted, and the EAPC plays a significantly lesser role today. Still, it could be that civil crisis management and disaster relief were among the most significant areas of NATO's activities between the end of the Cold War and 2014. Civil emergency planning in NATO did not fade out after the end of the Cold War. Instead, it changed character to emphasize civil crisis management and disaster relief. This policy area did, in fact, expand in the 1990s and served as the foundation for many of the partnership programs established during that time. The next chapter covers the years between 2014 and 2025. Here we can detect a "return" or re-inventing of civil emergency planning to its more traditional form, protecting the population and society from the effects of warfare—a challenge complicated by the hybrid nature of non-kinetic warfare and new vulnerabilities.

CHAPTER 8

The New Concept of Resilience

Although NATO is primarily understood as a defense alliance with a military principal focus, we have noted in previous chapters that the organization has always had an interest in various dimensions of security, including civil defense, civil emergency planning, and civil crisis management and disaster relief organization, either as explicit or implicit parts of its collective defense and deterrence capabilities. This may be motivated by the phrasing in Article Three of the North Atlantic Treaty: "In order more effectively to achieve the objectives of this Treaty, the Parties, separately and jointly, by means of continuous and effective self-help and mutual aid, will maintain and develop their individual and collective capacity to resist armed attack" (NAT 1949). Still, the framing and explicit linking of civil emergency planning to Article Three appears much more frequently in the period 2014–2025. Perhaps this was self-evident in the past, or that the current, extensive efforts to secure the entire society must find a concrete foundation in treaties and legal documents.

The basic idea behind the NATO mindset in these issues is the following: Weak societies create the possibility of ideological influence and of weakening, or even wrecking, the home front. It may lead to low morale among the fighting forces and weaken the much-needed support from society, and affect the nation's and, in extension, the alliance's ability to wage war. At the end of World War II and the foundation for NATO, it was clear that war-torn countries with weak economies and popular grievances could be fertile ground for communist expansion or

O. Larsson, *NATO's Approach to the Civil Dimensions of War*,
https://doi.org/10.1007/978-3-032-27871-5_8

the outburst of new military conflicts. The European states, the USA, and Canada feared the emergence of a new world war, and in different ways, NATO was created to prevent such a development. In the beginning, this was mainly due to economic and ideological concerns for the well-being and future security of Europe. The Marshall Plan preceded NATO and financially supported the reconstruction of European states after the World War II to facilitate a quick recovery of war-torn economies and to make them less vulnerable to communist influence, but it was not enough. The central purpose of creating NATO was to enhance psychological protection and to foster an ideological conviction to resist communism and halt potential Soviet aggression. Obviously, the civil administration and other "spheres" were seen as crucial to a credible military alliance and deterrence, allowing various articles of the North Atlantic Treaty to address such issues within member states. Interpretations and the importance of the articles in the treaty can differ depending on ambition, interests, and security concerns. Since 2014, however, there has been a high level of interest in the civil and non-military dimensions, with more personnel working in civil defense and crisis management than in military issues and operations at NATO headquarters. The build-up of credible deterrence and defense for Europe in the twenty-first century, along with the notion of grey zone and hybrid threats, has led NATO to adopt the concept of resilience to once again boost civil defense, or rather civil emergency planning and overall societal preparedness.

Obviously, this has sparked interest among scholars, and research on how NATO deploys resilience to counter hybrid threats is emerging. The idea is to make sense of the rediscovered "whole-of-society" approach for NATO. Paul Sigurd Hilde discusses the newly found interest in Article Three in the chapter "NATO and total defence - A framework for national efforts." It is important to note that NATO seldom use the concept of total defense, but, as Hilde points out, there is an unmistakable resemblance between the inherent meaning of total defense (whole-of-society) and the framework for national resilience that NATO has developed (Hilde 2025). He also notes that so far, there has been scant interest in the academic literature on NATO, civil emergency planning, and resilience (Hilde 2025). Frizzelle et al. (2022) welcome the initiative to build resilience at the national level and believe that "Resilient societies, and therefore a resilient alliance, is the antidote to hybrid warfare" (Frizzelle et al. 2022). They have several suggestions for further improvement of resilience. One is the need to establish standards and resilience metrics like those in military equipment that have enabled interoperability among the armed forces. Another one is the need to secure the democratic foundation within NATO: "Maintaining strong democratic institutions within member states is imperative to national and alliance resilience, including the resilience of NATO's partners from the alliance's southern and eastern flanks" (Frizzelle et al. 2022). Maria Mälksoo discusses the introduction of the concept of resilience in more cautious terms. She notes, similar to the discussion in Chap. 4 that "...resilience is analytically contested, because it occupies an uncomfortable foggy position vis-à-vis security as a logic of governmentality... the logic of resilience is consequently tied to controllability and manageability of risks" (Mälksoo 2025). She sets out to answer the "what, why, where, and how" of NATO's adoption of resilience, but the empirical focus is but a short part of her chapter. She concludes that resilience provides a conceptual bridge for NATO to tie together its "outside" to its "inside" and serves the purpose of deterrence (Mälksoo 2025). According to Zeynep Arkan "the notion of hybrid threats has become a cornerstone of European security discourse, encapsulating the ambiguities and complexities of modern conflict" (2025). This allows a narrative where NATO and the European Union can portray themselves as defenders of democracy and order and where the "east," foremost China, Russia, and Iran are revisionists threatening democratic values and international liberal order (Arkan 2025).

To understand the role and function of resilience as a key concept, we need to examine its emergence and its institutionalization within NATO. Our position in undertaking this analysis is strengthened by prior chapters, which demonstrate that resilience represents but the most recent phase in a broader historical context of civil defense and civil emergency planning, and can in fact be seen as a continuation of the vocabulary from the 1970s, crisis and war.

8.1 Resilience as a Key Policy Concept

The declaration from the 2012 NATO Summit in Chicago does not mention "resilience." Conversely, the 2014 Wales Summit incorporates the term twice, albeit in general terms. Only 2 years later, at the 2016 Warsaw Summit, however, it marked a significant escalation, with the term "resilience" appearing 15 times. Additionally, in Warsaw, allied leaders issued a separate statement entitled "Commitment to Enhance

Resilience," emphasizing that resilience constitutes an essential foundation for credible deterrence, defense, and the effective execution of NATO's core tasks. This sparked my interest as I have previously investigated the concept's entrance into civil crisis management, the environment, and national defense in Sweden, and noted its ambiguous role and meaning (Mingarini and Larsson 2025; Larsson 2021).

The declaration of the NATO Summit in Chicago 2012 is lengthy; while it does not mention resilience, it does mention Russia 33 times, indicating the deterioration of the relationship between Russia and NATO. Russia did engage in an invasion of Georgia in 2008 and maintained control over the separatist regions of South Ossetia and Abkhazia. This has been seen as directly linked to the Georgian willingness to "go West" and join the European Union and NATO. It may be that this turn of events is worrying for NATO, as 2012 marked the tenth anniversary of the establishment of the NATO-Russia Council (NRC) and the fifteenth anniversary of the NATO-Russia Founding Act (NATO 2012). In addition, most references to crisis management in the declaration concern the complementary functions of civil and disaster management in specific operations: "An appropriate but modest civilian crisis management capability has been established, both at the NATO Headquarters and within Allied Command Operations, in accordance with the principles and detailed political guidance we set out at our Summit in Lisbon" (NATO 2012). Still, there are no references to terms and concepts such as "civil defense" or "civil emergency planning." The only relevant aspects of these issues are references to cyber defense and a single mention of critical infrastructure.

The Wales summit in 2014 took place after the Russian attacks on the Crimean Peninsula in support of pro-Russian paramilitaries in the Donetsk and Luhansk regions. This is the start of one of the most severe military conflicts in Europe since World War II and effectively places NATO and Russia on a collision course. The response and tone capture the dire development:

> In order to ensure that our Alliance is ready to respond swiftly and firmly to the new security challenges, today we have approved the NATO Readiness Action Plan. It provides a coherent and comprehensive package of necessary measures to respond to the changes in the security environment on NATO's borders and further afield that are of concern to Allies. It responds to the challenges posed by Russia and their strategic implications. It also

> responds to the risks and threats emanating from our southern neighbourhood, the Middle East and North Africa. The Plan strengthens NATO's collective defence. It also strengthens our crisis management capability. The Plan will contribute to ensuring that NATO remains a strong, ready, robust, and responsive Alliance capable of meeting current and future challenges from wherever they may arise (NATO 2014).

Resilience is mentioned only twice, and both references are very general:

> NATO is both transparent and predictable, and we are resolved to display endurance and resilience (NATO 2014), and, "[t]he policy [in cyber security] reaffirms the principles of the indivisibility of Allied security and of prevention, detection, resilience, recovery, and defence" (NATO 2014).

There is no mention of civil defense or civil emergency planning, and crisis management is discussed only in the context of international crisis management in line with three overarching goals in the 2010 Strategic Concept. Similarly, disaster relief is not mentioned once. The Wales summit focused almost exclusively on the Russian aggression. Still, it might have been too early to draw any conclusions on the need to rebuild and reinstall civil defense or civil emergency planning as part of the preparation for classic deterrence and ultimately war.

The most significant change occurred in 2016, which is clearly a more workable timeline for an international organization with 30 member states to develop new policy directions.

It was at the Warsaw meeting in 2016 that NATO began discussing its efforts to strengthen *society's collective ability* to withstand crises, disruptions, and other challenges. NATO explicitly mentioned this theme in the communique that followed the summit, which emphasized the importance of a new holistic view of society's ability to deter and defend itself against a range of actors, threats, and disturbances. Here, resilience is identified as the ability to withstand an attack. NATO "builds" and "improves" its resilience to withstand an attack by an aggressor. Here, we can see a clear return to ideas of deterrence and defense from an aggressor against a NATO country, ideas that had been put on the shelf between 1989 and 2014.

There is also a section of *a commitment* to enhance resilience:

> Today we have made a commitment to continue to enhance our resilience and to maintain and further develop our individual and collective capacity to resist any form of armed attack. Civil preparedness is a central pillar of Allies' resilience and a critical enabler for Alliance collective defence. While this remains a national responsibility, NATO can support Allies in assessing and, upon request, enhancing their civil preparedness. We will improve civil preparedness by achieving the NATO Baseline Requirements for National Resilience, which focus on continuity of government, continuity of essential services, security of critical civilian infrastructure, and support to military forces with civilian means. In this context, we welcome the Resilience Guidelines approved by Defence Ministers in June 2016 (NATO 2016c).

Resilience is here connected to civil *preparedness*, but the communique does not mention the previous terms of civil defense or civil emergency planning. Resilience is also used to specify the endurance and resistance of armed forces and partners. It is thus used in multiple ways but must still be regarded as a central concept that conveys, foremost, the resistance and endurance of societies under distress.

At the Warsaw Summit, NATO also adopted the new steering document and specific guidelines for how the organization and its member states should work together to improve resilience. In a press release on July 8, NATO codified this as a "Commitment to enhance Resilience."

In the document, it is suggested that NATO and the member states share "… a commitment to continue to enhance our resilience against the full spectrum of threats, including hybrid threats, from any direction. Resilience is an essential basis for credible deterrence and defence and effective fulfilment of the Alliance's core tasks" (NATO 2016b).

This would also entail an understanding that a new geopolitical security environment is unfolding:

> We now face a broader and evolving range of military and non-military security challenges, which is the context for the Alliance's long-term adaptation. Being resilient against these challenges requires Allies to maintain and protect critical civilian capabilities, alongside and in support of military capabilities, and to work across the whole of government and with the private sector (NATO 2016b).

It is indeed telling that NATO emphasizes whole-of-government approaches and the inclusion of the private sector. What is more, this is not only efforts conducted during wartime but in the new security environment of grey zone and amid hybrid threats, and ultimately hybrid warfare (i.e., total war), indicating that this is ever-present. It always requires preparedness and alertness across the entire society, for peace and war. Or might we call it un-peace, the absence of war for the time being? For similar conclusions at the national level on the introduction of resilience, see (Larsson 2021; Ljungkvist 2024; Mingarini and Larsson 2025). It is also here that the theory of securitization becomes relevant. It is noted that Russia's aggression against Ukraine is a violation of international law and a disruption of peace in Europe. But without clear guidance and precision, it is difficult to see how building resilience across the entire society would, in fact, create the level of preparation needed for full-scale war. Everything can't be securitized at once. The risk is a shattered, spontaneous, and unclear structure, and difficulties in specifying who has the overarching responsibility for ensuring "resilience" in peacetime and during war.

Although NATO's resilience proposal acknowledges that this is primarily a national responsibility, as it always has been, looking back to the 1950s and 1960s. However, civil defense and emergency planning were different then, focused on preparing for war and more clearly separated between preparation and execution. This might be a mindset unsuitable for the twenty-first century and for notions of hybrid threats. NATO identifies itself as a coordinator and supervisor for resilience efforts:

> To complement and enable our military capabilities, we will continue to improve civil preparedness. Noting that civil preparedness is above all a national responsibility, we will strive to achieve the agreed requirements for national resilience. We will protect our populations and territory by strengthening continuity of government, continuity of essential services and security of critical civilian infrastructure; and we will work to ensure that our national and NATO military forces can at all times be adequately supported with civilian resources, including energy, transportation, and communications. This will include NATO support to assess and, upon request, facilitate national progress (NATO 2016b).

In the quote, we can see again that *civil preparedness* is used instead of civil defense or civil emergency planning. This approach to resilience and whole-of-society is comprehensive and programmatic. It opens and acknowledges NATO's role in specifying, coordinating, and evaluating the efforts of individual member states. It shows how the concept of resilience is adopted and adapted to NATO's security concerns and its other core tasks. As such, resilience is seen as having the potential to solve contemporary security challenges; being or becoming (ever more) resilient is essential, but it requires new security arrangements involving civil administration, the private sector, and civil society, and, lately, individuals. Here, I think it is important to consider the difference between civil defense and civil preparedness. Whereas civil defense more explicitly concerns the protection of the civil population in a war situation, civil preparedness indicates a more active, contributing role, a sense of readiness that is not about being protected from the horrors of war but about accepting them.

Military power and capabilities alone are no longer sufficient, as was later expressed in the General Report of 2021:

> …NATO recognises that the Alliance's military capacity and actions now depend to a large extent on civil sector support, expertise, and infrastructures. It also notes that the security threats it faces are no longer all of a military nature and tend to affect every aspect of Allied societies, requiring a combination of military and civilian responses (GR NATO 2021).

Why is resilience playing such a key role in NATO policy, whereas terms such as civil defense and civil emergency planning are no longer used? Resilience is also tied to a similar concept, civil preparedness, a relatively new term in this policy arena that emerged around the 1980s but has been used much more infrequently. Resilience and civil preparedness are both said to fall under NATO's original draft and purpose, Article 3 of the North Atlantic Treaty.

Article 3 has had a relatively unclear role since the end of the Cold War and was seldom explicitly mentioned during the Cold War. According to interviews with senior international staff, it did not seem viable in 2016 to return to the Cold War-era vocabulary of *civil defense and civil emergency planning*. Societies are today more complex and more interdependent than before, and in a way, more fragile to disruptions. This was also something that Covid-19 showed, according to interviews with Senior International Staff at the Defence Policy and Planning (DPP) Division. They both found the concept of resilience adequate and politically viable. It allowed NATO to pursue increased levels of "readiness" without blowing the war trumpet (Senior International Staff, "Head of the Enablement and Resilience Section in the Defence Policy and Planning Division," April 25, 2025, Brussels NATO HQ; The Head of the Joint Health Issues Group, "International Staff").

As a scholar deeply engaged with the concept of resilience including its philosophical foundations, its political implications and national applications, it puzzled me that an organization like NATO would consider this concept as functional, open, and pragmatic enough to organize what earlier would fall under the idea of civil defense and civil emergency planning simply because the old concept carried too much historical weight and might induce unease among the member states. However, a look in the rearview mirror also shows that civil defense and civil emergency planning were never fully embraced by the member states and, for the most part, were only reluctantly engaged with. Within a few years, the new concept of resilience would have gained both centrality and weight within NATO, but it is difficult to assess to what extent member states actually follow suit.

8.2 Formalizing Resilience and Civil Preparedness

In September 2016, delegates and experts from the member states met in Warsaw to exchange experiences and ideas on how NATO could withstand all forms of attack. They initiated the groundwork for how resilience would be conceptualized and strengthened in the NATO context. This resulted in the Seven Baseline Requirements complementing the three core functions:

1. the importance of ensuring political decision-making and central management functions,
2. securing important societal functions, and
3. civilian support for military operations.

We recognize these three core functions from previous chapters and the outline of civil emergency planning dating back to 1955. Similarly, the 7 baseline requirements are recognizable from earlier specifications of civil emergency planning, and the civil emergency planning questionnaire, which were also attempts to operationalize and measure the level of "readiness" and existing civil resources available.

1. Assured **continuity of government** and critical government services: for instance, the ability to make decisions and communicate with citizens in a crisis.
2. Resilient **energy supplies**: ensuring a continued supply of energy and having backup plans to manage disruptions.
3. Ability to deal effectively with the **uncontrolled movement of people** and to de-conflict these movements from NATO's military deployments.
4. Resilient **food and water resources**: ensuring resilient supplies that are safe from disruption or sabotage.
5. Ability to deal with **mass casualties and disruptive health crises**: ensuring that civilian health systems can cope and that sufficient medical supplies are stocked and secure.
6. Resilient **civil communications systems**: ensuring that telecommunications and cyber networks can function even under crisis conditions, with sufficient backup capacity. This also includes the need for reliable communications systems including 5G, robust options to restore these systems, priority access to national authorities in times of crisis, and thorough assessments of all risks to communications systems.
7. Resilient **transport systems**: ensuring that NATO forces can move across Alliance territory rapidly and that civilian services can rely on transportation networks, even in a crisis (NATO 2024c).

Ropke Wolf-Diether and Hasit Thankey who both work with these issues in the Defence Policy and Planning Division at NATO Headquarters, wrote an article in *NATO Review* (2019) suggestion that "…this commitment [of resilience] is based on the recognition that the strategic environment has changed, and that the resilience of civil structures, resources, and services is the first line of defence for today's modern societies" (Roepke and Thankey 2019). It is stated that resilient countries involving government, public, and private sectors have addressed vulnerabilities, making them less targetable and enhancing deterrence by denial—persuading adversaries that attacks will not succeed. Resilient societies recover quickly from crises, maintain essential services, and support NATO operations, including rapid reinforcement of allies. This resilience benefits responses to threats ranging from terrorism to collective defense, reinforcing the Alliance's deterrence and defense posture (Roepke and Thankey 2019).

However, by 2019, the concept and its organizing principles had already been circulating within NATO. For instance, in May 2017, the Allied Command of Transformation (ACT), in partnership with the City of Norfolk, Virginia, organized a conference titled "Interdependency in Resilience." This was supported by NATO members and partners, as well as representatives of the U.S. government, including the municipal and private sectors. The event aimed to stimulate collaboration among these actors and help build resilience across NATO in support of the ongoing activities of NATO Headquarters in the field of resilience (NATO 2017). A second conference held the same year in Prague, Czech Republic, followed up on the same theme. The NATO Advanced Research Workshop on "Resilience Capacity Building: Best Practices and Opportunities for NATO," took place on June 1–2, 2017. The workshop was organized by the Prague-based Institute of International Relations (IIR) together with the Finnish Institute of International Affairs (FIIA). The meeting aimed to broaden the existing network of civilian and military resilience experts from member states and partner countries, and to include experts who have not been involved in NATO's core resilience work (NATO 2017).

It was suggested in the conference report that *resilience* has always been a central part of the alliance:

> NATO's approach to resilience is enshrined in NATO's founding document, the Washington Treaty. In Article 3 of this Treaty, the Allies commit themselves to build capacities (individually and collectively) to resist an armed attack. It is no accident that Article 3 (preparedness) comes before Articles 4 and 5: the Allies are supposed to do their homework (Art. 3), and then ask for political consultations (Art. 4) and assistance from the other Allies (Art. 5) (NATO 2017).

Here we see a clear speech act of "responsibilization" discussed in Chap. 4, nations should cope on their own and only ask for help if necessary. Asking for a consultation, or even for assistance under Article Five, oddly appears to be a failure because it appears that you were not well-prepared. At the same time, what must be avoided at this point is the free-rider problem. Other aspects that are of interest here are the way in which the resilience effort is connected to the individual:

> Resilience starts with the citizens and communities, and then it spreads to regions, the national level, the private sector, NATO, and the EU…Building resilience from the top down is not necessarily the best approach. Often, grassroots solutions to building resilience are more effective. Citizens need to be empowered to drive resilience (NATO 2017).

It appears that the resilience approach pushes responsibility downward. Even though NATO is clearly mainly concerned with international and national security, the role and level of the individual are explicitly addressed. This is indeed something that has not been visible during earlier periods and under the concepts of civil defense and civil emergency planning. This seems to indicate a far more active and contributing role for civilians than would be under civil defense as a form of protection.

At the NATO Summit in Brussels in June 2021, Heads of State and Government pledged to enhance the national and collective resilience of the Member States through a Strengthened Resilience Commitment (NATO 2021c). "…that national and collective resilience are an essential basis for credible deterrence and defence and the effective fulfilment of the Alliance's core tasks, and vital in our efforts to safeguard our societies, our populations and our shared values" (NATO 2021c).

The continued need for strengthening resilience was because NATO continued to experience "…an increasingly complex security environment and the multiplication of military and non-military threats affecting all of our societies, it appears more vital than ever to consolidate our resilience through civil preparedness" (NATO 2021a).

An internal NATO report to the Committee on Democracy and Security in 2022 (an advisory body to the North Atlantic Council), entitled "Enhancing the resilience of allied societies through Civil preparedness," argues that during the Cold War, many of the civil and societal resources were managed by the states, enabling rapid recruitment and deployment of these resources. The document notes that during the 1990s, a common trend was the outsourcing and marketization of many sectors and critical infrastructure. Thus, civil preparedness requires cooperation and collaboration with many private actors. Most states today lack the capacity for control and thus the ability to govern in crises (NATO 2021a). In addition, the gaze also falls upon the civil population and the individual:

> The civilian population is arguably the most crucial and most often overlooked actor in resilience. It is the target and/or the main victim of many

> risks facing Allied countries. However, if properly prepared, it is also the first line of defence against these same threats (NATO 2021a).

As discussed in Chap. 4 on resilience, we can note how resilience can drive the focus to the smallest component and to induce a disciplinary and programmatic approach to activation and improvement. For instance: "Thus, it is crucial to place citizens at the heart of resilience-building efforts. They must be trained to deal with a crisis from its inception to its resolution, even if authorities are unable to provide their usual support. Public authorities must promote essential knowledge and skills among the population before a crisis erupts" (NATO 2021a). The report mentions the brochures Norway and Sweden distributed in 2018, which contained information on necessary food stocks, emergency communication lines, and first-aid training, and similar advice (NATO 2021a; Larsson 2021). In addition to such information campaigns, it is suggested that "the education system must be involved in training all youth, both girls and boys, in crisis response. Among other aims, these efforts should seek to develop young people's capacity to detect disinformation that undermines the authorities' ability to react and to gain citizens' trust in an emergency" (NATO 2021a). Another issue that is raised is the importance of continued trust in the democratic principles, even during large-scale crisis. It is thus:

> ...crucial to nourish a will among the civilian population to protect and defend the democratic principles that underpin our Allied societies. Security shocks can lead to a questioning of these principles, to political polarisation and social tensions, as was the case during the pandemic. Therefore, by developing more inclusive communication strategies and by involving the education system, authorities must constantly reaffirm and strengthen ties between citizens and their democratic values and institutions (NATO 2021a).

NATO imposes considerable requirements on the civilian population and individuals as central civil dimensions to be considered, modified and activated in the attempt to foster deterrence and resilience of NATO. Both public and private actors are expected to engage in these efforts and to develop close collaboration to facilitate and enhance resilience across sectors. Furthermore, the emerging and pivotal role assigned to individuals within the framework of national and societal resilience is recognized. The increased interest in, and mobilization of, citizens, along with the need to monitor and potentially enhance their behavior, represent a new dimension in security discourse following the Cold War era, an element absent during the Cold War. The relationship is reversed: under the idea of civil defense, the core principle was that civilians should be protected, whereas under the concepts of resilience and civil preparedness, they should be active and contributing to national and societal security.

On November 25, 2020, the independent Reflection Group released its report, titled "NATO 2030: united for a New Era. It was written by 10 leading figures appointed by NATO Secretary General Jens Stoltenberg following the decision at the December 2019 London Summit. It has been said that this report was a response to new tensions within the alliance after the French Statement about NATO being "brain dead" that was made with reference to the US withdrawal from northern Syria and the subsequent Turkish operation there, both apparently carried out without consultation within NATO (Tardy 2022). The Report is divided into three parts, looking in sequence at: the vision and main findings; the security and political environment; and recommendations (NATO n.d.). It is clear that NATO 2030 shares many similarities with "three wise men" and the "Harmel report," both of which aimed to address political tensions within NATO. Time will tell if the NATO 2030 report will achieve the same status as the previous politically oriented reports. The main focus of the report is the need for political leadership, cohesion, and improved consultation to avoid internal tensions within NATO. In accordance with its mandate, the report primarily addresses the political aspects of NATO's adaptation and only briefly mentions the military dimension and its current effort to build resilience across the alliance (NATO Parliamentary Assembly 2021; NATO n.d.).

In 2021, NATO continued its efforts in civil preparedness and formalized a more integrated, better-coordinated approach to strengthening resilience. This involved specifying resilience objectives to guide the development of nationally defined resilience goals and implementation plans, based on more precise, more measurable objectives within the seven baseline requirements. Senior officials responsible for resilience were appointed as consultants and experts whom member states could reach out to for advice to coordinate national efforts and streamline their crisis management and civil defense with NATO objectives (NATO 2024c). This was intended to allow NATO to advise and assess national resilience efforts in support of NATO's collective defense, thereby linking national efforts to NATO posture and plans. In NATO, it becomes inevitable that each country's resilience is seen as a building block for the alliance's overall capability and strength. Therefore, NATO has a considerable interest in ensuring that every country is resilient to withstand major disruptions such as natural disasters, destroyed infrastructure, various hybrid threats, and armed attacks. At the same time, it must engage in "governance from a distance" similar to the way it earlier attempted to govern countries in the era of civil emergency planning. The actual phase of realization of NATO policy in these areas is difficult to assess and would require a more detailed investigation of individual countries. What is developed is a similar questionnaire to assess the inventory, resources, and vulnerabilities of each member state for civil emergency planning.

The 2021 Brussels summit communique mentions resilience 27 times. It explicitly conveys ideas of "whole-of-society approaches and provides the suggestion of a resilience questionnaire":

> Noting that resilience remains a national responsibility, we will adopt a more integrated and better coordinated approach, consistent with our collective commitment under Article 3 of the North Atlantic Treaty, to reduce vulnerabilities and ensure our militaries can effectively operate in peace, crisis and conflict. Allies will develop a proposal to establish, assess, review, and monitor resilience objectives to guide nationally-developed resilience goals and implementation plans (NATO 2021b).

NATO indicates that it aims to take resilience seriously and to closely monitor development in each country. I am not sure whether lessons have been learned from the past, when NATO struggled to establish authority in civil defense and civil preparedness. Since NATO is based on collective defense, each country's potential vulnerability can become a weakness for the entire organization. NATO writes on its website, under the heading "Resilience, civil preparedness and Article 3," that strengthening the resilience of each society contributes to NATO's mission to protect societies, populations, and shared values (NATO 2024e). It is therefore not surprising that NATO representatives often emphasize the need for greater resilience. In a speech at a symposium in 2021, for example, Deputy Secretary General Mircea Geoană mentioned that resilience is a team sport that requires civil preparedness and military capacity but also the active participation of governments, the private sector, strong citizens, as well as close cooperation with partner countries and organizations, such as the EU. Still, it is difficult to see how such an open posture and policy could serve as a guide for improvement.

8.3 Establishing the Resilience Committee (RC)

In 2022, NATO adopted a new Strategic Concept at the Madrid Summit in June. The purpose was, as with previous strategic documents, "to define the security challenges facing the Alliance and outline the political and military tasks that NATO will carry out to address them" (NATO Strategic Concept 2022). The preface states the core purpose of the steering document:

> Our new Strategic Concept reaffirms that NATO's key purpose is to ensure our collective defence, based on a 360-degree approach. It defines the Alliance's three core tasks: deterrence and defence; crisis prevention and management; and cooperative security. We underscore the need to significantly strengthen our deterrence and defence as the backbone of our Article 5 commitment to defend each other (NATO Strategic Concept 2022).

It may seem strange that NATO continues with open strategic concepts and documents, even though it clearly identifies Russia and China as revisionist states, and that the strategy was adopted after Russia's full-scale invasion of Ukraine on February 24, 2024. This clearly establishes the document's geopolitical context and tone: serious, yet NATO prioritizes open policies. Of course, many policies and steering documents are kept under strict secrecy and remain classified.

This is the first time that resilience is explicitly mentioned in a strategic concept. It is mentioned 12 times, reflecting its key role in shaping the organization of civil dimension of defense and deterrence: "We will pursue a more robust, integrated, and coherent approach to building national and Alliance-wide resilience against military and non-military threats and challenges to our security, as a national responsibility and a collective commitment rooted in Article 3 of the North Atlantic Treaty" (NATO Strategic Concept 2022).

Resilience, whole-of-society, and a 360-degree approach all indicate an accentuated role for civil administration, society, private actors, and individuals who are seen as necessary contributors to the alliance. This, in turn, falls back on the notions of grey zone and hybrid threats that potentially target societies rather than states:

> Strategic competitors test our resilience and seek to exploit the openness, interconnectedness, and digitalization of our nations. They interfere in our democratic processes and institutions and target the security of our citizens through hybrid tactics, both directly and through proxies. They conduct malicious activities in cyberspace and space, promote disinformation campaigns, instrumentalise migration, manipulate energy supplies, and employ economic coercion (ibid).

When it comes to defining NATO's core task, it advocates that NATO "…will employ military and non-military tools in a proportionate, coherent and integrated way to respond to all threats to our security in the manner, timing and in the domain of our choosing."

> To that end, we will invest in crisis response, preparedness and management, through regular exercises and leverage our ability to coordinate, conduct sustain and support multinational crisis response operations. We will ensure the resources, capabilities, training and command and control arrangements to deploy and sustain military and civilian crisis management, stabilisation and counter-terrorism operations, including at strategic distance. Building on the lessons learned over the past three decades, including through our operations in Afghanistan, we will continue to improve our readiness, our military and civilian capabilities, and civil-military planning and coordination. We will further develop the Alliance's ability to support civilian crisis management and relief operations and to prepare for the effects of climate change, food insecurity and health emergencies on Allied security. This will allow us to respond to any contingency at short notice (NATO Strategic Concept 2022).

In the 2022 strategic concept, crisis management and disaster relief are tied to civil preparedness, suggesting a seamless connection between civil crisis management on the one hand and war preparations on the other. When a return to a more traditional approach to national and international security is called for, the language and old concepts are dated; instead of civil defense, we arrive at resilience and preparedness. At the same time, the new ideas and concepts, as well as the general approach to security, seem far more comprehensive than during the Cold War and the prime of civil defense efforts. This is most likely because grey zone and hybrid threats are ever-present security problems, even in the absence of war. Yet the connection between crisis and war, and the concepts of dual-use and an all-hazards approach, dates back to the early 1970s. At the same time, it is a security discourse on steroids in that it does not clearly distinguish between a peace and a war situation.

In 2022, NATO established a new Resilience Committee, which took over the functions and roles of the Senior Civil Emergency Planning Committee (SCEPC). The Resilience Committee provides strategic and policy direction and coordinates NATO's resilience activities. The Resilience Committee sets the priorities for *resilience activities* within the Alliance. It should translate NATO's ambition for national and collective resilience into specific actions and guidance and is responsible for maintaining the resilience planning and review cycle at NATO. This would include establishing, assessing, reviewing, and monitoring resilience objectives to guide the development of nationally defined resilience goals and related implementation plans. This may sound a lot like "implementation," even though NATO is understood as an interstate organization. In addition, it may appear likely that the current resilience effort will resemble previous efforts and attempts to govern member states during civil emergency planning.

The Committee should work to ensure a *whole-of-government* and *whole-of-society* perspective across the full range of resilience-related activities undertaken by NATO. It reports directly to the North Atlantic Council. It also coordinates with NATO military authorities and other NATO committees addressing the broader resilience agenda, providing relevant political-military advice and facilitating consideration of resilience aspects in NATO's defense planning, operations, and activities. The Resilience Committee also oversees the activities of the Euro-Atlantic Disaster Response Coordination Centre (EADRCC) at NATO Headquarters, established in 1998 (see Chap. 7). The Committee is also instructed to contribute to developing relations with partners and other relevant international organizations and institutions (NATO 2022d).

The Resilience Committee meets weekly, and countries are represented by their NATO delegations; this is again very similar to the plenary sessions with SCEPC. The day-to-day work is mainly carried out in working groups and the six specialized Planning Groups that support the resilience committee in specific areas. These are composed of subject-matter experts nominated by NATO Member states. Each Group is responsible for advising on resilience matters within its respective field of expertise (NATO 2022d). These groups have a similar function to NATO Civil Wartime Agencies, which were terminated in 2003 (see page 103 of the manuscript).

The six planning groups

- The Civil Communications Planning Group (CCPG) provides advice on building resilience in the communications sector;
- The Civil Protection Group (CPG) addresses ways to ensure continuity of government as well as the ability to deal effectively with uncontrolled movements of people; and
- The Energy Planning Group (EPG) is responsible for the oversight of resilient energy supplies;
- The Food and Agriculture Planning Group (FAPG) addresses resilience matters in the food and water sector;
- The Joint Health Group (JHG) covers Allies' ability to deal with mass casualties and disruptive health crises;
- The Transport Group (TG), subdivided across inland surface, maritime and aviation, supports resilient civil transport systems

NATO (2022d)

The Resilience Committee is thus very similar to its predecessor, SCEPC, in leading member states' efforts, with very similar methods and procedures. I explicitly asked about this during interviews with NATO staff members. Since resilience and former civil defense and civil emergency planning are national responsibilities, NATO still has limited ability to govern and control development, even though these areas are considered crucial for deterrence and defense within the alliance. The resilience committee conducts similar planning and review cycles that were previously performed by SCEPC, with civil emergency planning in mind. The new questionnaire has a similar structure and orientation to the previous ones. It is the member states themselves who answer a set of questions on their readiness, planning, and available resources related to the seven baseline requirements (Swedish representative, "National Delegation and representative at RC," April 25, 2025, Brussels NATO HQ). She believed that the closest thing to the more traditional civil defense committee was the Civil Protection Group (CPG) that works with the continuation of government and "refugees" but also the protection of populations.

According to Senior Staff, they have been able to place these questions in the same questionnaire as the NDPP, which should hopefully make a difference by elevating the issues of the civil dimensions (the general questionnaire regarding military development and readiness) (The Head of the Joint Health Issues Group, "International Staff" 2025; Senior International Staff, "Head of the Enablement and Resilience Section in the Defence Policy and Planning Division" 2025).

Senior Staff working on Health aspects of resilience set out the details of the questionnaire:

> Currently, we have approximately 120 questions covering seven baseline requirements. While I cannot disclose the specific measures and questions due to NATO classification, I can say that this content is continually refined through expert meetings, workshops, and similar activities to enhance our specificity. Although we may not achieve the same level of granularity as military planning metrics—such as the number of tanks or aircraft—we can still measure and compare countries' progress. This methodology allows us to track development over time within each nation, enabling a clearer understanding of each nation's readiness and level of resilience (The Head of the Joint Health Issues Group, "International Staff" 2025).

> This also allows us to report to military leadership and SAUCER that some countries are lagging. This review system recognizes that weaknesses in one member can impact the entire alliance. Ultimately, it incentivizes countries to improve their capabilities to avoid becoming a liability to the alliance." In addition to the four-year cycle, producing resilience reports for each country and for NATO as a whole, there are also regional resilience reports based on NATO's military areas. The last reports were in 2022, with the next in 2026 (ibid.).

Even though NATO cannot force countries to commit to certain levels of resilience or continued progress, the questionnaire and the reports provide a clear "naming-and-shaming" mechanism. An issue that has been repeatedly raised in interviews is that countries do not want to look bad in front of other NATO allies.

It was also the impression among senior staff that RC is much more active in producing policy documents, guidelines, and steering documents that are agreeable to all member states. Another thing that has changed is the number of international staff at its disposal. Whereas there were a few leading figures in the 1950s and 60s, international staff are today numerous and full-time employed professionals (Senior International Staff, "Head of the Enablement and Resilience Section in the Defence Policy and Planning Division" 2025). This is also said to produce better results and a stronger structure for the continued work.

There are also several centers of excellence that NATO is either the founding organization of, or an active member and supporter of. We may, for instance, consider the Euro-Atlantic Resilience Centre (E-ARC), which is a "centre of excellence in the field of resilience, a partner of NATO and the EU, acting for the benefit of these organisations, as well as Member States or partners." This was created and sanctioned by NATO at the NATO summit in Brussels 2021 and produces a significant number of reports, conferences, and content on its YouTube channel (Ghita 2024; NATO 2021b). Another similar center established in 2017 is the European Centre of Excellence for Countering Hybrid Threats (Hybrid CoE), an autonomous, network-based international organization founded by nine European Countries, the EU, and NATO to counter hybrid threats (Hybrid CoE—The European Centre of Excellence for Countering Hybrid Threats 2017). What we see here is a plethora of centers that support the discourse on hybrid threats and resilience and act as "knowledge producers" and policy entrepreneurs in the international security environment.

We might thus conclude that resilience is the current working concept that replaces civil defense and civil emergency planning. The fact that this concept has been included in policy documents and the Strategic Concept, and NATO even renamed SCPEC from 1955 to the "Resilience Committee 2022," further indicates the centrality of the change of vocabulary. The civil protection group has replaced the previous civil defense committee (later civil protection committee). And the other groups have similar but somewhat updated areas in civil emergency planning, now referred to as resilience.

The resilience concept has been identified as more viable than the old Cold War nomenclature and is frequently used in public communications. At the Washington summit, in June 2024, the communique stated:

> National and collective resilience are an essential basis for credible deterrence and defence and the effective fulfillment of the Alliance's core tasks in a 360-degree approach. Resilience is a national responsibility and a collective commitment, rooted in Article 3 of the Washington Treaty. Strengthening national and Alliance-wide preparedness for deterrence and defence requires a whole-of-government approach, public-private cooperation, and societal resilience considerations. We pledge to build on our ongoing efforts to strengthen national resilience by integrating civilian

planning into national and collective defence planning in peace, crisis and conflict (NATO 2024g).

In addition, NATO webpage features the same kind of message under the headline "Resilience, civil preparedness and Article 3":

> Each NATO member country needs to be resilient in order to withstand a major shock such as a natural disaster, failure of critical infrastructure, or a hybrid or armed attack. Resilience is the individual and collective capacity to prepare for, resist, respond to and quickly recover from shocks and disruptions, and to ensure the continuity of the Alliance's activities. Civil preparedness is a central pillar of Allies' resilience and a critical enabler for the Alliance's collective defence, and NATO supports Allies in assessing and enhancing their civil preparedness. Rooted in Article 3 of the North Atlantic Treaty, national and collective resilience are an essential basis for credible deterrence and defence, and are therefore vital to NATO's efforts to safeguard its societies, populations and shared values (NATO 2026d).[1]

8.4 Resilience and Military Support

There have been multiple conferences on resilience and its policies within NATO. One of the first major symposia was in 2017, followed by another in 2019, and then three consecutive years from 2022 to 2024. There has been an interesting development in the discourse on resilience within NATO over these years. In 2017, the concept was relatively open and encompassing.

In the report following the 2017 conference, it is stated that "Various aspects of resilience are interdependent, and it requires a 'whole community' and 'all hazard' approach to tackle all aspects of resilience." In addition, "There is only one kind of resilience; not a single private sector resilience, national resilience, NATO resilience, or EU resilience" (NATO 2017). Here, the conclusion is that "Resilience starts with the citizens and communities, and then it spreads to regions, the national level, the private sector, NATO, and the EU…Building resilience from the top down is not necessarily the best approach. Often, grassroots solutions

[1] This was also cited in Chap. 1, as a point of departure, thus, here we find the full circle, why we ended up with this particular vocabulary. In addition, this phrasing also survived the rebuilding of NATO webpage.

to building resilience are more effective. Citizens need to be empowered to drive resilience" (NATO 2017). Here we see clear evidence of what was discussed in Chap. 4: resilience tends to have a community and an individual focus. But also, the tendency for activation, fostering, and improvement directed toward the individual citizen. This discourse is certainly different from that which follows from civil defense and protection of populations and individuals.

After 2022, it is clear that NATO is returning to a more explicit military focus and is considering how to strengthen its efforts and capabilities. In the 2023 report, following the conference in Latvia, one of the key speakers, Vlasta Zekulic summarizes the situation:

> Russia's invasion of Ukraine in 2014 and resulting occupation of Crimea, and in particular the 2022 full-scale war of aggression against Ukraine, have once again refocused NATO efforts on deterrence, defence, and the necessity to be resilient against all threats. In 2016, Allies pledged to increase their resilience, noting that being resilient requires Allies to maintain and protect critical civilian capabilities, alongside and in support of military capabilities, and to work across the whole government and with the private sector… in the new security environment, deployed NATO troops may have to use the same resources and services as the local population. The Seven Baseline Requirements for resilience, defined in 2016 and revised in 2021, assigned qualitative and quantitative values to the most critical of these dual-need areas. However, in the ever-changing security environment where natural and adversary-driven crises can happen simultaneously, how much is enough? Who decides on prioritization? For the military authorities, the question is how NATO's current level of resilience affects Supreme Allied Commander Europe (SACEUR) military activities across the full spectrum of conflict (NATO 2023d).

Here, we find more emphasis on the role societal resilience has for the military troops, in support of the military operations. The final panel discussion of the 2024 *NATO Resilience Symposium* explored operationalizing resilience through civil-military planning. This panel brought together stakeholders from NATO enterprises and from the civilian and military sides of Allied nations. While sharing their perspectives on the expected opportunities and challenges of operationalizing civil-military planning, the speakers also focused on various elements of resilience planning, including authorities, resources, effects, processes, and best practices, which need to be in place and exercised to meet the expectations and realities of civil support to the military in a crisis or conflict (NATO 2024f). In addition, one of the main points of the concluding remarks was that NATO needs a "whole-of-government approach, supported by whole-of-society consideration. Only by involving all members of society can national resilience-building efforts be successful" (NATO 2024f).

In the same year, the Civil Protection Group held a conference in Stockholm on the topic of "Public-Private Cooperation in Securing Critical Supplies – Supporting Alliance Resilience." It could be that the topic sets the tone for what is later communicated in the conference report summary, but NATO emphasizes the need to recruit and align with the private sector to advance resilience and military support.

> Rooted in NATO's Article 3, resilience is both a national responsibility and a collective commitment. Each Ally must have national civil plans with the necessary public and private sector assets, capabilities, and resources to build societal resilience and support national military plans in close alignment with NATO's strategic goals. Public-private cooperation must therefore be strengthened in order not to be a weak link in the Alliance's core tasks of deterrence and defence, crisis prevention and management, and cooperative security. With the private sector owning and operating substantial portions of critical infrastructure and services, much of which enables military operations, public-private partnership is not a "nice to have" but a "must have." Partnering with the private sector is vital in maintaining an advantage over competitors and adversaries (NATO Civil Protection Group, MSB 2024).

The suggestion is also to "engage private sector representatives on NATO's public-private cooperation policy priorities" (NATO Civil Protection Group, MSB 2024).

In 2025, the first NATO Civilian Planning Conference was held in Stockholm, Sweden. In summary, the NATO webpage stated that "Civilian planning is the most important contribution to integrating civil and military planning in NATO." At the NATO Summit in The Hague, Allies committed to spend 5% of GDP on defence, with up to 1.5% allocated to defense- and security-related investments. This includes investments to protect critical infrastructure and networks, defend networks, and ensure civil preparedness and resilience (NATO 2025c).

Discussions during the Civilian Planning Conference were said to focus on promoting strong civil-military cooperation and on aligning NATO's defense plans with resilience planning. The conference gathered over 200 participants across civil and military stakeholders, policymakers, practitioners, and experts from member states, partners, and industry. The idea of the conference was to explore ways to strengthen NATO's resilience and readiness further (NATO 2025c).

NATO struggles with the meaning of resilience, which is a complex concept to define and apply. Several conferences feature very basic, broad discussions of the importance of resilience, but the sense is that NATO fails to make it practical. There has been a recent drift toward a military orientation and priority, a similar trend was visible for civil defense and civil emergency planning. Jan Hodicky and Wayne Buck (and others) find that "resilience is mostly about the measurement of capacity" (Hodicky et al. 2020). They aim to provide a "prototype of the resilience decision support model to be used by the NATO operational community to support their daily business" (Hodicky et al. 2020). The aim was to design a model that would enable NATO's resilience capacity to be measured more dynamically. Still, it illustrates how extremely complex whole-of-society approaches are: each hybrid threat must be prognosed, and the interactions among variables and their implications are infinite. The article demonstrates the difficulties in making resilience operational. Similar to past developments, rather than focusing on a few core tasks in civil defense and emergency planning, new elements and tasks are added to already ambiguous and complex issues.

In a policy brief capturing the latest development in NATO and the EU, authored by Christie and Berzina (2022), resilience is also given a more military orientation as it: "It involves not only the capacity of the armed forces to carry out their missions but also society's ability to withstand and recover from attacks. This ensures that harm to civilians is minimised, society can continue supporting military needs (enablement), and military resources are not excessively redirected toward civilian crises. Within NATO, this concept is known as "civil preparedness," while resilience refers to the combined impact of both civil preparedness and military capability" (Christie and Berzina 2022).

Again, we see how resilience is connected to military capacity and how preparedness is attached to recovery and later support for military missions. Again, the role and function of the population and the citizens are shifting from protection to contribution:

> NATO members should learn from the Finnish and Swedish approaches to engaging with citizens through government communications and in-person interactions to prepare them to be more helpful, self-sufficient, and resilient. Finland and Sweden have mandatory service requirements that may not be acceptable for all allies, but voluntary contributions to defense may be worth considering so as to create a positive relationship between military and civilian domains. Certainly, prioritizing communication and valuing citizen agency is a lesson applicable across NATO (Christie and Berzina 2022).

On February 14, 2025, the Resilience Committee introduced NATO's first Resilience Reference Curriculum (RRC) (a 144-page document) to assist NATO Allies and partners in enhancing their resilience against military and non-military threats and challenges to NATO security and their own national security. These threats include natural disasters, disruptions to critical infrastructure, and hybrid and armed attacks. This was the result of the work conducted by NATO's Defence Education Enhancement Programme (DEEP), the Resilience Section, and the Partnership for Peace Consortium, which involved collaboration with experts across member states and partner nations. The RRC is structured around four central thematic chapters, each targeting a distinct aspect of resilience. The curriculum opens with an executive summary that situates resilience within the contemporary landscape of uncertainty, disruption, and technological change. Four themes follow this.

1. Theme 1 introduces the concept of resilience within defense and security, providing analytical frameworks for understanding its levels, elements, and the threats it faces. It emphasizes the importance of context in assessing resilience, recognizing the diversity in how it is interpreted across different governance levels.
2. Theme 2 explores whole-of-government approaches, interdependence between resilience and instruments of national power, and the necessity of coordination among governmental agencies. The multinational dimension is highlighted, reflecting NATO's integrated security environment.
3. Theme 3 shifts focus on societal resilience, underlining the roles of civil society and the private sector. It specifies a whole-of-society approach, arguing that societal resilience is fundamental to national endurance and must be cultivated across all societal levels.

4. Theme 4 operationalizes the resilience concept, guiding users through the development, implementation, and assessment of resilience strategies in varied contexts.

The curriculum is intended as a toolkit for instructors, enabling them to design tailored courses and training sessions for both military and civilian audiences. The idea is to address resilience at the individual and multinational levels, and by integrating physical, psychological, governmental, and societal dimensions, the curriculum is said to offer a nuanced and adaptable framework for learning and further education (Resilience Committee 2025). NATO's Resilience Reference Curriculum represents an additional step in codifying and disseminating resilience education across NATO and its partners, alongside the existing seven baseline requirements and their respective codification in the questionnaire.

This is yet another example of how NATO hopes to influence understanding of resilience and how actors at all levels should incorporate it into their mindset and everyday operations.

8.5 Conclusions 2014–2025

The period from 2014 to 2025 entails a new approach to civil defense and emergency planning. First, these two "historical concepts" have given way to resilience and civil preparedness. We can also note that resilience has had a significant impact on the NATO context. It was adopted as a new approach that would allow mobilization of civil administration and civil society without blowing the "war trumpet." It was thus identified as a pragmatic and open concept that would allow heightened levels of security concerns in the wake of hybrid warfare and grey zone geopolitics that followed the 2014 Russian attack on Ukraine. Still, it might have appeared a bit too open, as extensive effort has been put into giving it a more precise meaning and purpose in the NATO context. At the beginning of the period, it was used to indicate a whole-of-society approach, with a broader purpose that encompassed everything from civil crisis management to disaster relief and, ultimately, war. The idea of a similar approach to cope with more minor civil crises and disasters, unavoidable elements of modern life, with the purposeful and harmful hybrid threats conducted by a capable enemy, with the purpose to disrupt and harm, seems a bit muddled. It is not necessarily the case that preparing for war and countering hybrid threats also enables the organization to cope with civil crisis management and disasters.

In this way, the concept of resilience and the "all-hazards" approach may lead NATO and other states astray. Resilience is an attractive concept and approach, but it may be a false promise; just as with other policy concepts, it must be filled with content and bracketed. It must also specify trade-offs between different priorities and values. There is no magic concept that allows us to have it all. In the latter part of the period, around 2022, at the same time as Russia's full-scale invasion of Ukraine, it is possible to detect an increased focus on defining resilience in terms of civil-military planning and on prioritizing military interests. In many ways, this emphasizes the support of NATO military planning and operations needed from the civil administration, civil society, and enterprises. Resilience is said to be all about adaptability and flexibility, but so too is the concept itself; it is open to new meanings and pragmatic. This chapter has shown the many ways in which NATO struggles to define and give meaning to the key concept of resilience, which is thought to replace the older, dated concepts of civil defense and civil emergency planning. The idea that this is a pragmatic and open concept might have made it easy to be put to use in policy texts, but it is much more challenging to see exactly what has been accomplished over the last 10 years. The new questionnaire is not publicly available, nor are the responses of the member states, as this would reveal all vulnerabilities and the lack of preparedness in their resilience efforts. NATO has, throughout its history, had difficulty influencing and governing its member states in the areas of civil defense and civil emergency planning. The concept of resilience seems to make this task even more difficult, as it is ambiguous about what it entails, how to prioritize, who is responsible, and related central, utterly important, and political dimensions of resilience. While all member states might agree that increased resilience is desirable, it remains unclear whether they are also willing to adhere to the general call for improvement, or whether Article 3 makes this field ungovernable from NATO's perspective.

CHAPTER 9

Conclusions and Further Challenges

The main aim of the book was to examine how NATO's approach to the civil dimensions of war and war preparedness, with a primary focus on the roles of populations and individuals, has changed over the organization's 75 years of existence. There are several reasons for this endeavor, and why it felt necessary to conduct such a study at this point in time.

The first is that, surprisingly, limited academic effort has been devoted to investigating the civil dimensions of defense and war preparations within NATO. This, despite the general understanding that modern war and thus war preparedness is total in the sense that modern war would affect and influence the entire state and society. No other book has attempted to recover the development in this area within NATO for the entire period, but there is, of course, research that analyzes individual member states or limited time periods (Cronqvist et al. 2022a, 2022c; Bjørnsson 2023; Collier and Lakoff 2021). By covering the entire period of NATO's existence, it is easier to account for the contingent developments in this area. There is a historical and empirical knowledge gap that could be filled by a detailed process tracing focusing on the vocabulary associated with the civil dimensions of war and war preparedness. The possibility to visit NATO HQ and the NATO archive in Brussels, and to access newly released documents from the 1950s to 1990s, along with unique interviews with former and current staff, enabled me to recapture the general trends and discussions on how NATO has viewed the role of populations and individuals throughout history. This book thereby

O. Larsson, *NATO's Approach to the Civil Dimensions of War*,
https://doi.org/10.1007/978-3-032-27871-5_9

offers a unique empirical contribution to the fields of civil defense, civil preparedness, and NATO research through its extensive archival research with access to previously classified documents in NATO's archive in Brussels, as well as through interviews of international staff working in NATO in its transitional phase at the end of the Cold War.

There is normative and political concern here as well. If we are to understand what NATO requires of the member states and the true costs of defense and war, we need to include the civil dimensions and resources. If we allow historical and contemporary security discourses to remain uncontested and fail to engage in their detailed construction and foundational ideas, we cannot see the full picture or the true costs of war and war preparedness. Thus, we need to engage in the deconstruction and unpacking of central policy concepts, such as civil defense, civil emergency planning, and resilience. In Chap. 2, I argued that security and securitization enable specific techniques of government, social, and political control to become more present, and with that, exclusions, violence, and other limits to democratic politics become more pronounced. Security *crowds out* other ways of thinking and alternative approaches to governance. This is why we need a more thorough and balanced understanding of the specific security discourses that shape our political environment. Obviously, we should not be naïve about the new geopolitical situation with an aggressive Russia, a militarily and economically strong China, and the USA, which is currently unpredictable and pursuing its own international political agenda amid substantial internal political turmoil. Still, how do we know we are preparing for the right kind of security challenges if we don't dismantle the current security discourse and vocabulary?

The second reason why this research felt important was the new geopolitical environment and the security discourse that has unfolded after the Russian annexation of Ukrainian territory in 2014, but also after the full-scale military invasion of Ukraine in 2022. NATO has actively and systematically been working to enhance the *resilience* of its member states since 2014. NATO indicates that this renewed focus on civil preparedness and a comprehensive, whole-of-society approach to security is driven by a new security paradigm. This paradigm emphasizes the importance of grey zone and hybrid threats, concepts that gained prominence and familiarity following Russia's annexation of the Crimean Peninsula in 2014. This shift has been identified as a crucial aspect of (Russian) hybrid warfare, although we may see similar tactics used by the USA in relation to Venezuela, Denmark, and Greenland, posing one of the greatest challenges to NATO unity in its entire history since 1949. This issue is not addressed in this book, but it marks a very interesting topic for future research, alongside similar political crises in the past, such as the Suez Canal crisis, the French withdrawal from the military structure, and the chaotic withdrawal from Afghanistan. NATO is certainly not without contemporary internal political crisis.

The focus of the book was not on large-scale political crises but on the new key policy concept of resilience and on whole-of-society approaches to national and international security. However, even if it was the adoption of the resilience concept that first caught my interest, I realized that this concept and the last period are only the latest development in how NATO has considered the civil dimensions and civil resources throughout history. I understood that this book needed to cover the entire period of NATO's existence to make the final turn of events understandable. There are important nuances in the vocabulary that NATO applies to the civil dimensions of defense and deterrence, and by examining the historical and conceptual development, we are in a better position to understand the current hype of resilience and the newly established Resilience Committee (RC), which is actually a renaming of the Senior Civil Emergency Planning Committee (SCEPC) that was established already in 1955.

I am not arguing that there is nothing new under the sun. Historical and conceptual development provides important insights into contemporary security discourses, but it is equally important to understand the security challenges NATO is formulating and addressing in the current era. As the world grows in technological dependency, more globally interconnected and complex, and with a wide range of actors capable of performing "attacks" that are not military or even physical, NATO, too, has converted its former military orientation to a broader understanding of security in the new security climate and geopolitical situation. However, all security and military efforts come at a monetary cost and involve trade-offs in prioritizing different political goals and values. Such commitments and priorities include serious obligations for member states that go well beyond strict military commitments. NATO proclaims that the organization and its allies now face threats and challenges from both state and non-state actors who use hybrid tactics to target political institutions, influence public opinion, and undermine the security of NATO citizens. Hybrid methods that operate just below the threshold of open hostility and warfare include propaganda, deception, cyber or physical sabotage, and other non-military tactics that may have been present all along to destabilize adversaries. However, in recent years, their speed, scale, and intensity, facilitated by rapid technological change and global interconnectivity, have increased and are therefore considered to pose serious security challenges to NATO and its member states. NATO has developed a comprehensive strategy for countering hybrid threats and hybrid warfare (NATO 2023a). NATO motivates its wider understanding of security and concern for member states' ability to withstand all kinds of shocks and disturbances in Article 3 of the North Atlantic Treaty (The North Atlantic Treaty 1949), which states:

> In order more effectively to achieve the objectives of this Treaty, the Parties, separately and jointly, by means of continuous and effective self-help and mutual aid, will maintain and develop their individual and collective capacity to resist armed attack (The North Atlantic Treaty 1949).

This article was part of the original 1949 treaty but has not received the same level of academic attention as the better-known Article 5. It has, on the other hand, not been as frequently mentioned as it has in the last period. Still, there are important nuances in how NATO has approached civil defense, later civil emergency planning, and, more recently, societal resilience. To contextualize the present, this book has traced the specific vocabulary and security discourses that have circulated across different eras and adopted a constructivist approach to NATO's civil dimensions and resources, which it has sought to secure and govern.

I therefore formulated the following research question to guide the book, for which the rest of the chapter provides a consolidated answer.

How has NATO approached the questions of civil defense and the role of the population and other civil dimensions of war and war preparedness throughout history?

9.1 Theoretical Premises

I have utilized two different theoretical approaches. One is the theory of securitization, as developed by the Copenhagen School of security. The theory of securitization holds that security is ultimately a matter of life and death, concerning our survival as individuals or as a collective. The logic of security would then state that existential threats in specific contexts can justify the use of extraordinary measures to address them, given that both threats and countermeasures are deemed credible. In fact, "by labeling it as security, an agent claims a need for and the right to treat it by extraordinary means" (Buzan et al. 1998), therefore: "[T]he exact definition and criteria for securitization is constituted by the intersubjective establishment of an existential threat with a saliency sufficient to have substantial political effects" (Buzan et al. 1998).

The importance here is the "speech-act," the talking about security. More critically, the theory specifies three elements in a security discourse: the referent objects, the securitizing actor, and the functional actors, which have been used in the research conducted. In this way, the analysis could recapture the central elements of how different NATO committees specified security problems, what needed protection, who should provide security, and the numerous tasks this entailed. More details on the theoretical approach of securitization can be found in Chap. 2. Here, I also discussed some important limitations of the theory. One such aspect is that there is seldom an audience to verify and approve of the suggested security threats and how to address them (Balzacq et al. 2016; Balzacq 2011, 2019; Côté 2016). Another one is to stay clear of the "Hobbesian trap" (Neal 2019). Neal suggests that security politics need not be as dramatic as the Copenhagen school proclaims. It does not always render a state of exception or transfer issues beyond the political realm. In fact, democratic institutions regularly handle both domestic and international security issues without declaring any state of exception (Neal 2019). In a setting such as NATO, it is clear that everything is related to national and international security in one way or another. Securitization theory identifies the logic and dynamics of security politics, even as it may appear much more mundane, granular, and incremental. In the NATO context, it is most often the case that security issues are handled by experts and finds its way into policy and governance without public debate (see also Bigo and McCluskey 2018).

The other theoretical premises for the book are discussed in Chap. 4, which focuses on the political dimensions of resilience. This discussion is important because I knew from the onset that NATO has adopted resilience as a key policy concept, replacing the historical vocabulary used in relation to civil dimensions and resources. Resilience often refers to the ability to cope with disturbances and disruptions and is therefore connected to a normative dimension; resilience is always good, and the more resilience, the better (Joseph 2018). In addition, a particular branch of resilience research invokes the sub-concept of *community resilience* and the adaptive capacity of local communities and individuals. Here, research identifies how communities use their social networks, communication, sense of belonging, social learning, and readiness to accept change to cope with disruptions (Berkes and Ross 2013; Koliou et al. 2015).

Why might resilience be problematic when it is adopted in the NATO context? My argument is that resilience is a concept that enables a specific form of governance. When resilience becomes attached to a security discourse, it facilitates security management and promotes programmatic approaches that view the whole society, including individuals, as a function or cog in a Foucauldian security apparatus (Foucault 2007; Foucault et al. 2008; Joseph 2018). Consequently, resilience is imbued with a specific set of priorities and content that is difficult to challenge. This is partly due to the prevailing notion that resilience is simply the desirable capacity of a unit or system to withstand shocks and disturbances and to quickly recover from adverse events and disruptions without clarifying costs and trade-offs.

In this book, I provide a lengthy discussion in Chap. 4 to illustrate the theoretical foundation for understanding resilience as a political concept that enables specific forms of social and political control, thereby potentially shaping the governance of security across NATO and its member states. Resilience is a key concept in the emerging security discourse, and in order to understand the current security arrangements within NATO, we need a clear theoretical understanding of it.

9.2 From Civil Defense to Resilience

A core observation is that there has never been a golden era of civil defense in NATO or any of the member states. Despite the immediate and substantial dangers of war and nuclear weapons, which were always a central part of the imagined war with the Soviet Union, NATO was never able to specify and "implement" any specified requirements or standards that would allow for NATO or its member states to care for the protection of the populations. It is difficult to understand why this is the case. We can recover partial explanations and clues in the material. The civil defense committee (CDC) was established in 1952, following the initial phase, as a working group. But by 1955, the CDC had already become a subcommittee of the Senior Civil Emergency Planning Committee (SCEPC). Civil Emergency Planning is a much broader approach, considering all civil dimensions and resources of societies and how they can be incorporated into war planning and preparedness. Thus, civil defense and the protection of the population and refugees were but a small part of Civil Emergency Planning and were thereafter not prioritized despite continued efforts by CDC. Another important aspect was the hydrogen bomb and the "new assumptions." Given the increased destructive ability of the hydrogen nuclear weapons (see for a detailed discussion in Chap. 5), there was little enthusiasm for improving civil protection on the margins. But NATO is not the only actor to blame for the bleak development in civil defense and the protection of populations and individuals. In fact, the responsibility for societal and civil preparedness falls under Article 3 and lies with the individual member states. NATO has had a coordinating and advisory role that lay in setting standards, issuing recommendations, and maintaining an inventory of development through the Civil Emergency Planning Questionnaire (CEPQ). In this, we can see that there has been a naming-and-shaming mechanism in the reports, but member states have been remarkably reluctant to follow NATO policy and recommendations.

Why is this? Given that NATO is often described as an intergovernmental rather than a supranational organization, the reluctance of member states to follow what must be understood as their own policy advice and directions appears contradictory. I believe it must be concluded that NATO might be better understood as a supranational organization (or a strong tendency toward one) with its own agency and agenda. It has been suggested that Lord Ismay, the first general secretary, was the one who put the O in NATO. With permanent international staff and expertise in complex issues, NATO appears to be in the driving seat. Sure enough, member states can veto decisions and are often active in shaping the wording of core policy documents. At the same time, NATO's international staff is the one who mainly formulates policy and controls everyday activities. In Chap. 7, it was noted that NATO staff in CDC and SCEPC highlighted the importance and feasibility of a civil crisis management focus and disaster relief after the end of the Cold War, making it a core feature of the Partnership for Peace program.

Still, it is puzzling that despite Lord Ismay's strong interest in civil defense and the notion of the important home front, which was part of the vocabulary in the 1950s and the 1960s, no member state seemed to live up to the basic requirements for civil defense and civil emergency planning as suggested by NATO. Rather, the material, in the form of documents and reports, tells a story of a policy field in constant crisis, always lagging behind. It could be that, after the end of World War II, all member states, not only the European ones, wanted to pursue other policies and welfare reforms, and simply could not motivate the extensive costs associated with military and civil preparedness domestically. Other political issues and reforms were simply more attractive and easier to pitch to the voters. It could also be the case that the goals of civil defense and civil emergency planning were, by themselves, never fully attainable; there could always be room for improvement and further preparations. Imagine telling your population that there are only shelters for 27% of the population, or that they expect people not to flee if there is a war, as was suggested during the "stay-put" policy. In addition, civil defense and civil emergency planning could easily expand beyond comprehension if they are not anchored by limited, clearly specified, and achievable goals. I believe it is possible to say that this is also what happened in the NATO context with CEPQ, which at one point covered over 200 questions, often with open-ended answers. It was overly ambitious and caved under its own pressure to do more rather than less (with higher precision and priority).

Rather than trying to do less with greater precision and clarity, NATO and the member states seem to have unconsciously opted to add more tasks and issues to an already complex policy area. Thus, rather than trying to solidify civil defense and the protection of civilian populations and individuals, it first expanded by introducing civil emergency planning and the Senior Civil Emergency Planning Committee (SCEPC). This added seven other permanent planning boards and committees, along with their operational counterparts in NATO Civil Wartime Agencies. Their joint purpose was to include civil resources critical to war preparedness and later assist in military operations. During the 1960s, this also included explicit policies for civilian logistics support during military operations, a key theme of large-scale exercises, CIVLOG 1965 and 1969. In 1969, NATO established the Committee on the Challenges of Modern Society (CCMS) to give the alliance a new "third dimension" and incorporate societal aspects of security. This added a mix of civil crisis management and disaster relief to the already-stretched civil defense and civil emergency planning. It can be added that NATO's role in disaster management was discussed throughout its existence, following severe natural disasters that struck member states in the 1950s and 1970s. Thus, it was possible to detect that, already in the 1970s, NATO's vocabulary included "modern" ideas such as "all-hazards-approach," "dual-use," civil-military collaboration, and the idea that it was possible to combine civil crisis management and war preparedness to address a wide range of societal contingencies on a single scale. All these elements were sustained through the 1980s and sometimes referred to civil preparedness, with occasional references to total defense, thus covering all the above aspects under a single heading, showcasing the integrated approach to crisis *and* war.

The end of the Cold War could have led to NATO's dissolution, as its original purpose was to safeguard Europe against the Soviet Union's ideological and military influence. But NATO immediately identified new security challenges that must be addressed. The quote from Javier Solana in 1999 captures NATO's new outlook: "Now that the Cold War is over, we are faced not with a single all-embracing threat but with a multitude of new risks and challenges." After the end of the Cold War and during the 1990s, as the immediate threat of large-scale war and nuclear attacks was removed, NATO swiftly reoriented itself to include international crisis management and out-of-area operations, also known as non-article five operations, engaging in many military operations in the region. Also, in these operations, ideas of civil dimensions and civil support were included, but they were not oriented toward civil defense and the protection of populations as such. Such ideas would, however, partly return after 9/11 and the identification of international political terrorism targeting populations.

This did not mean that the Civil Defense Committee (renamed the Civil Protection Committee in the mid-1990s) or the SCEPC was disbanded. Rather, what occurred could almost be described as bureaucratic activism in which international staff found ways to "secure" and expand the role of civil protection and civil preparedness. For instance, civil crisis management and disaster relief became a diplomatic means to initiate collaboration with Eastern European countries, including Russia. It was one of the main themes of the Partnership for Peace (PfP) and eventually led NATO to accept a proposal from Russia to establish the Euro-Atlantic Disaster Response Coordination Center (EADRCC) in 1998, which was initially placed under the Euro-Atlantic Partnership Council and SCEPC and remains active to this day, but Russia is, of course, excluded from its program.

In 2014, Russia invaded Ukrainian territory, seizing the Crimean Peninsula in February–March and then supporting pro-Russian paramilitaries in the Donetsk and Luhansk regions of eastern Ukraine. In 2022, Russia launched a full-scale invasion that has led to a 4-year-long war (and counting in 2026) at the very borders of NATO. Perhaps NATO should have acted differently already when Russia invaded Georgia in 2008. Both cases might be seen as Russian aggression against countries in the Russian "sphere of interest" that wish to join NATO and the European Union. This new geopolitical situation reintroduces concerns about civil defense and emergency planning, as traditional war preparation becomes crucial. In 2014, we saw the first mention of resilience as a new concept in this policy field, but it was in 2016 that it became a key policy concept in the area of civil defense and emergency planning, with a specific declaration of "commitment to resilience." In September 2016, NATO also finalized the "seven baseline requirements of resilience," which serve as evaluation criteria in the new resilience questionnaire that is but a new variant of the CEPQ. In 2022, NATO adopted its eight Strategic Concept, which explicitly mentions resilience. In addition, in 2022, the Senior Civil Emergency Planning Committee changed its name (but not its functions) to the Resilience Committee.

Why did NATO change its vocabulary, and what does it mean? One reason was that international staff did not believe it would be possible to return to "old" Cold War-era vocabulary. Instead, resilience was a fashionable and pragmatic concept to which similar issues could be attached. The other one was that it is also partly a new and more advanced security situation, with new and hyper-modern hybrid threats and grey-zone tactics. The interconnected world and the extensive civil-state collaboration and management concerning many of the critical infrastructure, civil dimensions, and resources of war and hybrid war, would also demand a new take for "whole-of-society."

Resilience recognizes NATO's role in defining, coordinating, and assessing member states' efforts when it comes to Article 3. It is also a more comprehensive, programmatic approach to the civil dimensions than during the Cold War, because it explicitly calls for the active participation of civil actors, populations, and even individuals in peacetime and war. In fact, we could see that NATO explicitly identified communities and individuals as actors in the new defense posture. Resilience is viewed as vital for addressing modern security challenges, requiring new arrangements with civil authorities, the private sector, civil society, and individuals. There is one important difference from the ideas present in civil defense and emergency planning. Whereas these latter concepts concern the protection of populations, civilian and non-combatants in war situations, resilience seems to emphasize constant preparedness, active readiness, and acceptance of wartime hardships. There is the Civil Protection Group (CPG), but in the documents analyzed, there is little evidence of the idea or the efforts to *protect* against the hardships of war and nuclear attacks.

This is the answer to the question posed at the beginning of the book, and Chaps. 5–8 provide all the details, twists, and turns for the initiated reader to support this summary.

9.3 Limitations of the Study and Future Research

I have focused on the empirical material found in the NATO archives and identified and recovered sources on NATO and its policies toward the civil dimensions that have never been analyzed before. A unique material that has provided insights into NATO's understanding of the civil dimensions of defense and war preparedness throughout history. Still, I focused foremost on the development and vocabulary related to civil defense and the protection of the population and individuals. There are other aspects of civil emergency planning that could be explored to gain knowledge of other civil dimensions of war preparedness, such as petroleum, aviation, shipping, food and agriculture, communications, or similar areas. In addition, it might be worth pursuing research on these and other specific topics, such as refugees, environmental security, disaster relief, and civil crisis management, to further examine the civil dimensions and the resources NATO has included in its policy and planning, with the caveat that some research has already been conducted.

In addition, this book spans 75 years, allowing it to tell "the full story." It enabled a focus on the development and unfolding vocabulary of security discourses, circulating the civil dimensions of war in NATO's view. The focus has been on aligning the major trends and events with the more fine-grained planning within NATO's machinery. It has been more difficult to follow up on the "implementation" of NATO policies in the member states. What has actually been achieved on the ground? Country reports in the archives could be studied in more detail to further nuance the general conclusion that most member states did very little. Comparisons between countries, explaining why member states were reluctant to adhere to NATO policies in civil defense, the formulation of CEPQ, and the review cycles are worth exploring in more detail, not only noting their format and functions. Historical CEPQ can be contrasted with the new, similar method, which relates to resilience and the resilience committee. At the same time, it is important to remember that information on contemporary policy on these issues is scarce. We must first ensure that we have access to accurate and trustworthy information, which is difficult given the current secrecy and vulnerability of open sources, and the potential for information on weaknesses within member states to be used by an adversary.

9.4 Theoretical Discussion and Concluding Remarks

One central issue throughout the study has been NATO's ability to govern and control issues it deems important to its plans and policies. It is identified as an intergovernmental organization. Thus, by definition, NATO cannot force member states to do anything they are unwilling to do. In the areas of civil defense, civil emergency planning, and, lastly, resilience, most, if not all, aspects fall under Article 3, providing member states with even greater independence to address these issues in ways they find optimal, or simply not follow NATO recommendations despite naming-and-shaming mechanisms. Civil defense and the protection of populations from the hardships of war were clearly not prioritized, and member states seemed reluctant to take such matters seriously despite NATO's and the Civil Defense Committee's coordinating efforts. The discussion in Chap. 4, on the political aspects of resilience, suggested that the resilience concept could generate substantial social and political control.

Resilience has been suggested to form the basis for a specific version of governmentality that would generate new instruments and strategies for governing both national and societal security by creating specific subjects, or individuals (Bergström 2018; Chandler 2013; Davoudi 2018; Evans and Reid 2014). Furthermore, resilience has been said to allow for the securitization of an ever-widening range of threats, coupled with a preemptive approach to crises and risks (Comfort et al. 2010). This would, in a strict sense, require a population consisting of self-reliant and capable citizens who would willingly support the state authorities during crises. This, in turn, enables interventionism, that aim to transform individual citizens into "resilient" neoliberal subjects (Bergström 2016, 2017; Chandler 2013; Chandler and Reid 2016; Davoudi 2018).

Although we can note similar tendencies and ideas in NATO's policy and vocabulary, such as improving citizens and altering their behaviors and attitudes, we see little evidence that NATO has been able to solidify conformity among member states since adopting the resilience concept. Why is that?

First, states and people are not the same, even if resilience may create an individual subjectivity; states certainly express far more autonomy in relation to the concept. Second, I have foremost been investigating the policy and the vocabulary, or the "discourse." Obviously, policy is a blueprint that outlines desired ways to govern and the subjects that follow. What happens in "reality," or outside the discourse, is a different matter worth exploring further in governmentality studies. It still points to one crucial aspect of NATO: who governs the intergovernmental organization, and to what extent member states are willing to follow "their" own policies?

NATO is described as the world's most powerful and enduring alliance, but we know remarkably little of its inner life and political dimensions. This book has offered a historical and discursive account of the development of civil defense into resilience, but it is clear that we need more critical studies and scrutiny of how NATO governs and is governed.

Literature

Adey, Peter, and Ben Anderson. 2012. Anticipating Emergencies: Technologies of Preparedness and the Matter of Security. *Security Dialogue* 43 (2): 99–117.

Adler, Emanuel. 1997. Seizing the Middle Ground:: Constructivism in World Politics. *European Journal of International Relations* 3 (3): 319–363. https://doi.org/10.1177/1354066197003003003.

Aldrich, Daniel P. 2012. *Building Resilience: Social Capital in Post-Disaster Recovery*. University of Chicago Press.

Aldrich, Daniel P., and Michelle A. Meyer. 2015. Social Capital and Community Resilience. *American Behavioral Scientist* 59 (2): 254–269.

Alexander, David E. 2013. Resilience and Disaster Risk Reduction: An Etymological Journey. *Natural Hazards and Earth System Sciences* 13 (11): 2707–2716.

Allison, Roy. 2014. Russian 'Deniable' Intervention in Ukraine: How and Why Russia Broke the Rules. *International Affairs* 90 (6): 1255–1297.

Aradau, Claudia. 2004. Security and the Democratic Scene: Desecuritization and Emancipation. *Journal of International Relations and Development* 7 (4): 388–413.

Arkan, Zeynep. 2025. *European Security and Hybrid Threats: A Narrative in the Making*. Springer Nature.

Bacchi, Carol Lee. 1999. *Women, Policy and Politics: The Construction of Policy Problems*.

Baele, Stephane J., and Diana Jalea. 2023. Twenty-Five Years of Securitization Theory: A Corpus-Based Review. *Political Studies Review* 21 (2): 376–389.

Baker, Natalie D., and Lisa Grant Ludwig. 2018. Disaster Preparedness as Social Control. *Critical Policy Studies* 12 (1): 24–43.

Balzacq, Thierry. 2011. Securitization Theory. In *How Security Problems Emerge and Dissolve*.

O. Larsson, *NATO's Approach to the Civil Dimensions of War*,
https://doi.org/10.1007/978-3-032-27871-5

Balzacq, Thierry. 2019. Securitization Theory: Past, Present, and Future. *Polity* 51 (2): 331–348.

Balzacq, Thierry, Sarah Léonard, and Jan Ruzicka. 2016. 'Securitization' Revisited: Theory and Cases. *International Relations* 30 (4): 494–531.

Bartelson, Jens. 1995. *A Genealogy of Sovereignty*. No. 39. Cambridge University Press.

Bartelson, Jens. 2001. *The Critique of the State*. Cambridge University Press.

Behnke, Andreas. 2000. The Message or the Messenger? Reflections on the Role of Security Experts and the Securitization of Political Issues. *Cooperation and Conflict* 35 (1): 89–105.

Bergström, Johan. 2018. An Archaeology of Societal Resilience. *Safety Science* 110:31–38.

Berkes, Fikret, Johan Colding, and Carl Folke. 2008. *Navigating Social-Ecological Systems: Building Resilience for Complexity and Change*. Cambridge University Press.

Bigo, Didier. 2006. Internal and External Aspects of Security. *European Security* 15 (4): 385–404.

Bigo, Didier. 2012. Security, Surveillance and Democracy. In *Routledge Handbook of Surveillance Studies*. Routledge.

Bigo, Didier, and Emma McCluskey. 2018. What Is a PARIS Approach to (in) Securitization? Political Anthropological Research For. In *The Oxford Handbook of International Security*, 116.

Bjørnsson, Iben. 2023. Negotiating Armageddon: Civil Defence in NATO and Denmark 1949–59. *Cold War History* 23 (2): 217–238.

Bondesson, Sara. 2022. *Empowerment and Social Justice in the Wake of Disasters: Occupy Sandy in Rockaway After Hurricane Sandy, USA*. Taylor & Francis.

Bourbeau, Philippe. 2015. Resilience and International Politics: Premises, Debates, Agenda. *International Studies Review* 17 (3): 374–395.

Bourbeau, Philippe. 2018. *On Resilience: Genealogy, Logics, and World Politics*. Cambridge University Press.

Brady, Michelle. 2014. Ethnographies of Neoliberal Governmentalities: From the Neoliberal Apparatus to Neoliberalism and Governmental Assemblages. *Foucault Studies* 11–33.

Brand, Fridolin Simon, and Kurt Jax. 2007. Focusing the Meaning (s) of Resilience: Resilience as a Descriptive Concept and a Boundary Object. *Ecology and Society* 12 (1).

Buzan, Barry, Ole Wæver, Ole Wæver, and Jaap De Wilde. 1998. *Security: A New Framework for Analysis*. Lynne Rienner Publishers.

Canadian War Museum. 2023. Canada and NATO. Canadian War Museum, November 27. https://www.warmuseum.ca/articles/canada-and-nato.

Chandler, David. 2013. Resilience and the Autotelic Subject: Toward a Critique of the Societalization of Security. *International Political Sociology* 7 (2): 210–226.
Chandler, David, and Julian Reid. 2016. *The Neoliberal Subject: Resilience, Adaptation and Vulnerability*. Rowman & Littlefield.
Chmutina, Ksenia, Gonzalo Lizarralde, Andrew Dainty, and Lee Bosher. 2016. Unpacking Resilience Policy Discourse. *Cities* 58:70–79.
Christie, E. H., and K. Berzina 2022. NATO and Societal Resilience: All Hands on Deck in an Age of War. The German Marshall Fund of the United States (GMF). https://www.coe-civ.eu/kh/nato-and-societal-resilience-all-hands-on-deck-in-an-age-of-war.
Civil Defense Committee. 1953. RECORD OF MEETING-CDC AC/23-R/5. NATO Archives Online. https://archives.nato.int/record-of-meeting-378.
Civil Defense Committee. 1954a. Civil Defense Committee 1954, 4 December, AC/2 5-R/13. NATO Archives Brussels.
Civil Defense Committee. 1954b. RECORD OF MEETING—Civil Defense Committee 14–15 November—AC/23(CD) R /4. NATO Archives Online. https://archives.nato.int/record-of-meeting-1959.
Civil Defense Committee. 1955a. DRAFT REPORT ON CURRENT WORK IN THE LIGHT OF THE NEW ASSUMPTIONS AC/23(CD)D/110-REV1. NATO Archives Online. https://archives.nato.int/draft-report-on-current-work-in-the-light-of-the-new-assumptions-5.
Civil Defense Committee. 1955b. RECORD OF MEETING—Civil Defense Committee AC 23 CD R/6. NATO Archives Online. https://archives.nato.int/record-of-meeting-1961.
Civil Defense Committee. 1955c. Summary Record of Civil Defense, 22nd and 23rd November, 1955, AC 23 CD. NATO Archives Brussels.
Civil Defense Committee. 1962. PREPARATION OF THE 1963 YEARLY REVIEW QUESTIONNAIRE—AC/23(CD)D/420. NATO Archives Online. https://archives.nato.int/preparation-of-the-1963-yearly-review-questionnaire-3.
Civil Defense Committee. 1965. AC 23 CD 505. NATO Archives Brussels.
Civil Defense Committee. 1968. AC 23 CD—D 555. NATO Archives Brussels.
Civil Defense Committee. 1970a. AC 23 (CD) D 604. NATO Archives Brussels.
Civil Defense Committee. 1970b. AC 23 CD D 611. NATO Archives Brussels.
Civil Defense Committee. 1971a. NATO CO-OPERATION FOR EMERGENCY DISASTER RELIEF IN PEACE TIME AC 23 WP 20. NATO Archives Brussels.
Civil Defense Committee. 1971b. Progress Report to SCEPC for 1970–1971—AC 23 D 633. NATO Archives Brussels.
Civil Defense Committee. 1971c. REPORT TO THE CIVIL DEFENCE COMMITTEE BY THE AD-HOC STUDY GROUP ON THE STATE OF

CIVIL DEFENSE PREPEREDNESS WITHIN MEMBER STATES—As OF 1st APRIL 1971—AC 23 D 625. NATO Archives Brussels.

Civil Defense Committee. 1972a. AC/23-D/641 EXTRACTS FROM THE SENIOR COMMITTEE'S DECISIONS TAKEN AT THE 71ST MEETING. NATO Archives Online. https://archives.nato.int/extracts-from-the-senior-committees-decisions-taken-at-the-71st-meeting-3.

Civil Defense Committee. 1972b. PROGRAMME OF THE BRIEFING SESSION OF THE CIVIL DEFENCE COMMITTEE MEETING TO BE HELD ON 13TH SEPTEMBER 1972. NATO Archives Online. https://archives.nato.int/programme-of-the-briefing-session-of-the-civil-defence-committee-meeting-to-be-held-on-13th-september-1972.

Civil Defense Committee. 1972c. WORKING GROUP ON REFUGEES—AC 23 D 653. NATO Archives Brussels.

Collier, Stephen J., and Andrew Lakoff. 2008. Distributed Preparedness: The Spatial Logic of Domestic Security in the United States. *Environment and Planning D: Society and Space* 26 (1): 7–28.

Collier, Stephen J., and Andrew Lakoff. 2021. *The Government of Emergency: Vital Systems, Expertise, and the Politics of Security*. Vol. 25. Princeton University Press.

Comfort, Louise K., Arjen Boin, and Chris C. Demchak. 2010. In *Designing Resilience: Preparing for Extreme Events*, edited by Louise K. Comfort, Arjen Boin, and Chris C. Demchak. University of Pittsburgh Press.

Corry, Olaf. 2014. From Defense to Resilience: Environmental Security beyond Neo-Liberalism. *International Political Sociology* 8 (3): 256–274.

Côté, Adam. 2016. Agents without Agency: Assessing the Role of the Audience in Securitization Theory. *Security Dialogue* 47 (6): 541–558.

Cote, Muriel, and Andrea J. Nightingale. 2012. Resilience Thinking Meets Social Theory: Situating Social Change in Socio-Ecological Systems (SES) Research. *Progress in Human Geography* 36 (4): 475–489.

Cronqvist, Marie, Rosanna Farbøl, and Casper Sylvest, eds. 2022a. *Cold War Civil Defence in Western Europe: Sociotechnical Imaginaries of Survival and Preparedness*. Springer International Publishing. https://doi.org/10.1007/978-3-030-84281-9.

Cronqvist, Marie, Rosanna Farbøl, and Casper Sylvest, eds. 2022b. Conclusion: Civil Defence Futures (Re)Imagined. In *Cold War Civil Defence in Western Europe: Sociotechnical Imaginaries of Survival and Preparedness*. Springer International Publishing. https://doi.org/10.1007/978-3-030-84281-9.

Cronqvist, Marie, Rosanna Farbøl, and Casper Sylvest, eds. 2022c. Order on Their Home Fronts: Imagining War and Social Control in 1950s NATO. In *Cold War Civil Defence in Western Europe: Sociotechnical Imaginaries of Survival and Preparedness*. Springer International Publishing. https://doi.org/10.1007/978-3-030-84281-9.

David, Baldwin. 1997. The Concept of Security. *Review of International Studies* 23 (1): 5–26.
Davoudi, Simin. 2018. Resilience and Governmentality of Unknowns. In *Governmentality after Neoliberalism*. Routledge.
Dean, Mitchell. 2007. *Governing Societies*. McGraw-Hill Education (UK).
Dean, Mitchell M. 2009. *Governmentality: Power and Rule in Modern Society*.
Dean, Mitchell. 2013. *The Signature of Power: Sovereignty, Governmentality and Biopolitics*. Sage.
Dillon, Michael, and Andrew Neal. 2015. *Foucault on Politics, Security and War*. Springer.
Dillon, Michael, and Julian Reid. 2001. Global Liberal Governance: Biopolitics, Security and War. *Millennium* 30 (1): 41–66.
Edström, H., J. Matlary, and M. Petersson. 2011a. In *NATO: The Power of Partnerships*, New Security Challenges, edited by H. Edström, J. Matlary, and M. Petersson. Palgrave Macmillan UK. https://doi.org/10.1057/9780230297500.
Edström, Håkan, Janne Haaland Matlary, and Magnus Petersson. 2011b. *NATO: The Power of Partnerships*. Springer.
Eichler, Jan. 2021. *NATO's Expansion after the Cold War*, Global Power Shift. Springer International Publishing AG. https://doi.org/10.1007/978-3-030-66641-5.
Evans, Brad, and Julian Reid. 2014. *Resilient Life: The Art of Living Dangerously*. Wiley.
Fjäder, Christian. 2014. The Nation-State, National Security and Resilience in the Age of Globalisation. *Resilience* 2 (2): 114–129.
Flockhart, Trine. 2016. The Coming Multi-Order World. *Contemporary Security Policy* 37 (1): 3–30. https://doi.org/10.1080/13523260.2016.1150053.
Folke, Carl, Stephen R. Carpenter, Brian Walker, Marten Scheffer, Terry Chapin, and Johan Rockström. 2010. Resilience Thinking: Integrating Resilience, Adaptability and Transformability. *Ecology and Society* 15 (4).
Foucault, Michel. 2007. *Security, Territory, Population: Lectures at the Collège de France, 1977–78*. Springer.
Foucault, M. 2010. *The Birth of Biopolitics: Lectures at the Collège de France, 1978–1979*. Palgrave Macmillan. https://books.google.se/books?id=Or8NDgAAQBAJ.
Foucault, Michel, Arnold I. Davidson, and Graham Burchell. 2008. *The Birth of Biopolitics: Lectures at the Collège de France, 1978–1979*. Springer.
Frizzelle, Bryan, Julie Garey, and Isak Kulalic. 2022. NATO's National Resilience Mandate: Challenges and Opportunities. *Defence Studies* 22 (3): 525–532.
German, Tracey. 2017. NATO and the Enlargement Debate: Enhancing Euro-Atlantic Security or Inciting Confrontation? *International Affairs* 93 (2): 291–308.

Ghita, Cristian. 2024. *E-ARC Mission Statement—Centrul Euro-Atlantic Pentru Rezilienţă—E-ARC*. March 18. https://e-arc.ro/en/2024/03/18/e-arc-mission-statement/.
Goldgeier, James M., and Joshua R. Itzkowitz Shifrinson. 2023. *Evaluating NATO Enlargement: From Cold War Victory to the Russia-Ukraine War*. Springer.
Hagström, Linus. 2021. Disciplinary Power: Text and Body in the Swedish NATO Debate. *Cooperation and Conflict* 56 (2): 141–162.
Hallams, Ellen, Luca Ratti, and Benjamin Zyla. 2013. *NATO beyond 9/11: The Transformation of the Atlantic Alliance*. Springer.
Hamblin, Jacob Darwin. 2010. Environmentalism for the Atlantic Alliance: NATO's Experiment with the "Challenges of Modern Society". *Environmental History* 15 (1): 54–75. https://doi.org/10.1093/envhis/emq008.
Hansen, Lene. 2013. *Security as Practice: Discourse Analysis and the Bosnian War*. Routledge.
Hatzivassiliou, Evanthis. 2017. *The NATO Committee on the Challenges of Modern Society, 1969–1975: Transatlantic Relations, the Cold War and the Environment*. Springer.
Hayek, Friedrich August, and Bruce Caldwell. 2014. *The Road to Serfdom: Text and Documents: The Definitive Edition*. Routledge.
Hellström, Agnes. 2023. *Fredsfittan—Nato-Beslutet Som Förändrade Sverige*. Bazar.
Hilde, Paal Sigurd. 2025a. NATO and Total Defence: A Framework for National Efforts. In *European Total Defence*. Routledge.
Hilde, Paal Sigurd. 2025b. "NATO and Total Defence: A Framework for National Efforts." 1st Ed. United Kingdom: Routledge, 2025. 239–260. In *European Total Defence. Ed. by Gjermund Forfang Rongved*. Routledge.
Hodicky, Jan, Gökhan Özkan, Hilmi Özdemir, Petr Stodola, Jan Drozd, and Wayne Buck. 2020. Dynamic Modeling for Resilience Measurement: NATO Resilience Decision Support Model. *Applied Sciences* 10 (8): 2639. https://doi.org/10.3390/app10082639.
Holling, Crawford S. 1973. Resilience and Stability of Ecological Systems. *Annual Review of Ecology and Systematics* 4 (1): 1–23.
Hope, Ian. 2024. NATO, 1968–1989. In *Routledge Handbook of NATO*, edited by John Andreas Olsen. Routledge.
Huysmans, Jef. 2008. The Jargon of Exception—On Schmitt, Agamben and the Absence of Political Society. *International Political Sociology* 2 (2): 165–183.
Huysmans, Jef. 2014. *Security Unbound: Enacting Democratic Limits*. Routledge.
Hybrid CoE—The European Centre of Excellence for Countering Hybrid Threats. 2017. Hybrid CoE—The European Centre of Excellence for Countering Hybrid Threats. https://www.hybridcoe.fi/about-us/.

Ismay, Lord. 1954. *NATO—The First 5 Years 1949–1954—By Lord Ismay, Secretary General of the North Atlantic Treaty Organization*. NATO Archives Online.

Ismay, Lord. 1955. The North Atlantic Treaty Organization. *Royal United Services Institution. Journal* 100 (597): 1–10.

Jabri, Vivienne. 2006. War, Security and the Liberal State. *Security Dialogue* 37 (1): 47–64.

Johns, Fleur. 2005. Guantánamo Bay and the Annihilation of the Exception. *European Journal of International Law* 16 (4): 613–635.

Joseph, Jonathan. 2013a. Resilience as Embedded Neoliberalism: A Governmentality Approach. *Resilience* 1 (1): 38–52.

Joseph, Jonathan. 2013b. Resilience in UK and French Security Strategy: An Anglo-Saxon Bias? *Politics* 33 (4): 253–264. https://doi.org/10.1111/1467-9256.12010.

Joseph, Jonathan. 2018. *Varieties of Resilience: Studies in Governmentality*. Cambridge University Press.

Kaplan, Lawrence S. 1999. *The Long Entanglement: NATO's First Fifty Years*. Praeger.

Kaplan, Lawrence. 2007. NATO Review—History: The 40th Anniversary of the Harmel Report. NATO Review, January 1. https://www.nato.int/docu/review/articles/2007/01/01/history-the-40th-anniversary-of-the-harmel-report/index.html.

Kennan, George. 1944. *The Long Telegram*. Moscow. https://nsarchive2.gwu.edu/coldwar/documents/episode-1/kennan.htm.

Kennedy, Thomas J. Jr. 1984. *NATO Politico-Military Consultation*.

Kinnvall, Catarina, and Jennifer Mitzen. 2020. Anxiety, Fear, and Ontological Security in World Politics: Thinking with and beyond Giddens. *International Theory* 12 (2): 240–256.

Korosteleva, Elena A., and Trine Flockhart. 2020. Resilience in EU and International Institutions: Redefining Local Ownership in a New Global Governance Agenda. *Contemporary Security Policy* 41 (2): 153–175. https://doi.org/10.1080/13523260.2020.1723973.

Larsson, Oscar L. 2021. The Connections between Crisis and War Preparedness in Sweden. *Security Dialogue* 52 (4): 306–324.

Lentzos, Filippa, and Nikolas Rose. 2009. Governing Insecurity: Contingency Planning, Protection, Resilience. *Economy and Society* 38 (2): 230–254.

Lizarralde, Gonzalo, Ksenia Chmutina, Lee Bosher, and Andrew Dainty. 2015. Sustainability and Resilience in the Built Environment: The Challenges of Establishing a Turquoise Agenda in the UK. *Sustainable Cities and Society* 15:96–104.

Ljungkvist, Kristin. 2024. The Military-Strategic Rationality of Hybrid Warfare: Everyday Total Defence under Strategic Non-Peace in the Case of Sweden.

European Journal of International Security 1–20. https://doi.org/10.1017/eis.2024.18.

MacKinnon, Danny, and Kate Driscoll Derickson. 2013. From Resilience to Resourcefulness: A Critique of Resilience Policy and Activism. *Progress in Human Geography* 37 (2): 253–270.

Mälksoo, Maria. 2025. Risk, Resilience, and Resistance. In *The Oxford Handbook of NATO*, edited by Mark Webber and James Sperling. Oxford University Press.

Manyena, Siambabala Bernard. 2006. The Concept of Resilience Revisited. *Disasters* 30 (4): 434–450.

Marshall Plan. 1948 [2026]. Milestones in the History of U.S. Foreign Relations—Office of the Historian. https://history.state.gov/milestones/1945-1952/marshall-plan.

McGreavy, Bridie. 2016. Resilience as Discourse. *Environmental Communication* 10 (1): 104–121.

Milestones in the History of U.S. Foreign Relations—Office of the Historian. n.d.. https://history.state.gov/milestones/1953-1960/sputnik. Accessed 23 January 2026.

Military Committee. 1958. THE MILITARY PROGRESS OF THE NORTH ATLANTIC TREATY ORGANIZATION—REPORT NO. 11. MC 0005/13. NATO Archives Online. https://archives.nato.int/the-military-progress-of-the-north-atlantic-treaty-organization-report-no-11.

Military Committee. 1959. THE MILITARY PROGRESS OF THE NATO REPORT NO. 12—MC 0005/14. NATO Archives Online. https://archives.nato.int/the-military-progress-of-the-nato-report-no-12.

Military Committee. 1963. BASIC ASSUMPTIONS FOR CIVIL EMERGENCY PLANNING IPT 055/41/D. NATO Archives Online. https://archives.nato.int/basic-assumptions-for-civil-emergency-planning.

Military Committee. 1964. MC 0043/14 FINAL—NATO FALL EXERCISE 1962 Military Committee Series. NATO Archives Online.

Military Committee. 1965. MCM-0110-1965—REPORT ON EX CIVLOG '65 Military Committee Memorandum (MCM) Series. NATO Archives Online.

Military Committee. 1972. FINAL REPORT ON EXERCISE WINTEX 1971—MC 0043/26 DRAFT REV 2 Final. NATO Archives Online. https://archives.nato.int/final-report-on-exercise-wintex-1971.

Milloy, John C. 2006. *The North Atlantic Treaty Organization, 1948–1957: Community or Alliance?* McGill-Queen's Press-MQUP.

Mingarini, Noa Melin, and Oscar Larsson. 2025. Resilience Is Everywhere, but What Does It Mean? A Study of the Use of the Term Resilience in Swedish Public Policy. *Critical Policy Studies* 1–17.

National Security Archive. 2017. September 12 Two-Plus-Four Ministerial in Moscow: Detailed Account [Includes Text of the Treaty on the Final Settlement with Respect to Germany and Agreed Minute to the Treaty on the Special Military Status of the GDR after Unification] |. https://nsarchive.gwu.edu/document/16139-document-25.

National Security Archives. 2017. NATO Expansion: What Gorbachev Heard | National Security Archive. https://nsarchive.gwu.edu/briefing-book/russia-programs/2017-12-12/nato-expansion-what-gorbachev-heard-western-leaders-early.

NATO. 1949. The North Atlantic Treaty. https://www.nato.int/en/about-us/official-texts-and-resources/official-texts/1949/04/04/the-north-atlantic-treaty.

NATO. 1950. "The Strategic Concept for the Defense of the North Atlantic Area" (DC 6/1). NATO Archives Brussels.

NATO. 1955a. DRAFT RESOLUTION ON THE ESTABLISHMENT OF A STEERING COMMITTEE FOR CIVIL EMERGENCY PLANNING—The North Atlantic Council Ad Hoc Committees Working Group to Examine the United States Proposal for Reorganization of the Civil Emergency Planning Structure. NATO Archives Online. https://archives.nato.int/draft-resolution-on-the-establishment-of-a-steering-committee-for-civil-emergency-planning.

NATO. 1955b. REPORT BY THE COMMITTEE ON CIVIL ORGANIZATION IN TIME OF WAR ON THE ORDER OF PRIORITY OF CIVIL DEFENCE MEASURES—NATO Archives Online. NATO Archives Online. https://archives.nato.int/report-by-the-committee-on-civil-organization-in-time-of-war-on-the-order-of-priority-of-civil-defence-measures.

NATO. 1956. Report of the Committee of Three. https://www.nato.int/en/about-us/official-texts-and-resources/official-texts/1956/12/13/report-of-the-committee-of-three.

NATO. 1967a. *MC 14/3 Overall Strategic Concept for the Defense of the North Atlantic Treaty Organization Area*. https://www.nato.int/docu/stratdoc/eng/a680116a.pdf.

NATO. 1967b. THE NORTH ATLANTIC COUNCIL AND ITS COMMITTEE SYSTEM—NATO Archives Online. https://archives.nato.int/the-north-atlantic-council-and-its-committee-system.

NATO. 1968. *The Harmel Report*. NATO Archives Online.

NATO. 1980. DECLASSIFICATION AND DOWNGRADING OF DOCUMENTS—The North Atlantic Council Ad Hoc Committees Senior Civil Emergency Planning Committee Food and Agriculture Planning Committee / Committee on Wartime Commodity Problems AC/25-N/260. NATO Archives Online. https://archives.nato.int/declassification-and-downgrading-of-documents-3.

NATO. 1989. NATO Summit March 1989. https://www.nato.int/cps/en/natohq/official_texts_23554.htm?
NATO. 1990. NATO DEFENCE PLANNING—MINISTERS' DECISIONS 22ND AND 23RD MAY 1990—NATO Archives Online. https://archives.nato.int/nato-defence-planning-ministers-decisions-22nd-and-23rd-may-1990.
NATO. 1991. The Situation in Yugoslavia. NATO. https://www.nato.int/cps/en/natohq/official_texts_23849.htm.
NATO. 1994. NATO Summit Brussels 1994. https://www.nato.int/cps/en/natohq/official_texts_24470.htm?mode=pressrelease.
NATO. 1995. Study on NATO Enlargement. https://www.nato.int/cps/en/natohq/official_texts_24733.htm.
NATO. 1997a. Founding Act on Mutual Relations, Cooperation and Security between NATO and the Russian Federation. https://www.nato.int/cps/en/natohq/official_texts_25468.htm.
NATO. 1997b. Madrid Declaration on Euro-Atlantic Security and Cooperation Issued by the Heads of State and Government at the Meeting of the North Atlantic Council. https://www.nato.int/cps/en/natohq/official_texts_25460.htm.
NATO. 1997c. NATO Logistics Handbook: Chapter 11: Civil Emergency Planning. https://www.nato.int/docu/logi-en/1997/lo-1101.htm.
NATO. 1999. "An Alliance for the 21st Century" Washington Summit Communiqué Issued by the Heads of State and Government Participating in the Meeting of the North Atlantic Council in Washington, D.C. on 24th April 1999. https://www.nato.int/cps/en/natohq/official_texts_27440.htm.
NATO. 2002. NATO-Russia Relations: A New Quality Declaration by Heads of State and Government of NATO Member States and the Russian Federation. https://www.nato.int/cps/en/natohq/official_texts_19572.htm.
NATO. 2004. Istanbul Summit Communiqué Issued by the Heads of State and Government Participating in the Meeting of the North Atlantic Council. https://www.nato.int/cps/en/natohq/official_texts_21023.htm.
NATO. 2006a. Backgrounder—NATO's Role in Civil Emergency Planning. NATO Public Diplomacy Division.
NATO. 2006b. Comprehensive Political Guidance Endorsed by NATO Heads of State and Government on 29 November 2006. NATO. https://www.nato.int/cps/en/natohq/official_texts_56425.htm.
NATO. 2008. NATO Archives. NATO Civil Organisation Records 1952–1974. https://www.nato.int/archives/a5258.htm#01.
NATO. 2012. Chicago Summit Declaration Issued by NATO Heads of State and Government (2012). NATO. https://www.nato.int/cps/en/natohq/official_texts_87593.htm.

NATO. 2013. NATO in Focus—An Introduction to the Transatlantic Alliance—NATO Archives Online. https://archives.nato.int/nato-in-focus-introduction-to-transatlantic-alliance.
NATO. 2014. Wales Summit Declaration Issued by NATO Heads of State and Government (2014). NATO. https://www.nato.int/cps/en/natohq/official_texts_112964.htm.
NATO. 2015. Comprehensive Political Guidance (Archived). NATO. https://www.nato.int/cps/en/natohq/topics_49176.htm.
NATO. 2016a. NATO's Home. https://www.nato.int/cps/en/natohq/declassified_136208.htm.
NATO. 2016b. Press Release: Commitment to Enhance Resilience. https://www.nato.int/cps/fr/natohq/official_texts_133180.htm?selectedLocale=en.
NATO. 2016c. Warsaw Summit Communiqué Issued by NATO Heads of State and Government (2016). NATO. https://www.nato.int/cps/en/natohq/official_texts_133169.htm.
NATO. 2017. Resilience Capacity Building Implications for NATO Conference Report June1–2, 2017. NATO.
NATO. 2021a. 2021—REPORT—ENHANCING THE RESILIENCE OF ALLIED SOCIETIES THROUGH CIVIL PREPAREDNESS. https://www.nato-pa.int/document/2021-enhancing-resilience-allied-societies-through-civil-preparedness-garriaud-maylam.
NATO. 2021b. Brussels Summit Communiqué. https://www.nato.int/en/about-us/official-texts-and-resources/official-texts/2021/06/14/brussels-summit-communique.
NATO. 2021c. Strengthened Resilience Commitment. https://www.nato.int/cps/en/natohq/official_texts_185340.htm.
NATO. 2022a. Defence Planning Committee (1963–2010). https://www.nato.int/cps/em/natohq/topics_49201.htm.
NATO. 2022b. Harmel Report. NATO. https://www.nato.int/cps/en/natohq/topics_67927.htm.
NATO. 2022c. NATO and Nuclear Planning Group (NPG). https://www.nato.int/cps/em/natohq/topics_50069.htm.
NATO. 2022d. Resilience Committee. https://www.nato.int/cps/en/natohq/topics_50093.htm.
NATO. 2022e. Strategic Concepts. NATO. https://www.nato.int/cps/en/natohq/topics_56626.htm.
NATO. 2022f. Strategic Concepts. Official Texts and Resources | NATO. https://www.nato.int/en/about-us/official-texts-and-resources/strategic-concepts.
NATO. 2023a. NATO—Countering Hybrid Threats. https://www.nato.int/cps/en/natohq/topics_156338.htm.

NATO. 2023b. NATO—Relations with Russia. https://www.nato.int/cps/en/natolive/topics_50090.htm#relations.
NATO. 2023c. NATO—Resilience, Civil Preparedness and Article 3. August 2. https://www.nato.int/cps/en/natohq/topics_132722.htm.
NATO. 2023d. NATO Resilience Symposium 25-27 April 2023 Riga, Latvia.
NATO. 2024a. NATO and IMS. https://www.nato.int/cps/en/natohq/topics_64557.htm?
NATO. 2024b. NATO-Russia Council. https://www.nato.int/cps/en/natohq/topics_50091.htm.
NATO. 2024c. No TitleResilience, Civil Preparedness and Article 3. https://www.nato.int/cps/en/natohq/topics_132722.htm.
NATO. 2024d. Peace Support Operations in Bosnia and Herzegovina (1995–2004). NATO. https://www.nato.int/cps/en/natohq/topics_52122.htm.
NATO. 2024e. Resilience, Civil Preparedness and Article 3. Site Name Seo. https://www.nato.int/en/what-we-do/deterrence-and-defence/resilience-civil-preparedness-and-article-3.
NATO. 2024f. Resilience Symposium 2024, "NATO at 75: Delivering Resilient Deterrence and Defence". https://www.act.nato.int/activities/resilience-symposium/.
NATO. 2024g. Washington Summit Declaration. https://www.nato.int/en/about-us/official-texts-and-resources/official-texts/2024/07/10/washington-summit-declaration.
NATO. 2025a. Euro-Atlantic Disaster Response Coordination Centre. https://www.nato.int/cps/en/natohq/topics_52057.htm?
NATO. 2025b. NATO and France—NATO Declassified. https://www.nato.int/cps/en/natohq/declassified_160672.htm.
NATO. 2025c. NATO Civilian Planning Conference, Stockholm November 2025. North Atlantic Treaty Organization (NATO). https://www.nato.int/en/news-and-events/articles/news/2025/11/04/deputy-secretary-general-addresses-the-first-nato-civilian-planning-conference.
NATO. 2025d. NATO Response Force (2002–2024). NATO. https://www.nato.int/cps/en/natohq/topics_49755.htm.
NATO. 2026a. A Short History of NATO. NATO History | NATO. https://www.nato.int/en/about-us/nato-history/a-short-history-of-nato.
NATO. 2026b. Committee on Civil Organization in Time of War—NATO Archives Online. NATO Archives Online. https://archives.nato.int/committee-on-civil-organization-in-time-of-war-2.
NATO. 2026c. NATO Member Countries. Organization | NATO. https://www.nato.int/en/about-us/organization/nato-member-countries.
NATO. 2026d. Resilience, Civil Preparedness and Article 3. NATO Webpage. https://www.nato.int/en/what-we-do/deterrence-and-defence/resilience-civil-preparedness-and-article-3.

NATO. 2026e. Senior Civil Emergency Planning Committee—Series AC/98—Senior Civil Emergency Planning Committee. NATO Archives Online. https://archives.nato.int/senior-civil-emergency-planning-committee.

NATO. n.d. *NATO 2030—Fact Sheet*.

NATO and Swedish Civil Contingency Agency. 2009. *International CEP 2009 Civil Emergency Planning in the NATO/EAPC Countries*. Stockholm.

NATO Archives Online. 2026. Civil Protection Committee—NATO Archives Online. NATO Archives Online. https://archives.nato.int/civil-protection-committee-2.

NATO CCMS Report. 1988. NATO. The Challenges of Modern Society—NATO Archives Online. https://archives.nato.int/nato-challenges-of-modern-society-2.

NATO Civil Protection Group, MSB. 2024. NATO Civil Protection Group Seminar 2024—Public-Private Cooperation in Securing Critical Supplies—Supporting Alliance Resilience.

NATO, Committee on Civil Organization in Time of War. 1953. RECORD OF MEETING—Committee on Civil Organization in Time of War AC/23-R/8. NATO Archives Online. https://archives.nato.int/record-of-meeting-381.

NATO CPG. 2006. Comprehensive Political Guidance Endorsed by NATO Heads of State and Government on 29 November 2006. NATO Archives Brussels.

NATO, IMS, Working Group Memorandum. 1968. MILITARY REPRESENTATION IN NATO CIVIL WARTIME AGENCIES—NATO Archives Online. NATO. https://archives.nato.int/military-representation-in-nato-civil-wartime-agencies-7.

NATO, IMS, Working Group Memorandum. 1969. REPORT ON EXERCISE CIVLOG 69—NATO Archives Online IMSWM-159-69. NATO. https://archives.nato.int/report-on-exercise-civlog-69.

NATO Information Service. 1959. *Facts about NATO*. NATO Information Service, Printed by Bosch, Utrecht in the Netherlands.

NATO Information Service. 1994. The Concept of Combined Joint Task Forces (CJTF) 1994 Press Release. NATO Archives Brussels.

NATO Lisbon Summit Declaration. 2010. NATO. https://www.nato.int/cps/en/natohq/official_texts_68828.htm.

NATO Military Committee. 1952. MC 14/1, NORTH ATLANTIC MILITARY COMMITTEE DECISION ON M.C. 14/1 A REPORT BY THE STANDING GROUP on STRATEGIC GUIDANCE. NATO Archives Brussels.

NATO Military Committee. 1969. SYMPOSIUM ON CIVIL EMERGENCY PLANNING (10–14 FEBRUARY 1969)—Meeting Records for 31 of January NATO Archives Online. https://archives.nato.int/symposium-on-civil-emergency-planning-10-14-february-1969.

NATO NAC. 1990. Verbatim Record of the Special Meeting of the North Atlantic Council in Ministerial Session, Held at NATO HQ, Brussels, 3 May 1990. Speech by Secretary Baker USA NATO Archives Online. https://archives.nato.int/verbatim-record-of-the-special-meeting-of-the-north-atlantic-council-in-ministerial-session-held-at-nato-hq-brussels-3-may-1990-compte-rendu-de-la-de-la-reunion-extraordinaire-du-conseil-en-session-ministerielle-tenue-au-siege-de-lotan.

NATO NAC. 1991. ACTION SHEET—REVIEW OF CIVIL EMERGENCY PLANNING ACTIVITIES IN VIEW OF THE CHANGING NEEDS OF THE ALLIANCE—NATO PO(91)67-AS1. NATO Archives Brussels. https://archives.nato.int/action-sheet-review-of-civil-emergency-planning-activities-in-view-of-the-changing-needs-of-the-alliance.

NATO, North Atlantic Council. 1957. MC 14/2 3rd Strategic Concept "OVERALL STRATEGIC CONCEPT FOR THE DEFENSE OF THE NORTH ATLANTIC TREATY ORGANIZATION AREA". NATO.

NATO Parliamentary Assembly. 2021. NATO 2030: A MORE UNITED AND STRONGER ALLIANCE ON THE GLOBAL STAGE* DECLARATION 460. https://natolibguides.info/nato2030/officialtexts.

NATO Press Release on CCMS. 1972. CCMS PROGRESS IN 1972—NATO Archives Online. NATO. https://archives.nato.int/ccms-progress-in-1972.

NATO Public Diplomacy Division. 1959. Know Your NATO. North Atlantic Treaty Organization. Shield of Freedom, 1949–1959—NATO Archives Online. NATO Archives Online. https://archives.nato.int/know-your-nato-north-atlantic-treaty-organization-shield-of-freedom-1949-1959.

NATO, Public Diplomacy Division. 1971. Allied Defence in the Seventies / Défense de l'Alliance 1970–1980—NATO Archives Online. NATO. https://archives.nato.int/allied-defence-in-seventies-defense-de-lalliance-1970-1980.

NATO, Public Diplomacy Division. 1972. Aspects of NATO. Chronology (1945–1973)—NATO Archives Online. https://archives.nato.int/aspects-of-nato-chronology-1945-1973.

NATO, Public Diplomacy Division. 1976. Aspects of NATO. The Challenges of Modern Society—NATO Archives Online. https://archives.nato.int/aspects-of-nato-challenges-of-modern-society.

NATO, Public Diplomacy Division. 1982. Aspects of NATO Series 1 - N° 6. Civil Emergency Planning—NATO Archives Online. NATO. https://archives.nato.int/aspects-of-nato-series-1-n-6-civil-emergency-planning.

NATO, Public Diplomacy Division. 1988. CP Civil Preparedness—The Way Ahead/PC Etat de Préparation Civile—La Voie à Suivre—NATO Archives Online. https://archives.nato.int/cp-civil-preparedness-way-ahead-pc-etat-de-preparation-civile-la-voie-suivre.

NATO Public Diplomacy Division. 1991. The Challenges of Modern Society 1991—NATO Archives. NATO Archives Brussels. https://archives.nato.int/challenges-of-modern-society.

NATO Public Diplomacy Division. 1994. NATO Logistics Handbook Chapter 7: Civil Emergency Planning. NATO Archives Brussels. https://archives.nato.int/nato-logistics-handbook.

NATO Public Diplomacy Division. 2001. NATO Handbook 2001. NATO Public Diplomacy Division. https://archives.nato.int/nato-handbook-7.

NATO, Public Diplomacy Division. 2003. NATO Handbook 1971—NATO Archives Online. NATO. https://archives.nato.int/nato-handbook-1970.

NATO Public Diplomacy Division. 2006. NATO Handbook 2006. NATO Public Diplomacy Division.

NATO Public Diplomacy Division. 2008. Backgrounder—Civil Support for Military Operations and Emergency Responses—NATO Archives Online. https://archives.nato.int/backgrounder-civil-support-for-military-operations-and-emergency-responses.

NATO Public Diplomacy Division. 2009. Minimum Standards and Non-Binding Guidelines for First Responders Regarding Planning, Training, Procedure and Equipment for Chemical, Biological, Radiological and Nuclear (CBRN) Incidents. Modalities for the Advisory Support Team—NATO Archives Online. https://archives.nato.int/minimum-standards-and-non-binding-guidelines-for-first-responders-regarding-planning-training-procedure-and-equipment-for-chemical-biological-radiological-and-nuclear-cbrn-incidents-modalities-for-the-advisory-support-team.

NATO Review. 1989. NATO Review. NATO Archives Online. https://archives.nato.int/nato-review-106.

NATO SCEP. 1989. CIVIL EMERGENCY PLANNING SYMPOSIUM 1989—NATO Archives Online. https://archives.nato.int/civil-emergency-planning-symposium-1989-2.

NATO SCEPC. 1990a. DRAFT INTERIM MINISTERIAL GUIDANCE FOR CIVIL EMERGENCY PLANNING 1991–1993—NATO Archives Online. NATO Archives Online. https://archives.nato.int/draft-interim-ministerial-guidance-for-civil-emergency-planning-1991-1993.

NATO SCEPC. 1990b. SCEPC LIST OF TASKS—NATO Archives Online. NATO Archives Online. https://archives.nato.int/scepc-list-of-tasks.

NATO SCEPC. 1990c. STATUS OF CIVIL EMERGENCY PLANNING—NATO Archives Online. https://archives.nato.int/status-of-civil-emergency-planning-2.

NATO SCEPC. 1990d. THE FUTURE OF CIVIL EMERGENCY PLANNING DISCUSSION PAPER BY THE DIRECTOR, CIVIL EMERGENCY PLANNING—NATO Archives Online. https://archives.nato.int/the-future-of-civil-emergency-planning-discussion-paper-by-the-director-civil-emergency-planning.

NATO SCEPC. 1991a. ADAPTATION OF CIVIL PREPAREDNESS TO THE CHANGING NEEDS OF THE ALLIANCE AC/98-WP/289-REV2—NATO Archives. https://archives.nato.int/adaptation-of-civil-preparedness-to-the-changing-needs-of-the-alliance-3.

NATO SCEPC. 1991b. CIVIL EMERGENCY PLANNING AND REVIEW CYCLE AC 98 N/572—NATO Archives. https://archives.nato.int/civil-emergency-planning-and-review-cycle.

NATO SCEPC. 1991c. POSSIBLE CO-OPERATION IN THE FIELD OF CIVIL EMERGENCY PLANNING WITH THE COUNTRIES OF CENTRAL AND EASTERN EUROPE (THE HAND OF FRIENDHSIP)—AC/98-WP/293-REV1 NATO Archives. https://archives.nato.int/possible-co-operation-in-the-field-of-civil-emergency-planning-with-the-countries-of-central-and-eastern-europe-the-hand-of-friendhsip.

NATO SCEPC. 1991d. REVIEW OF CIVIL EMERGENCY PLANNING ACTIVITIES IN VIEW OF THE CHANGE NEEDS OF THE ALLIANCE AC/98-WP/297—NATO Archives. NATO Archives Brussels. https://archives.nato.int/review-of-civil-emergency-planning-activities-in-view-of-the-change-needs-of-the-alliance.

NATO SCEPC. 1991e. REVIEW OF CIVIL EMERGENCY PLANNING ACTIVITIES IN VIEW OF THE CHANGING NEEDS OF THE ALLIANCE AC/98-D/1308. NATO Archives Brussels. https://archives.nato.int/review-of-civil-emergency-planning-activities-in-view-of-the-changing-needs-of-the-alliance.

NATO SCEPC. 1991f. REVIEW OF THE NATO CIVIL WARTIME AGENCIES AC/98-N/575—NATO Archives. https://archives.nato.int/review-of-the-nato-civil-wartime-agencies.

NATO SCEPC. 1991g. THE CIVIL EMERGENCY PLANNING AND REVIEW CYCLE (CEPRC) AC/98-WP/298. NATO Archives Online. https://archives.nato.int/the-civil-emergency-planning-and-review-cycle-ceprc.

NATO Secretary General. 1958. NATO CO-OPERATION FOR DISASTER RELIEF IN PEACETIME—NATO Archives Online. https://archives.nato.int/nato-co-operation-for-disaster-relief-in-peacetime.

NATO Secretary General. 1969. CONDUCT OF CIVLOG 69—NATO Archives Online-Information Release by Secretary General. NATO Archives Online. https://archives.nato.int/conduct-of-civlog-69.

NATO Secretary General. 1976. THE STATE OF CIVIL EMERGENCY PLANNING—NATO Archives Online. NATO. https://archives.nato.int/the-state-of-civil-emergency-planning.

NATO Secretary General. 1977. A NATO PEACETIME DISASTER RELIEF ORGANIZATION—NATO Archives Online. https://archives.nato.int/a-nato-peacetime-disaster-relief-organization.

NATO Secretary General. 1983. 1982 ASSESSMENT OF THE MILITARY IMPLICATIONS OF THE STATE OF CIVIL PREPAREDNESS—NATO Archives Online. NATO. https://archives.nato.int/1982-assessment-of-the-military-implications-of-the-state-of-civil-preparedness.

NATO Strategic Concept. 1991. The Alliance's 1991 Strategic Concept. NATO. https://www.nato.int/cps/en/natohq/official_texts_23847.htm.

NATO Strategic Concept. 1999. The Alliance's Strategic Concept (1999). Official Texts and Resources | NATO. https://www.nato.int/en/about-us/official-texts-and-resources/official-texts/1999/04/24/the-alliances-strategic-concept-1999.

NATO Strategic Concept. 2010a. Active Engagement, Modern Defence—Strategic Concept for the Defence and Security of the Members of the North Atlantic Treaty Organisation. NATO. https://www.nato.int/cps/en/natohq/official_texts_68580.htm.

NATO Strategic Concept. 2010b. NATO Strategic Concept 2010 Active Engagement, Modern Defence Strategic Concept for the Defence and Security of the Members of the North Atlantic Treaty Organization. https://www.nato.int/cps/en/natohq/topics_82705.htm.

NATO Strategic Concept, NATO. 2022. NATO Strategic Concept 2022. https://natolibguides.info/nato2030/2022strategicconcept.

Neal, Andrew W. 2019. *Security As Politics*. Edinburgh University Press.

Neocleous, Mark. 2008. *Critique of Security*. Edinburgh University Press.

Nobel Price Committee. 2024. Nobel Prize. https://www.nobelprize.org/prizes/peace/1953/marshall/facts/.

North Atlantic Council. 1955. RESOLUTION ON THE ESTABLISHMENT OF A SENIOR CIVIL EMERGENCY PLANNING COMMITTEE—C M 1955-100. NATO Archives Online. https://archives.nato.int/resolution-on-the-establishment-of-a-senior-civil-emergency-planning-committee.

North Atlantic Council. 1956. PUBLIC RELATIONS ASPECTS OF POLITICAL CONSULTATIONS IN NATO C/M 56/25. NATO Archives Online. https://archives.nato.int/public-relations-aspects-of-political-consultations-in-nato.

North Atlantic Council. 1959. CIVIL EMERGENCY PLANNING—1959 YEARLY REVIEW—C-M(60)1. NATO Archives Online. https://archives.nato.int/civil-emergency-planning-1959-yearly-review.

O'Grady, Nathaniel, and Duncan Shaw. 2023. Resilience, Responsibility and State Abandon: The Changing Role of the Government in Emergencies. *Political Geography* 100:102796.

Pedlow, Gregory. 1997a. *NATO Strategy Documents: 1949–1969*. Brussels: NATO.

Pedlow, Gregory. 1997b. *The Evolution of NATO Strategy, 1949–1969*. Brussels: NATO.

Pike, Andy, Stuart Dawley, and John Tomaney. 2010. Resilience, Adaptation and Adaptability. *Cambridge Journal of Regions, Economy and Society* 3 (1): 59–70.

Poast, Paul, and Alexandra Chinchilla. 2020. Good for Democracy? Evidence from the 2004 NATO Expansion. *International Politics* (University of Chicago, Chicago, USA (GRID:grid.170205.1) (ISNI:0000 0004 1936 7822); University of Chicago, Chicago, USA (GRID:grid.170205.1) (ISNI:0000 0004 1936 7822)) 57 (3): 471–490. https://doi.org/10.1057/s41311-020-00236-6.

Porter, Libby, and Simin Davoudi. 2012. The Politics of Resilience for Planning: A Cautionary Note. *Planning Theory and Practice* 13 (2): 329–333.

Pouliot, Vincent. 2010. *International Security in Practice: The Politics of NATO-Russia Diplomacy*. Vol. 113. Cambridge University Press.

Prior, Tim, and Florian Roth. 2014. The Boundaries of Building Societal Resilience: Responsibilization and Swiss Civil Defense in the Cold War. *Behemoth—A Journal on Civilisation* 7 (2): 103–123.

Public Diplomacy Division. 1961. FINAL COMMUNIQUE—NAC SPRING MINISTERIAL IN OSLO FROM 8TH MAY TO 10 MAY 1961 PRESS RELEASE M1(61)6. NATO Archives Online. https://archives.nato.int/final-communique-nac-spring-ministerial-in-oslo-from-8th-may-to-10-may-1961.

Rådestad, C., and O. Larsson. 2018. Responsibilization in Contemporary Swedish Crisis Management: Expanding "Bare Life" Biopolitics through Exceptionalism and Neoliberal Governmentality. *Critical Policy Studies* 14 (1): 86–105. https://doi.org/10.1080/19460171.2018.1530604.

Rådestad, Carl, and Oscar Larsson. 2020. Responsibilization in Contemporary Swedish Crisis Management: Expanding "Bare Life" Biopolitics through Exceptionalism and Neoliberal Governmentality. *Critical Policy Studies* 14 (1): 86–105.

Rae, Gavin. 2019. *Critiquing Sovereign Violence: Law, Biopolitics and Bio-Juridicalism*. Edinburgh University Press.

Reichborn-Kjennerud, Erik, and Patrick Cullen. 2016. *What Is Hybrid Warfare?* JSTOR.

Reid, Julian. 2012. The Disastrous and Politically Debased Subject of Resilience. *Development Dialogue* 58 (1): 67–79.

Renz, Bettina. 2016. Russia and "Hybrid Warfare". *Contemporary Politics* 22 (3): 283–300.

Renz, Bettina. 2018. Russia and "Hybrid Warfare". In *Russia, the West, and the Ukraine Crisis*. Routledge.

Resilience Committee. 2025. Resilience Reference Curriculum. NATO Information Service. https://www.nato.int/en/news-and-events/articles/news/2025/02/21/nato-launches-the-resilience-reference-curriculum.

Risse-Kappen, Thomas. 2016. Collective Identity in a Democratic Community. In *Içinde Domestic Politics and Norm Diffusion in International Relations: Ideas Do Not Float Freely, Thomas Risse*, 78–113.

Roepke, Wolf-Diether, and Hasit Thankey. 2019. Resilience: The First Line of Defence. *NATO Review* 27 (2).

Rose, Nikolas, and Peter Miller. 2010. Political Power beyond the State: Problematics of Government. *The British Journal of Sociology* 61:271–303.

Rynning, Sten. 2024. *NATO: From Cold War to Ukraine, a History of the World's Most Powerful Alliance*. Yale University Press. http://ebookcentral.proquest.com/lib/fhs-ebooks/detail.action?docID=31223293.

Salter, Mark B. 2010. When Securitization Fails: The Hard Case of Counter-Terrorism Programs. In *Securitization Theory*. Routledge.

Salter, Mark B. 2019. Security Actor-Network Theory: Revitalizing Securitization Theory with Bruno Latour. *Polity* 51 (2): 349–364.

Sarotte, Mary Elise. 2021. *Not One Inch: America, Russia, and the Making of Post-Cold War Stalemate*. Yale University Press.

Saxi, Håkon Lunde, Bengt Sundelius, and Brett Swaney. 2020. Baltics Left of Bang: Nordic Total Defense and Implications for the Baltic Sea Region. *Strategic Forum* 304:1–19.

SCEPC. 1956a. ASSUMPTIONS FOR CIVIL EMERGENCY PLANNING—SCEPC AC/98-D/14. NATO Archives Online. https://archives.nato.int/assumptions-for-civil-emergency-planning-7.

SCEPC. 1956b. MAINTENANCE OF GOVERNMENTAL CONTROL AC/98-D/12. NATO Archives Online. https://archives.nato.int/maintenance-of-governmental-control.

SCEPC. 1956c. RECORD OF MEETING—AC 98/1 First Meeting of Senior Civil Emergency Planning Committee. NATO Archives Online. https://archives.nato.int/record-of-meeting-1984.

SCEPC. 1956d. SCEPC Yearly Review Report AC 98-D/17, Report for Year 1956. NATO Archives Brussels.

SCEPC. 1957a. CIVIL EMERGENCY PLANNING REVIEW OF PROGRESS IN 1957—REPORT BY THE CIVIL DEFENCE COMMITTEE—AC/98-D/53. NATO Archives Online. https://archives.nato.int/civil-emergency-planning-review-of-progress-in-1957-report-by-the-civil-defence-committee.

SCEPC. 1957b. MEASURES T O IMPLEMENT THE STRATEGIC CONCEPT M C 14/2 (Revised) SCEPC A 98. NATO Archives Brussels.

SCEPC. 1967. AC-98 D 330. NATO Archives Brussels.

SCEPC. 1970a. AC 98 D 471. NATO Archives Brussels.
SCEPC. 1970b. AC 98 D 476.
SCEPC. 1970c. AC 98 D 486. NATO Archives Brussels.
SCEPC. 1970d. AC 98 D 488. NATO Archives Brussels.
SCEPC. 1970e. AC 98 D 513. NATO Archives Brussels.
SCEPC. 1970f. Annual Report from Civil Defense Committee AC 98 D 501. NATO Archives Brussels.
SCEPC. 1970g. Decision Sheet for the SCEPC Plenary Session of the 19th and 20th November 1970—AC 98 DS 65. NATO Archives Brussels.
SCEPC. 1970h. INPUT BY THE CEP DIRECTORATE TO THE WORK OF THE EXECUTIVEWORKING GROUP ON THE STUDY ON ALLIANCE DEFENCE PROBLEMS FOR THE 1970S—AC/98-D/497. NATO Archives Online. https://archives.nato.int/input-by-the-cep-directorate-to-the-work-of-the-executiveworking-group-on-the-study-on-alliance-defence-problems-forthe-1970s.
SCEPC. 1970i. Norwegian Proposals for Increasing the Efficiency of Civil Emergency Planning in NATO—AC 98 D512. NATO Archives Brussels.
SCEPC. 1970j. REPORT TO THE COUNCIL ON THE EFFECTS OF THE SHORTCOMINGS IN CIVIL EMERGENCY PREPAREDNESS ON THE DEFENCE CAPABILITIES OF THE ALLIANCE-AC/98-D/516. NATO Archives Brussels. https://archives.nato.int/report-to-the-council-on-the-effects-of-the-shortcomings-in-civil-emergency-preparedness-on-the-defence-capabilities-of-the-alliance.
SCEPC. 1970k. THE REVIEW OF NATO CIVIL EMERGENCY ARRANGEMENTS IN TIME OF CRISIS OR WAR—AC 98 D 498. NATO Archives Online. https://archives.nato.int/the-review-of-nato-civil-emergency-arrangements-in-time-of-crisis-or-war.
SCEPC. 1971a. 2ND REPORT OF THE INFORMAL AD HOC GROUP ON THE FOLLOW-UP TO THE AD 70 STUDY—AC 98 D 554. NATO Archives Online. https://archives.nato.int/2nd-report-of-the-informal-ad-hoc-group-on-the-follow-up-to-the-ad-70-study.
SCEPC. 1971b. Danish Comments on the Norwegian Proposal in AC 98 D 512—AC 98 D 570. NATO Archives Brussels.
SCEPC. 1971c. INTERIM REPORT BY THE INFORMAL AD HOC GROUP ON THE FOLLOW-UP TO AD 70 STUDY—AC 98 D 543. NATO Archives Online. https://archives.nato.int/interim-report-by-the-informal-ad-hoc-group-on-the-follow-up-to-ad-70-study.
SCEPC. 1971d. Report of the Special Group of Expert on Civil Emergency Planning AC 98 D 555. NATO Archives Brussels.
SCEPC. 1972. AD 70: SCOPE AND FORMAT OF THE MAY 1972 REPORT TO MINISTERS—AC 98 D 592. NATO Archives Online. https://archives.nato.int/ad-70-scope-and-format-of-the-may-1972-report-to-ministers.

SCEPC. 1973. REPORT TO THE PLENARY SESSION ON CIVIL SUPPORT TO MILITARY PREPAREDNESS IN NATO—AC/98-D/673. NATO Archives Online. https://archives.nato.int/report-to-the-plenary-session-on-civil-support-to-military-preparedness-in-nato.

SCEPC. 1974a. HILEX-6: REPORT BY THE CENSHADCOM—NATO Archives Online. NATO Archives Online. https://archives.nato.int/hilex-6-report-by-the-censhadcom.

SCEPC. 1974b. UNITED STATES PRESENTATION ON CIVIL SUPPORT OF MILITARY PREPAREDNESS IN NATO-AC/98-D/695. NATO Archives Online. https://archives.nato.int/united-states-presentation-on-civil-support-of-military-preparedness-in-nato.

SCEPC. 1976a. Senior Civil Emergency Planning Committee in Plenary Session—Report by Selected Group Part 1 AC 98 D 802. NATO Archives Brussels.

SCEPC. 1976b. Senior Civil Emergency Planning Committee in Plenary Session—Report by the Selected Group Part 2-5 Ac 98 D 803. NATO Archives Brussels.

SCEPC. 1977. Senior Civil Emergency Planning Committee Plenary Session July 1977 Decision Sheet AC 98 DS 121. NATO Archives Brussels.

SCEPC. 1978. NATO Civil Emergency Questionnaires AC 98 D 875. NATO Archives Brussels.

SCEPC. 1979a. Civil Emergency and Review Cycle—Report to the Council on the State of Civil Preparedness AC 98 D 911. NATO Archives Brussels.

SCEPC. 1979b. PROPOSED CEP SYMPOSIUM: 1980 WORKING PAPER. Note by the Director, Civil Emergency Planning AC/98-WP/146. NATO Archives Brussels.

SCEPC. 1979c. Summary Report on the State of Civil Preparedness Note by the Directore—AC 98 WP 144. NATO Archives Brussels.

SCEPC. 1981. NATO CIVIL EMERGENCY PLANNING AND REVIEW CYCLE Note by the Director. Civil Emergency Planning—AC 98 D 1022. NATO Archives Brussels.

SCEPC. 1983. Civil Emergency Planning Questionnaire—Approved Information Request—AC 98 D 1091. NATO Archives Brussels.

SCEPC. 1986. Compendium of Technical Information for the Basic Protection of Populations—AC 98 D 1184. NATO Archives Brussels.

SCEPC. 1987a. National CEP Organisation, Activities, and Efforts. Presentation of Italy AC 98 N 481. NATO Archives Brussels.

SCEPC. 1987b. REPORTING OF DISASTERS Note by the Director AC 98 D 1189. NATO Archives Brussels.

SCEPC. 1988. Ministerial Guidance for Civil Emergency Planning 1989–1993 AC 98 D 1243. NATO Archives Brussels.

Schmitt, Carl. 2005. *Political Theology: Four Chapters on the Concept of Sovereignty*. University of Chicago Press.
Schumann, Anna. 2022. Fact Sheet: Thermonuclear Weapons. Center for Arms Control and Non-Proliferation, November 18. https://armscontrolcenter.org/fact-sheet-thermonuclear-weapons/.
Secretary-General. 1971. NATO CO-OPERATION FOR EMERGENCY DISASTER ASSISTANCE IN PEACETIME—REVISION OF DOCUMENT C-M(58)102 -. NATO Archives Online. https://archives.nato.int/nato-co-operation-for-emergency-disaster-assistance-in-peacetime-revision-of-document-c-m-58-102.
Seery, Mark D., E. Alison Holman, and Roxane Cohen Silver. 2010. Whatever Does Not Kill Us: Cumulative Lifetime Adversity, Vulnerability, and Resilience. *Journal of Personality and Social Psychology* 99 (6): 1025.
Snegovaya, Maria. 2023. Why Russia's Democracy Never Began. *Journal of Democracy* 34 (3): 105–118.
Sperling, Valerie. 2018. *Building the Russian State: Institutional Crisis and the Quest for Democratic Governance*. Routledge.
Standing Group. 1965. SGM-0379-65—REPORT ON EX CIVLOG '65 Standing Group Memeorandum Series.
Stoltenberg, Jens. 2025. *On My Watch*. W. W. Norton & Company.
Tardy, Thierry. 2022. *'NATO 2030. United for a New Era': A Digest*. JSTOR.
The North Atlantic Council. 1952a. Committee on Civil Organization in Time of War—AC/23-D/17. NATO Archives Online. https://archives.nato.int/committee-on-civil-organization-in-time-of-war-2.
The North Atlantic Council. 1952b. COMPOSITION OF THE WORKING GROUP AC/23-N/1. NATO Archives Online. https://archives.nato.int/composition-of-the-working-group.
The North Atlantic Council. 1953. Progress Report by the Chairman of the Committee of Civil Organization in Time of War' C-M(53)148. NATO Archives Brussels.
The North Atlantic Council. 1954. APPOINTMENT OF TECHNICAL ADVISERS ON CIVIL DEFENCE PROBLEMS—C-M(54)11. NATO Archives Online. https://archives.nato.int/appointment-of-technical-advisers-on-civil-defence-problems.
The North Atlantic Council. 1962a. ANNUAL POLITICAL APPRAISAL—SPECIAL REPORT BY THE SECRETARY GENERAL ON NATO DEFENCE POLICY C-M(62)48 -. NATO Archives Online. https://archives.nato.int/annual-political-appraisal-special-report-by-the-secretary-general-on-nato-defence-policy.
The North Atlantic Council. 1962b. Civlog 65—North Atlantic Council Decision—C/M 62 152'. NATO Archives Brussels.
The North Atlantic Treaty. 1949.

Tocci, Nathalie. 2020. Resilience and the Role of the European Union in the World. *Contemporary Security Policy* 41 (2): 176–194. https://doi.org/10.1080/13523260.2019.1640342.

Truman, S. Harry. 1947. *Truman Doctrine—Congress Speak.* https://www.archives.gov/milestone-documents/truman-doctrine.

US Historical Archive. 2025. Milestones in the History of U.S. Foreign Relations—Office of the Historian SALT 1 and 2. Office of the Historian. https://history.state.gov/milestones/1969-1976/salt.

Van Heuven, Marten H. A. 1970. Civil Emergency Planning in NATO. *The International Lawyer* 4 (2): 391–398. JSTOR.

Vinx, Lars. 2025. Carl Schmitt. In *The Stanford Encyclopedia of Philosophy*. Stanford University. https://plato.stanford.edu/entries/schmitt/.

Walker, Rob B. J. 2010. *After the Globe, before the World.* Routledge.

Welsh, Marc. 2014. Resilience and Responsibility: Governing Uncertainty in a Complex World. *The Geographical Journal* 180 (1): 15–26.

Williams, Michael C. 2003. Words, Images, Enemies: Securitization and International Politics. *International Studies Quarterly* 47 (4): 511–531.

Williams, Michael. 2007. *Culture and Security: Symbolic Power and the Politics of International Security*. Routledge.

Williams, Michael C. 2011. Securitization and the Liberalism of Fear. *Security Dialogue* 42 (4–5): 453–463.

Williams, Nicholas. 2023. NATO Operations. In *Research Handbook on NATO*, Elgar Handbooks in Political Science. Edward Elgar Publishing. https://doi.org/10.4337/9781839103391.00028.

Wilson, Lee, and Laurens Bakker. 2016. Cutting off the King's Head: Security and Normative Order beyond the State. *Conflict, Security & Development* 16 (4): 289–300.

Wither, James Kenneth. 2020. Back to the Future? Nordic Total Defence Concepts. *Defence Studies* 20 (1): 61–81.

Yost, David S. 2010. NATO's Evolving Purposes and the Next Strategic Concept. *International Affairs* 86 (2): 489–522.

Index

0–9
9/11, 33, 148, 149, 176, 217

A
AD 70 report, 122, 123
Article 2, 60–62, 114
Article 3, 4, 36, 40, 50, 59, 72, 87, 91, 110, 117, 186, 189, 193, 194, 199, 200, 202, 206, 212, 215, 218, 220
Article 5, 1, 2, 4, 33, 143, 148, 152, 155, 173, 176, 194, 212

B
Berlin Wall, 30, 55, 68, 93, 97, 137, 138, 159

C
Civil crisis management, 5, 111, 124, 129, 134, 146, 157, 159, 161, 163–165, 168, 170–172, 176, 177, 179, 182, 195, 205, 206, 215–217, 219
Civil defense, 1, 3, 5–10, 18, 25, 39, 40, 50, 55, 61, 67, 68, 71–91, 94, 96, 98, 101–105, 109–111, 113, 115–123, 125–135, 138, 141, 147, 151, 153, 157, 159, 161–163, 165, 177, 179–187, 190, 192, 193, 195, 197, 199, 201, 203, 205, 206, 210, 212, 214–221
Civil Defense Committee, 10, 71, 74–78, 80–82, 86, 88, 102–104, 106, 109, 110, 117–120, 122, 125, 126, 132, 133, 168, 197, 199, 214, 217, 220
Civil emergency planning, 3, 5, 8, 10, 80, 82, 83, 87–89, 91, 94, 98, 103–105, 107, 110, 111, 114–116, 119, 121–135, 157–167, 169, 170, 172, 174, 177, 179–187, 190, 193, 196, 197, 199, 203, 206, 210, 212, 215, 216, 219, 220
Civil Emergency Planning Questionnaire, 130, 133, 135,

O. Larsson, *NATO's Approach to the Civil Dimensions of War*,
https://doi.org/10.1007/978-3-032-27871-5

159, 162, 167, 168, 172, 187, 215, 216, 218, 219
Civil-military cooperation, 111, 147, 160, 171, 202
Civil preparedness, 3–6, 8, 39, 83, 87, 123, 124, 128–131, 133, 134, 158, 160–163, 175, 184–187, 190, 192, 193, 195, 200, 202, 203, 205, 210, 215–217
Committee on the Challenges of Modern Society (CCMS), 113–115, 119, 134, 164, 216
Crisis and war, 85, 120, 123, 124, 126, 128, 160, 161, 165, 181, 196, 217
Crisis management, 2, 5, 21, 22, 30, 41–43, 49, 51, 103, 105, 107, 113, 115, 116, 123, 128, 145–147, 150, 152–156, 158–160, 167, 174–176, 180, 182, 183, 192, 195

D
Democracy, 6, 14–16, 19, 22, 23, 26, 28, 29, 45, 116, 139, 148, 153, 181
  democratization, 26, 33, 138
Détente, 98–102, 104, 112, 122, 133, 142
Disaster relief, 2, 103, 111, 115, 116, 119, 126, 129, 132, 134, 138, 146, 155, 158, 161, 163, 166, 168, 170–172, 174, 175, 177, 179, 183, 195, 205, 215–217, 219
Dual-use, 94, 110, 111, 132, 134, 196, 216

E
Euro-Atlantic Disaster Response Coordination Center (EADRCC), 171, 172, 175, 177, 196, 217

F
Flexible approach, 96, 98
Foucault, Michel, 8, 47–49, 214

G
Governmentality, 40, 45–50, 53, 181, 220, 221
Grey zone, 2, 3, 22, 35, 51, 52, 98, 180, 185, 195, 205, 210, 218

H
Harmel report, 59, 99–101, 122, 192
Hobbes
  Hobbesian trap, 20, 213
Homefront, 135
Hybrid threats, 2–4, 20, 22, 23, 35, 39, 44, 51, 52, 98, 158, 180, 181, 184, 185, 193, 195, 196, 199, 205, 210, 212, 218
  hybrid war, 2, 218

I
Individuals, 1, 5, 7, 14, 16, 22, 34, 40, 44, 46, 49, 52, 55, 78, 107, 109, 118, 170, 186, 191, 194, 201, 209, 212, 214–216, 218–220
International crisis management, 5, 7, 31, 33, 138, 139, 141, 142, 146, 151, 152, 154, 183, 217
Ismay, Lord, 26, 58–61, 72, 73, 75, 79, 81, 94, 215

K
Kosovo, 142, 156, 168
 Kosovo crisis, 31, 172

L
Logistics, 107, 110, 117, 126, 147, 157, 159, 166
 logistics support, 103, 110, 134, 216

N
NATO Archives, 10, 88, 102, 103, 132, 133, 157, 219
NATO enlargement, 28, 32, 146
New assumptions, 79, 82, 85, 90, 103, 110, 215
Nuclear weapons, 9, 64, 68, 69, 71, 76, 77, 84, 90, 93, 94, 96–98, 103, 108, 110, 111, 113, 214, 215

O
Out-of-area operations, 1, 141, 148, 150, 151, 153, 154, 165, 176, 217

P
Partnership for Peace (PfP), 30, 144, 147, 161, 167–171, 177, 215, 217
Pearson, Lester B., 26, 58, 60, 62
Population(s), 1, 3–5, 7–9, 23, 33, 48, 49, 55, 68, 69, 71–74, 77, 78, 81, 82, 84–86, 89–91, 96, 98, 103, 109, 110, 115, 118, 120–124, 126, 128, 131–133, 138, 141, 154, 157, 158, 161, 167–169, 172, 173, 175, 177, 185, 186, 190, 191, 193, 197, 200, 201, 203, 209, 212, 214–220

R
Resilience, 2–5, 7, 11, 18, 23, 35, 36, 39–53, 59, 134, 158, 175, 180–206, 211–214, 218, 220, 221
 resilience and society, 42
 resilience as governmentality, 47
Resilience Committee, 10, 40, 104, 194, 196–199, 204, 205, 211, 218, 220

S
SACEUR, 59, 108, 201
Schmitt, Carl, 16, 17, 48
Secretary General, 26, 60, 79, 109, 116, 127, 128, 131, 137
Securitization, 9, 16–19, 22, 49, 52, 185, 210, 212, 213, 220
 securitization theory, 15–21, 213
Security, 1–7, 9, 10, 13–23, 25–29, 31–36, 39–53, 55, 56, 58, 59, 61, 62, 64–66, 84, 91, 94, 97, 101–103, 111, 122, 133, 134, 137, 139, 140, 143, 144, 146–149, 151–155, 157, 159, 161, 164, 165, 169, 171, 173–177, 179–186, 190, 192, 194–196, 199, 201, 202, 204, 205, 210–214, 216–220
Security community, 26, 32, 137, 145, 176
Security politics, 6, 7, 9, 13, 15, 17–23, 55, 213
Senior Civil Emergency Planning Committee, 10, 40, 74, 79–89, 91, 102, 104, 105, 107, 109–111, 113, 115, 117–133,

157–165, 170, 171, 173, 196, 197, 211, 214–218
(Sir) John Hodsoll, 73–77, 79, 80, 90
Sputnik, 64
Strategic concept, 9, 10, 39, 53, 65–69, 71, 82, 97, 98, 104, 131, 139–141, 143, 145, 146, 152, 154, 156, 157, 164, 194, 195

T

Terrorism, 15, 33, 52, 137, 138, 146, 147, 149, 150, 154, 157, 159, 175, 176, 188, 195, 217
(the) Balkans, 31, 141, 142, 147–150, 152, 156, 176
The Marshall Plan, 57, 180
The Monroe Doctrine, 36
The North Atlantic Treaty, 4, 25, 28, 58, 60, 65, 67, 87, 94, 97, 99, 101, 114, 179, 180, 186, 193, 194, 200, 212
Three Wise Men (report), 59, 62, 63, 173, 192

U

Ukraine, 20, 28, 31, 33–35, 101, 146, 147, 150, 152, 156, 185, 194, 201, 205, 206, 210, 217

FSC
www.fsc.org
MIX
Papier | Fördert gute Waldnutzung
FSC® C083411

Kolibri 360 GmbH
Ferdinand-Jühlke-Straße 7
99095 Erfurt, Deutschland
produktsicherheit@kolibri360.de